The Mozambican Modern Ghost Story
(1866–2006)

RECONFIGURING IDENTITIES IN THE PORTUGUESE-SPEAKING WORLD

Edited by
Paulo de Medeiros and Cláudia Pazos-Alonso

VOL. 16

PETER LANG
Oxford • Bern • Berlin • Bruxelles • New York • Wien

Peter J. Maurits

The Mozambican Modern Ghost Story (1866–2006)

The Genealogy of a Genre

PETER LANG
Oxford • Bern • Berlin • Bruxelles • New York • Wien

Bibliographic information published by Die Deutsche Nationalbibliothek.
Die Deutsche Nationalbibliothek lists this publication in the Deutsche Nationalbibliografie; detailed bibliographic data is available on the Internet at http://dnb.d-nb.de.

A catalogue record for this book is available from the British Library.

Library of Congress Cataloging-in-Publication Data

Names: Maurits, Peter J., 1981– author.
Title: The Mozambican modern ghost story (1866-2006) : the genealogy of a genre / Peter J. Maurits.
Description: Oxford ; New York : Peter Lang, [2022] | Series: Reconfiguring identities in the Portuguese-speaking world, 2235-0144 ; vol no. 16 | Includes bibliographical references and index.
Identifiers: LCCN 2021055745 (print) | LCCN 2021055746 (ebook) | ISBN 9781789975413 (paperback) | ISBN 9781789975420 (ebook) | ISBN 9781789975437 (epub)
Subjects: LCSH: Ghost stories, Mozambican (Portuguese)—History and criticism. | Mozambican fiction (Portuguese)—19th century—History and criticism. | Mozambican fiction (Portuguese)—20th century—History and criticism. | LCGFT: Literary criticism.
Classification: LCC PQ9934 .M38 2022 (print) | LCC PQ9934 (ebook) | DDC 869.3/08733099679—dc23/eng/20220124
LC record available at https://lccn.loc.gov/2021055745
LC ebook record available at https://lccn.loc.gov/2021055746

Cover image: The Banco de Moçambique building in Maputo, with ruins in the foreground. Photograph by Boris Kester (October 2015). Permission granted by <www.traveladventures.org>.

Cover design by Peter Lang Ltd.

ISSN 2235-0144
ISBN 978-1-78997-541-3 (print)
ISBN 978-1-78997-542-0 (ePDf)
ISBN 978-1-78997-543-7 (ePub)

© Peter Lang AG 2022

Published by Peter Lang Ltd, International Academic Publishers,
52 St Giles, Oxford, OX1 3LU, United Kingdom
oxford@peterlang.com, www.peterlang.com

Peter J. Maurits has asserted his right under the Copyright, Designs and Patents Act, 1988, to be identified as Author of this Work.

All rights reserved.
All parts of this publication are protected by copyright.
Any utilisation outside the strict limits of the copyright law, without the permission of the publisher, is forbidden and liable to prosecution.
This applies in particular to reproductions, translations, microfilming, and storage and processing in electronic retrieval systems.

This publication has been peer reviewed.

Capital comes [into this world] dripping from head to foot, from every pore, with blood and dirt.

– Karl Marx

Everything resolves. That is the function of contradiction.

– Three-Headed Spirit

Contents

Preface	ix
Acknowledgements	xiii
CHAPTER 1 Thesis and terms	1
CHAPTER 2 The modern ghost story	41
CHAPTER 3 Emergence of the Mozambican modern ghost story	75
CHAPTER 4 The Mozambican modern ghost story	115
CHAPTER 5 Re-emergence of the Mozambican modern ghost story	153
Conclusion	189
Bibliography	193
Index	213

Preface

This book will argue that a Mozambican modern ghost story exists and that it registers primitive accumulation. It shows how literary form – a genre – can alter when it moves, temporally and spatially, through the world-literary system, and reacts with different forms and raw materials. In conducting this study, several complexities relative to periodization, selection, categories and scope were encountered. It is important to highlight them here to clarify why certain choices were made. For its periodization, this study uses the colonialism–post-independence–civil war–post-civil-war timeline. Levy has argued, because Mozambique has 'undergone dizzying cycles of back-and-forth institutional changes in political and economic orders since independence' – and, it can be added, before independence – that such a relatively 'clear periodization' of Mozambican history is possible (Levy 113). Yet as Arrighi writes, periodizing 'risks doing violence to reality' because the structure it provides is 'imposed' on history (Arrighi 30). Nevertheless, as Arrighi also suggests, the clarifying potential may outweigh such violence.

The selection of this book's primary corpus relied on an attempt to read all Mozambican literary works, in order to see if modern ghost story forms, in different guises, exist, and to understand possible relations between those guises. Practically, this meant traveling to different libraries and reading all the available books. Such an approach is bound to fail because even a 'small literature' as the Mozambican one is large and, evidently, it is not possible to access those works that were lost or never published. It even proved difficult, for different reasons, to access some of the works that have been preserved. Moreover, even if all works could have been accessed – and, indeed, even all the works that were accessed – they cannot possibly be addressed in a book of this size, and certainly not all at length. Thus, throughout this study, as Mozambican literature proliferates and works get longer and more complex – transitioning from poetry to the short story to the novel as dominant form – this book will rely on fewer and fewer works to make its case. Chapter 4 attempts to mediate this using short readings but Chapter 5 only uses Mia Couto's complex 2006 novel *O Outro Pé da Sereia*. In anticipation of criticisms hereof, I can only show comprehension.

Most of the authors discussed in this book are men and Couto's work is overwhelmingly present. If the selection method addressed above is indiscriminate, then this must say something about what Mozambican authors get to be published, which works get access to circulation and which do not and about who engages with the form at stake in this book. These dynamics, however, lie beyond the scope of this book.

The category of 'Mozambican' is problematic because it is neither homogeneous nor straightforward. Even in 1996, Chabal wrote 'Mozambique is not yet a country in any meaningful sense of the word' (79). Much has changed since then, but, in 2020, the differences between rural and urban areas are still significant. For example, scholars have argued consistently that Mozambican literary production is predominantly located in the urban centres in the south of the country – and particularly in the capital, Maputo, where most political elites are also located. Many, if not most of the authors that write modern ghost stories as discussed in this book, belong to the 'south' in some way or other and belong, not seldom, to the *assimilado* class, which may have helped them in studying abroad and tap into other literary ecologies more easily. As this book is being written, fundamentalist cells are operating in the north of Mozambique (particularly in Mocimboa da Praia). Analysts have begun to claim the success of these cells lies, in part, in the same neglect of the north by the (political elites in the) south that formed the conditions of the civil war in the 1970s and 1980s. Hence, even if this is a book about the Mozambican modern ghost story, 'Mozambican' may address a different region or group than that specifier could imply.

Finally, scope. This book has five chapters, starting in the nineteenth and ending in the twenty-first century. The first chapter discusses the main thesis and unpacks the central terms – how are modernity, register, primitive accumulation and the modern ghost story understood in this book. The second chapter shows how Walter Scott shaped a modern ghost story genre in the nineteenth century – which registered the financial crisis of 1825 – and how it remained prominent. The third chapter analyses Campos

Preface xi

de Oliveira's 1866 poem 'Uma Visão' [An Apparition] and Orlando Mendes' 1965 *Portagem* [Toll] as respectively a Gothic predecessor and as an early version of the Mozambican modern ghost story. It argues that *Portagem* registered primitive accumulation of the Mozambican labour market in the nineteenth century. Chapter 4 demonstrates that in the 1980s, a more explicitly Mozambican modern ghost story registered Mozambique's capitalist restoration of that period. The main case study, Couto's 'A História dos Aparecidos' ['The Tale of two Apparitions'], is followed by short readings of several Mozambican modern ghost stories. Chapter 5 claims that the Mozambican modern ghost story re-emerged in the first decade of the twenty-first century, and registered primitive accumulation as mediated by the globalization and world-literature debates. Using the example of Couto's *O Outro Pé da Sereia* (2006), it shows how genre traditions are modified in this period by drawing on narrative strategies of globalization.

With a scope of these proportions, some aspects are emphasized and others will inevitably get lost. This unsettling thought is eased only by the awareness of all the outstanding work being done on Mozambican literature. This book aims to be a minor contribution to the field.

Acknowledgements

This study was initially conducted as doctoral research in the context of the Deutsche Forschungsgemeinschaft (DFG) research and training group, 'Globalization and Literature: Representations, Transformations, Interventions', at the University of Munich (LMU). Robert Stockhammer led this group and Tobias Döring was its co-speaker and part of the thesis committee. Their support made this book possible, and I am grateful for it. My colleagues and friends in the research group, as well as my 'confriends' in Lusophone studies, advised me on numerous occasions, and I am thankful to them. I thank Nathaniel Ngomane, for making me feel at home in Maputo and its libraries, and Livia Apa, whom I have never met but who introduced me to the work of Aníbal Aleluia. Andrés Romero Jodar generously read an early version of the thesis, and Babs Paz consistently provided the much-needed structure to continue the project, even after the PhD period. Natalya Bekhta and Gero Guttzeit edited an earlier version of Chapter 2 for the journal *Anglistik*, and their advice improved the text considerably. Vera Peixoto generously helped me out with some translation problems I had. Hrvoje Tutek and Jernej Habjan changed the way I understand literature. Their friendship and knowledge helped make this book into what it is today. Paulo de Medeiros has supported me from the day I entered university. The direction he provided, even long after both of us had left Utrecht University, has decisively determined the work I have done and am doing. I cannot thank him enough. While revising this book, I started working at the University of Erlangen-Nuremberg, where Heike Paul, Katharina Gerund and Stephen Koetzing welcomed me even before I joined their department. I learned much from them, and this book is better than it was because of them. I am forever indebted to Bani L. Dodor and Iris U. S. Divé for their tolerance, patience and comradeship.

Of course, all flaws are my own, and I look forward to learning from them.

xiv

Acknowledgements

Chapter 2 is an expansion and modification of my previous publication. Universitätsverlag Winter GmbH granted me non-exclusive permission to reprint it here. The initial bibliographical reference is: Maurits, Peter J., '(Haunted) Cosmopolitan Spaces: World-Literature, the Modern Ghost Story, and the Structure of Debt', in Heinz Antor and Julia Hoydis (eds), *Anglistik: International Journal of English Studies* 30/3 (Heidelberg: Universitätsverlag Winter, 2019), 57–72.

CHAPTER I

Thesis and terms

Notable of literary works in which the supernatural plays a central role is that scholars often approach them differently when they are produced by African authors. This is understandable in part because of the necessity to historicize but may lead to confusions. 'Madhaianhoca', the opening story of Aníbal Aleluia's short story collection *Contos do Fantástico* (2011 [1988]), illustrates this well. Its narrator recalls the bloody Battle of Chicungussa and articulates that, in the present of the story, the battle's beating drums and rattling maracas are still heard at the site of the conflict, because those who died return to dominate those they conquered and to take revenge on those who mistreated them in life.

Two characters, Portuguese settler colonialists called administrator and secretary, are sceptical of the supernatural phenomenon and a 'régulo' [local leader] invites them on a trip to witness it for themselves (16). During the trip, the administrator asks the secretary if he believes the stories to be true and the latter answers denigratingly that

> [c]laro que não. Quem não conhece a mentalidade supersticiosa do preto? Eles inventam estas histórias porque aqui morreu muita gente no século passado. Para eles, onde morreu alguém é um lugar mistérioso. (Aleluia 2011: 16)
>
> [of course not. Isn't the superstitious mentality of Negroes well known? They invent these stories because, a century ago, many people died here. For them, a place where someone died is mysterious.]

The trio arrives at its destination, hears nothing, and the Portuguese hoot and declare the locals crazy. The régulo is hurt but inspirits when he hears the distant sound of maracas. The Portuguese continue their mocking and opprobriously ask him, 'não conheces a cigarra africana, régulo' [don't you recognize the African cicada, régulo]? Yet the sound amplifies and even the secretary has to admit that they are dealing with a 'mistério' [mystery] (17). The administrator, however, does not budge. This is not a 'mistério' or 'milagre' [miracle] he scoffs. It is an 'acusma' [acousma], a 'sugestão auditiva colectiva' [collective auditory hallucination] (18).

The residents of the nearby village laugh at the 'incongruência' [incongruence] and the 'mera hipocrisia' [mere hypocrisy] of the two 'brancos' [Whites], who believe in 'seres alados que conviviam com Deus' [winged creatures who live with God], and in 'anjos que ninguém jamais viu ou ouviu' [angels who no one has ever seen or heard], but who 'negavam a realidade dos *sicuembos* [spirits] que se faziam ouvir nitidamente' [deny the reality of the *sicuembos*, which clearly make themselves heard] (18–19). The villagers have no such doubts. They believe in the existence of 'fantasmas e bruxos, de curandeiros e mau olhado, de vacinas contra serpentes' [ghosts and warlocks, healers and the evil eye, vaccines against snakes], and so on (19).

The villagers comment specifically on the colonial racism of the Portuguese characters; the position that structurally similar beliefs are inferior based on those who hold them. Yet the argument that they and thus the story put forward has implications beyond the diegetic world and on the level of literature. 'Madhaianhoca' uses the trope of the haunted location resulting from unnatural death, a narrative device that the secretary foregrounds by ridiculing it intradiegetically. However, this trope is also common to Portuguese, and European more generally, folklore and literature, and specifically to the genre of the ghost story. It even appears in one of the most iconic Portuguese novels of the nineteenth century, Eça de Queiroz' 1875 *O Crime do Padre Amaro* [The Crime of Padre Amaro], in the form of a nun who died of heartbreak and who on 'certas noites' [certain nights] roams the corridors of the Aveiro convent screaming 'Augusto! Augusto!' (1912: 83). A narrator in Hugo Rocha's 1969 *Histórias Fantasmagóricas* [Ghost Stories] writes that abandoned houses in which 'alguém morreu em circumstâncias anormais' [someone died under abnormal circumstances] are haunted (125). The chamber in Walter Scott's

'The Tapestried Chamber' is haunted because 'in yon fatal apartment incest and unnatural murder were committed' (Scott 1900: 45).

Scholars generally do not consider 'Madhaianhoca' a ghost story, which is understandable for the same reason that De Queiroz' *Padre* is not argued to be one: the haunted location trope is not determinative of the plot. Yet even 'Um Pequeno em Chibuto' ['A Kid in Chibuto'], a short story that appears later in Aleluia's collection, is not considered a ghost story, although its plot of a house that is haunted because it is built on a 'cemitério' [cemetery] is archetypal of that genre (Aleluia 2011: 37).

At the very least, then, *Fantástico* raises questions about the ghost story genre in the context of Mozambican literature: are there Mozambican ghost stories, when are they published, how did they take shape? These questions motivate this book and lead to its main thesis.

Thesis and overview

The main thesis of this book is *there exists a Mozambican modern ghost story and it registers primitive accumulation*. In brief, this book shows how a modern ghost story, which complexly registers the British 1825 financial crisis, takes shape in the early nineteenth century. The form circulates throughout the world-literary system, including Mozambique, where Gothic literature is already published in the late nineteenth century and where a first Mozambican modern ghost story, which registers the transition to colonial capitalism, is published in 1960. The modern ghost story genre then disappears but re-emerges in the 1980s, registering Mozambique's post-independence capitalist restoration. It disappears again at the beginning of the 1990s and reappears in 2006, registering now the same and arguably ongoing capitalist restoration, but now mediated by debates on globalization and world-literature.

Before unpacking this, it is first necessary to elucidate the different terms that make up the main thesis of this book, which is the task of this chapter. In brief, this chapter explicates how modernity is understood relative to capitalism, that primitive accumulation is understood as the recurring and continuing 'original sin' of capitalism and that register signifies the relation between literary form and social reality. For its understanding of the modern ghost story, it draws on a tradition of scholarship that started in the nineteenth century to argue that, rather than any work with spirits or ghostly figures, the genre consists of a set of formal conventions and is distinct from supernatural predecessors, such as the Gothic novel. The genre has an important point of beginning in Britain but circulated throughout the world-literary system, during which its conventions modified as a result of interaction with local materials and forms.

Modernity

'The problem of modernity is the focal issue, the problem *par excellence* of contemporary social theory', writes Heller in 1984 (44). While there is a consensus that a 'new type of society was born' around the time of the French Revolution, she argues – which was dynamic, future oriented and based on economic expansion, industrialization and science rather than religion, and in which traditions disappear and are destroyed or created – there is significant disagreement on how to explain these issues (Heller 1984: 44–5). Almost forty years later, no consensus has formed on how to conceptualize 'modernity'. Prominently, the term is used in- and outside the academy to signal contemporaneity or technological progress, to contrast with the perceived traditional or primitive past and, perhaps most importantly, to signify modernization.

The vastness of modernity debates precludes an exhaustive discussion of the term. Instead, it must suffice to say that this study understands, with Wallerstein, 'modernity' as having emerged around the time of the French Revolution. This did not occur in a vacuum but was 'connected with and stimulated struggles for liberation of various kinds and nascent nationalisms throughout Europe and around its edges – from Ireland to Russia, from Spain to Egypt' and Haiti (Wallerstein 1995: 473). Importantly, it could thus consolidate the 'geoculture' that was necessary to 'sustain and reinforce' the capitalist world economy, which had been emerging since the

Thesis and terms 5

middle of the fifteenth century (Wallerstein 1995: 473). Hence, as Jameson has argued, 'the only satisfactory semantic meaning of modernity lies in its association with capitalism' (Jameson 2002: 13).

It is essential to such a conception of modernity that there is one modernity rather than a plurality of modernities, as Neil Lazarus and Crystal Bartolovich (relying on the work of Harry Harootunian) argue. The latter proposed that 'modernization [...] has obscured [...] the idea of modernity as a specific cultural form and a consciousness of lived historical time that differs according to social forms and practices' (2000: 62). In other words, he argues, there are 'differing inflections of the modern', which is to say:

> not alternative modernities but coeval or, better yet, peripheral modernities (as long as peripheral is understood only as a relationship to the centers of capitalism before World War II), in which all societies shared a common reference provided by global capital and its requirements. Each society, however, differed according to specific times and places, the 'not quite the same'. (Capitalism always differed wherever it established its regime, despite the putative similarity of its procedures and processes.) In this regard, modernity provided a framework of temporal imminence in which to locate all societies. (Harootunian 2000: 62–3)

For Harootunian, then, modernity is 'driven by the desiring machine of capitalism [...] everywhere' (63). Elaborating on Harootunian's claims, Lazarus and Bartolovich (2002) write that modernity is usually and 'erroneously' understood as a '"cultural" dilemma', grasped in terms of 'Westernization', which facilitates notions of alternative modernities (15). For them, however, 'modernity and capitalism are inextricably bound up with each other in the world as we, collectively – though heterogeneously – live it' (15). Modernity is, in Jameson's terms, *singular* (Jameson 2002), even though it is constituted through 'uneven and combined development' (Lazarus and Bartolovich 2002: 10).

Warwick Research Collective (WReC) later reformulated this; modernity for them – as for this book – refers to 'the way in which capitalism is "lived" – wherever in the world-system it is lived – [and not to] "however a society develops"' (WReC 2015: 24). Consequently, the modern ghost story thus registers an aspect of the capitalist world-system.

6   CHAPTER I

Primitive accumulation

The aspect of modernity that the modern ghost story registers, according
to this book, is primitive accumulation. Having explained how capital
creates surplus value, and how surplus value subsequently creates capital,
Marx points to a problem. This 'whole movement', he writes,

> seems to turn in a vicious circle, out of which we can only get by supposing a primi-
> tive accumulation [...] preceding capitalist accumulation; an accumulation not the
> result of the capitalist mode of production, but its starting-point. (Marx 2008a: 363)

He continues that this primitive accumulation plays 'in Political Economy
about the same part as original sin in theology'; that is, an 'anecdote of
the past', in which there were two types of people: intelligent and non-
intelligent. According to this narrative, the latter – branded as 'lazy' –
were passive, while the former accumulated wealth, which supposedly
explains the capital/labour contradiction under capitalism (2008a: 363).
Marx emphasizes that this narrative does not conform to historical truth;
in 'actual history', he writes, 'it is notorious that conquest, enslavement,
robbery, murder, briefly force, play the great part' in starting the cycle
of capitalist accumulation (364). When a capitalist system emerges, with
its separation (but unity) of capital(ist) and labour(er) – those who own
the modes of production and those who must sell their labour power to
reproduce themselves – capitalism not only maintains this separation
but also 'reproduces it on a continually extending scale' (364). For Marx,
primitive accumulation is thus

> nothing else than the historical process of divorcing the producer from the means
> of production [...], those moments when great masses of men are suddenly and
> forcibly torn from their means of subsistence, and hurled as free and 'unattached'
> proletarians on the labour-market. (364–5)

For Marx, primitive accumulation thus involves the 'expropriation' of
those who still own the means of subsistence.

Primitive accumulation does not occur just once. Marx vaguely addresses this when speaking of the 1848 revolution in France which, he

Thesis and terms 7

wrote, 'moves in a descending line. It finds itself in this state of retrogressive motion' (2008b: 43). Lenin more clearly warned, after the October Revolution, how 'the capitalists may return to Russia and may grow stronger than we are [because] there is a firmer economic basis for capitalism in Russia than for communism. That must be borne in mind' (2014: 564). Lenin was right, of course, and Esherick, with the power of hindsight, discusses that the 'restoration of capitalism' indeed occurred in 'Yugoslavia, in the Soviet Union, and [...] in China' (Esherick 1979: 41) and, as this book shows, in Mozambique. More broadly, Federici (2017) states that the process of primitive accumulation is thus 'not a one-time historical event confined to the origins of capitalism', the point of departure of 'accumulation proper', but rather an 'eternally recurrent' aspect of the capitalist system of production, which is 'always contemporaneous with its expansion'.

In line with this, Arendt illustrates the recurrence of primitive accumulation using the example of British imperialism. In the 1860s and 1870s, she writes, Britain dealt with a depression that resulted from the 'overproduction of capital' (1976: 148). Consequently, capitalists were forced to realize

> for the first time that the original sin of simple robbery, which centuries ago had made possible 'the original accumulation of capital' (Marx) and had started all further accumulation, had eventually to be repeated lest the motor of accumulation suddenly die down. (Arendt 1976: 148)

The laws of their 'production system', capitalists understood, 'from the beginning had been calculated for the whole earth', and to prevent a 'catastrophic breakdown' it was necessary to export capital from Britain, which lacked raw materials and had a saturated home market (Arendt 148–9). Harvey, building on Arendt and Luxemburg and making a parallel to his contemporaneity, argues that primitive accumulation is still a 'continuing force' in the world-system (Harvey 2003: 143). He emphasizes that primitive accumulation also includes the commodification and privatization of public sectors and land, and the 'conversion of various forms of property rights (common, collective, state, etc.) into exclusive private property rights' (2003: 145). Making the parallel explicit, he adds that the 'scenario' Arendt describes 'sounds all too familiar given the experience of the 1980s and 1990s' (Harvey 2003: 145).

8 CHAPTER I

This book, then, understands primitive accumulation as the process that occurs with capitalist expansion and that can be a continuing force. Chapter 2 deals with this process as a continuing force in early nineteenth-century Britain, which eventually affects publishing; Chapter 3 with the incorporation of the Portuguese colonial system into the capitalist world-system in the late nineteenth century; and Chapters 4 and 5 with the primitive accumulation of the 1980s and 1990s in the form of Mozambique's capitalist restoration.

Register

The social realm does not express itself in literary form in an unmediated way. This book understands this relation of mediation as 'registering', a term it borrows from the WReC's 2015 landmark publication on world-literature. Scholars have understood the relation between the literary and the social in vastly different and contradictory ways. One theoretical approach used the concept of *reflection*, and Dasgupta argued of Lenin – while admitting that it 'would be useless to look for a consistent system of literary criticism or of aesthetics' in Lenin's work – that 'art [for Lenin was] a reflection of the whole of objective reality' (1970: 22). Macherey and Lanser complicated this idea by arguing that art functions as a mirror, or reflects, only in the way that ideology does (1976: 14–15). Bakhtin (2008) prefers the term *refraction* – a distortion that mediates the text to the reader as water distorts rays of light – and Spivak, similarly, argues that 'the line between aesthetics and politics is neither firm nor straight' (2013: 67).

In the wake of such accounts, critics suggested that – rather than reflect, or even refract – literature processes, produces, shapes or labours works from the raw materials of social or lived experience, which are, in turn, shaped by the social relations of their context (e.g. Hartley 2017). Eagleton attempted to clarify this using the analogy of automobile production, arguing that, although a car is made from certain raw materials, it is 'clearly more than a reflection' of those materials (2002: 48); rather, the 'car reproduces the materials of which it is built' (2002: 48).

Thesis and terms 9

Eagleton's imagery is usefully clear, yet the term 'reproduction' may suggest a larger intactness and directness of conveyance of these raw materials than is accurate. The WReC circumvents such issues. They suggest that literary forms are 'mediations or formally encoded registrations of the "lived experience of capitalism's bewildering creative destruction (or destructive creation)"', and they use 'registration' to discuss this 'relation between literary form and social reality' (2016: 544). Emphasizing the 'complexity and intricacy' of the term 'register', they argue it includes the 'difficult Schwarzian understanding of literary form as "the abstract of social relationships"', as well as Adorno's argument that there is

> no content, no formal category of the literary work that does not, however transformed and however awarely, derive from the empirical reality from which it has escaped. It is through this relationship, and through the process of regrouping its moments in terms of its formal law, that literature relates to reality. (WReC 2016: 545)

Avoiding accusations of positivism, the WReC emphasizes how this process of understanding registration is an ever 'unfinished and open-ended process of disclosing and interpreting what perpetually remains "still-to-be-known" in a literary work' (2016: 545). In short, for them, there exists a 'single, but radically uneven world-system; a singular modernity, combined and uneven; and a literature that variously registers this combined unevenness in both its form and content to reveal itself as, properly speaking, world-literature' (WReC 2016: 535).

It is in this sense of the term 'register' – as a mediation between literary form and social realm – that this book argues the modern ghost story 'registers' primitive accumulation.

The ghost story

There are competing ways of understanding the central category of this book: the modern ghost story. It is therefore necessary to delineate the most consequential understandings at some length. Most important, in this context, are conceptions of the modern ghost story as omnipresent,

10   CHAPTER I

particularly modern and defined by a ghostly presence. The remainder of
this chapter addresses these issues and discusses how this literary form
circulates and adapts. Finally, the chapter distinguishes between the
modern ghost story tradition, on the one hand, and the supernatural traditions of what will be called the *traditional field*, on the other.

The omnipresence thesis

If Aleluia's 'Madhaianhoca' presents the opportunity to examine a part
of Mozambican literature in light of a supernatural tradition that is not
exclusively national, despite its unmistakably Mozambican elements,
Aleluia's preface of *Contos* even more explicitly invites doing so. Starting
from a description of the ritual of providing food for a deceased person
in his own village – a decidedly 'local' tradition of the Linga-Linga pen-
insula – the introduction explains how that tradition has been inflected
by various elements. Influential, Aleluia argues, are '[o] Cristianismo'
[Christianity], which arrived in the region in the sixteenth century, 'sete
séculos de proselitismo islâmico' [seven centuries of Islamic proselytism]
and 'muitos séculos' [many centuries] of interaction with people from the
east of the Indian Ocean (6). He continues to enumerate Luther, Zoroas-
trianism, Saint Paul, Moses, Mozambican medicine men, theosophy and
psychopathology as important for the ghost stories and (extra-literary)
practices that involve ghost figures (6–12). In his view, a 'universal' notion underpins these and all other supernatural traditions: the existence
of a 'duplo em cada homem' [double in every human], from which 'deriva
a crença em anjos, demónios, génios e fantasmas' [the belief in angels,
demons, genies and ghosts is derived] (6–7).

Aleluia consciously inscribes his work into what he considers a universal and supranational tradition.[1] He also participates, arguably uncon-
sciously, in what this chapter calls the *omnipresence thesis* of the ghost

---

1   The full extent to which the book is inscribed in a literary ecology that is not ex-
     clusively national cannot be addressed here; it is worth noting, however, that it
     opens with an epigraph by Aldous Huxley.

story. This thesis has formed a standard part of ghost-story debates for at least four generations of ghost-story scholars, and posits that the genre has existed for an exceptionally long time – possibly even since the beginning of humanity. Scarborough, 'pioneer of the [ghost story] genre' (Sullivan 1978: 32), popularized the omnipresence thesis in her milestone study on the ghost story, published just after the end of the genre's so-called golden age (1880–1914). She writes that the 'supernatural is an ever-present force in literature' (1917: 15) and that the ghost is 'absolutely indestructible' (95), as it appears to be 'unapologetically at home in twentieth-century fiction [as well as] in classical mythology, Christian hagiology, medieval legend, or Gothic Romance' (81). Although Scarborough's focus is the Anglophone realm, the ghost, for her, is therefore the 'permanent citizen of the world' (81). Later, Penzoldt claims that the 'ghost […] appears from the beginning of literature' and references the first book of Samuel, Homer's *Odyssey*, Pliny the Younger's haunted-house ghost story and Lucian's haunted-house stories before also turning to British fiction (1952: 32). Hugo Rocha writes that the 'histórias de fantasmas' [ghost stories] are encountered in the 'Biblia, nas grandes epopeias homéricas, em Plínio o Moço' [Bible, the great Homeric epics, in Pliny the Younger] (1969: 18). Briggs writes that ghost stories are 'as old and older than literature' before she turns to Anglophone literature (1977: 25). Wolfreys claims 'ghosts are always with us, and perhaps now more than ever before', and subsequently turns to Anglophone works (2001: 1).

The omnipresence thesis creates several problems, which Aleluia does not fully escape. In this context, it is clarifying to ask what its function is, particularly because its utterance is almost invariably followed by discussions of modern, predominantly British or Anglophone fiction. A possible answer is found in the ghost-story collection of Casares, which formulates the omnipresence thesis as follows: 'las ficciones fantásticas son anteriores a las letras. Los aparecidos pueblan todas las literaturas: están en *el Zendavesta*, en *la Biblia*, en *Homero*, en *Las Mil y una Noches*' [fantastic fictions precede literature. Apparitions populate all the literatures of the world: *The Zendavesta*, *The Bible*, Homer, and *Arabian Nights*] (1940: 5). Casares classifies this narrative of the omnipresence thesis as background 'history' for the stories in his collection (1940: 5). Yet this possible aim of providing a historical account is in stark contrast with the amount of time

12   CHAPTER I

and lack of sources spend on the omnipresence thesis (5). In her book on
ghost stories in Antiquity, Felton argued that only 'few specific studies of
ancient ghost stories exist' (1999: 1),[2] and it could be added that those that
do exist are seldom cited. Characteristically, Casares – like Scarborough,
Penzoldt, Briggs and Wolfreys – narrates the omnipresence thesis and
dedicates eleven more quick sentences to the possible itinerary of the ghost
story before it appears 'en el idioma inglés' [in the English language] in the
fourteenth century, after which 200 pages of almost exclusively modern
works follow (Casares 1940: 5).

A first problem of the omnipresence thesis, then, is that ghost-story
scholars *understate* their case with a focus on the modern – or even the
modern Anglophone – realm. Their scope could be widened – and increasingly has been since the 2010s – by adding ghost stories from almost
all of what, in retrospect, can be called literatures: along synchronic and
diachronic axes, including the modern and premodern, stretching from
Japanese ghost stories (Drazen 2011) to the Egyptian folkloric tale of
Nebusemekh (Bunson 2002), from North American and Australian Indigenous ghost stories (Boyd and Thrush 2011; Borwein 2018) to the Per-
sian epic of *Gilgamesh* (George 2003). It is possible to consider these stories
generically related through narrative devices, motifs and plots. For example,
the film *American Haunting* (Solomon 2005), the story of Nebusemekh,
Elpenor's return in the *Odyssey* (Homer 1871: 270–1), Patroclus' return in
the *Iliad* (Homer 1851: 418) and Aleluia's 'Madhaianhoca', to name just
a few, all concern improper burial and the restless deceased. Motifs like
the haunted property/mansion, and the use of the narrative device of suspense, as Felton shows, can be traced back to at least Pliny the Younger's
Letters (Felton 38), and have remained prominent in ghost stories ever
since (including in Aleluia's *Contos*). The motif of the cold gust of air an-
nouncing the ghost's presence, which is found in *Gilgamesh* (relative to
Enkidu's ghost), also plays a prominent role in blockbuster film *The Sixth
Sense* (Shyamalan 1999).

2   Another option would be that it is, in fact, a justification of the use of the ghost
     story – a form which has been perceived as non-literary, as genre fiction – as pri-
     mary material. This approach strikes me as self-defeating, as the act of justification
     justifies the perceived demand for justification.

Thesis and terms   13

A second problem of the omnipresence thesis, however, is that ghost-story scholars *overstate* their case, relying on the ideological construct of so-called 'Western civilization', which is supposedly rooted in Greek (or even Mesopotamian) civilizations and from which a direct line can supposedly be drawn to the British, and later US-American, empires (Aleluia only rewrites this to a certain extent). It might thus appear that a direct line can also be drawn from *Gilgamesh*, through Pliny the Younger, all the way to contemporary ghost-story films, which might lead to the idea that, in Smajić's formulation, the 'study of ghosts and stories about them can (and perhaps should) escalate into a project with an ever-retreating horizon' (2010: 13). Such an ever-retreating horizon might produce knowledge about the 'coincident beliefs or delusions' of mankind over time (Lang 1885: 624) and insights into the way literary form inherits into later literary works. As Felton has demonstrated, 'some of the best ghost story writers [...] had traditional classical educations and had probably read Pliny in the original Latin' (Felton 111). However, it also creates the risks of being ahistorical; as Lazarus has argued in a different context, the 'radically continuist' argument in which 'Europe' is a 5,000-year-old civilizational unit (2011: 9) 'flatten[s] out history, [thus] failing to register the necessary distinctions between qualitatively different moments, epochs and determinate universes of meaning' (2011: 15).

If a work of literature results from the raw materials of social or lived experience, which are shaped in turn by the social relations of their context, which it thus registers, it would follow that ghost stories differ during different epochs. Expectedly, Bown, Burdett and Thurschwell argue that the ghost story 'signif[ies] differently at different historical moments' (12), Hay argues that the 'the ghost story changes over time' (2011: 21) and even Smajić acknowledges that ghost stories can be identified as the 'expression of culturally and historically specific concerns, beliefs, or values' (2010: 13). The radical continuism of the omnipresence thesis disavows this; the differences in form, signification and so on are lost in an ever-retreating horizon. Because this book claims there is a specificity to the modern ghost story due to its situatedness within modernity, it rejects the omnipresence thesis, at least in part. This, then, necessitates further outlining how the modern ghost story *is* understood.

14   CHAPTER I

The modern ghost story

Debates on the modern ghost story unfold over more than two centuries
and have at least three recurring aspects: the distinction from the preceding Gothic genres, the emphasis on the ghost story as literary form
and the reliance on (changing) conceptions of modernity. Walter Scott's
'On the Supernatural in Fictitious Composition' (1827) is arguably the
first theorization of the genre. It outlines how there is a clear formal break
between the modern ghost story and its predecessors, most immediately
the Gothic novel and the Gothic romance. Scott, whose experience of
modernity was influenced by the end of (some) oppressive regimes and
the rise in dominance of (liberal) capitalist ones,[3] stipulates that, unlike
in the Gothic novel, where exaggerated ghosts appear throughout the
narrative, in the modern ghost story the appearance of the ghost should
be restricted, and the

> exhibition of supernatural appearances in fictitious narrative ought to be rare, brief,
> indistinct, and such as may become a being to us so incomprehensible, and so dif-
> ferent from ourselves, of whom we cannot justly conjecture whence he comes, or
> for what purpose, and of whose attributes we can have no regular or distinct per-
> ception. (Scott 1827: 64)

In contrast to the talkative Gothic supernatural creatures (Scarborough
97), Scott has 'great doubts' about whether it is 'wise' for an author to
'permit [...] his goblin to speak at all' (Scott 1827: 60). The supernatural,
he continues, is 'of a character which is extremely difficult to sustain' and,
in order for 'modern authors' not to 'exhaust' it, the 'imagination of the
reader is to be excited if possible, without being gratified' (60–4).

Scott's article, cited much less often in modern ghost story scholarship than one might expect, is essential for twentieth-century ghost-story
scholars – even though their conception of modernity, and thus the modern
ghost story, is inflected by their acute present and, particularly, by the

---

3   For a detailed discussion of Scott's supernatural works, see Chapter 2 of this book.
     For an account of Scott and modernity, see Lincoln (2007).

Thesis and terms

modernization theory of modernity (cf. Wallerstein 1995). Scarborough argues, for example, that the modern ghost story tradition is distinct from its earlier counterparts, such as the 'Gothic romance' (1917: 6), because in 'modernity' supernatural figures are more terrifying as well as more humorous (72). For her, 'modern' ghost story plots are deeply grounded in the development of science and technology (73), which can be 'more marvelous than the imagined. [...] Dante would write a new *Inferno* if he could see the subway at rush hour' (3–4). Van Doren Stern claims the modern ghost story results from the shift from 'ancient ways of thinking' to a 'fierce, new technological civilization' – including the replacement of the 'horse' by the 'automobile', the invention of the aeroplane, and so on – and that technology seemed to bring 'horrors of its own' (1947: xvi–xvii). Penzoldt says the modern ghost story 'must be treated as a separate genre' because 'Gothic novelists [...] exaggerated in their use of ghosts and other apparitions' (1952: 13) and, following Weber's notion of *disenchantment*, that the genre is a remnant of 'ancient [...] beliefs' that, although 'modern man disavows' those 'superstition[s]', are still expressed in the ghost story (6). For him, the modern ghost story is ultimately a specific set of conventions that includes titles, motifs and – arguably most importantly – a 'climax', as opposed to a 'plot', in the form of the apparition for which the entire story prepares (13–28). Briggs says the modern ghost story serves to 'exorcize, in controlled circumstances, fears which in solitude or darkness might become unmanageable', including technological developments (1977: 11). Emphasizing the importance of form, she shows the genre does not rely on the ghost figure but can evolve around 'possession and demonic bargains, spirits other than those of the dead, including ghouls, vampires, werewolves, the "swarths" of living men and the "ghost-soul" or Doppelgänger' (12). Penzoldt also includes such creations in his definition, and both echo Scott's use of 'goblin'. Briggs explicates that these creatures are 'generically related' through the formal conventions of 'suspense and the unknown' and their 'common intention of inducing fear by the use of the supernatural' (13). Finally, Sullivan argues that the modern ghost story occurs 'when things appear to be falling apart' (1978: 3), which he connects to the climactic structure, 'the sense of a gradual building of uncontainable forces' (3). In a variation of Briggs's argument on form, he writes that 'even stories where we never see a ghost' can be ghost stories (9). Finally, he suggests that there is '[r]arely [...] an end of it'; that is, the genre resists narrative closure (3).

Modern ghost-story scholars, despite their conceptions of the genre, have thus understood the genre as a set of conventions – rather than a narrative form pivoting on the figure of the ghost – which is distinct from the preceding, more exaggerated genres of the Gothic romance/novel, and which is somehow connected to, or thematizes, the social transition to modernity. Scholarship of the genre changed in the twenty-first century under the influence of the emergence of cultural, gender, postcolonial and similar studies – and, most importantly (as unpacked further below), in the wake of Jacques Derrida's 1993 *Specters of Marx* (henceforth *Specters*). Hay's study on the modern ghost story, however, rather than departing from nineteenth- and twentieth-century scholarship, builds on it and refines and explicates some of its arguments.[4] Three aspects of his study are particularly important in the context of this book.

First, Hay – although not specifying this as such – notices the prominence of transition in nineteenth- and twentieth-century modern ghost-story scholarship, and posits it as the genre's most important aspect. For him, the genre as a whole can be read as 'the traumatic transition [...] from feudalism to capitalism lived out over and over again' (Hay 2011: 2).

Second, Hay provides a periodization within the modern ghost-story genre. Starting from Scott – for Hay, the first modern ghost-story author – he characterizes the first modern ghost stories as failed modernity narratives: a narrative concerned with (not) being modern (enough), a specifically modern concern. Hay explains how, in modernity, the past is generally experienced as distinct from the present, as no longer accessible; and yet, the past appears in the present. This double relationship to the past is 'complexly up for grabs' in the ghost story, which, for him, demonstrates a kinship with the historical novel because both 'stage history for us by bringing the dead before us as a spectacle' (Hay 29). However, where the inability to separate the inaccessible past from the present appears as nostalgia in the historical novel, in the modern ghost story it takes on

---

4   Arguably, like the current study, Hay's work must nevertheless be seen in the context of *Specters*.

Thesis and terms 17

the form of horror. A brief look at Scott's 1829 'The Tapestried Chamber' shows how convincing this argument is. The story is set in a landscape with only 'few marks of modern improvement' (Scott 1900: 34); the castle has a 'modern Gothic lodge' (36) and its haunted chamber is devoid of 'modern habits' (38). The failure to be modern thus structures the narrative from its outermost layers to its innermost chambers, where it explodes as haunting, as horror. Importantly, Hay argues, even though the ghost story maintains the same general characteristics, over time, as the genre travels, the historical novel connection is lost and the genre becomes associated with realism (for him, following Lukács, the mapping of social totality), naturalism (around 1880) and finally so-called magical realism. Thus, Hay shows the genre is both coherent and changes over time.

Third, like nineteenth- and twentieth-century scholars, Hay insists that to understand the genre scholars must pay attention to its form: its 'structural logic' (2). He adds five aspects to those mentioned above: (a) Ghost stories deal with issues with the law and, because lawyers can erase the past, they are in his view 'indistinguishable from an exorcist' (3); (b) Something returns – often something traumatic that has not been worked through – and he stresses his understanding of 'trauma as social' and 'historical' rather than 'psychoanalytical' (4–6)[5]; (c) '[M]odern ghost stories are fundamentally narratives of class identity' (see also Dickerson 1996; Lynch 2004), which may take shape as conflicts around private property, attitudes towards servants and so on (Hay 2011: 8, see also chapter two of this book on 'Green Tea'); (d) Ghost stories are connected to empire; and (e) The modern ghost story 'negotiates in its narrative the contradiction between

---

5   The Freudian understanding of the modern ghost story is among the most prominent. However, Mark Edmundson showed that, for Freud, 'the psyche, however else he may describe it, is centrally the haunted house of terror Gothic. Freud's remarkable achievement is to have taken the props and passions of terror Gothic – hero-villain, heroine, terrible place, haunting – and to have relocated them inside the self' (32; see also Castle 1995: 175). Hay therefore says that using Freud's theory of the psyche – which is modelled on the ghost story – to explain the ghost story would be a 'circularity that will get us nowhere' (Hay 5). Of course, it may be that authors writing after Freud were influenced by the psychoanalytical haunted-house trope (and the associated concept of the uncanny).

the [...] two relationships with the past, questioning how the present inherits that past, how it relates to it, how it follows from that past, how we get from there to here' (15). Learning to read the ghost story, he argues, is thus learning to 'see objects as characterized not just by their physical characteristics, but rather as embedded in social and historical relations' (17).

Hay's resituating of nineteenth- and twentieth-century ghost-story scholarship is convincing but leaves unanswered the question of why the modern ghost story keeps re-emerging – why is what he calls the traumatic transition from feudalism to capitalism lived out in modern ghost stories over and again, at what periods and why then? Shapiro addresses these questions, asking: 'If everyday life in capitalist societies is a ghoulish hell, why do generic inscriptions of Gothic narratives and devices tend to re-emerge [...] at certain discrete periods[?]' (2008: 30). Based on the date of the highest density of Gothic works, he observes that the Gothic occurs in moments when capitalism divorces labourers from those means of production 'that might sustain them outside of or in tension with a system that produces commodities only for their profit-generating potential' (30). Moreover, he argues, '[h]eightened supernaturalism' not only 'emerges as a cultural marker of a region's initial appropriation by liberal political economy' but also 'reappears with each new turn of the screw' – when a further integration of a region into the capitalist world-system occurs (32). For him, this is the case because, in those 'conjunctural moments, capitalism's gruesome nature is most sensationally revealed' (44).

Shapiro writes about the Gothic in general, of which the modern ghost story is a sub-genre.[6] His claim is important here because it shows the ghost story re-emerges specifically when humans are separated from their means of subsistence and are created as wage labourers. In different terms, for Shapiro the ghost story (re-)emerges with primitive accumulation, the incorporation into capitalism or the further integration – the 'continuing force', in Harvey's words (2003: 143) – into that system. This book maintains that Hay and Shapiro can best be understood in conjunction – the ghost story re-emerges in different moments and plays out the traumatic

---

6 'The ghost story is in all sorts of ways a sub-genre of the gothic [...] a paradigmatic gothic narrative' (Hay 2011: 23).

Thesis and terms 19

transition to capitalism over and again, certainly; but it particularly does so in the form of primitive accumulation, at moments in which primitive accumulation occurs in one of its forms. As will be discussed in the following chapters, the genre also *registers* primitive accumulation in ways not accounted for by either Hay or Shapiro. Before discussing this, however, it is necessary to specify further how the genre of the modern ghost story is understood – by indicating how it is *not* understood.

The influence of Specters of Marx

The publication of Derrida's *Specters of Marx* in 1993 was of paramount importance to the critical reception of the ghost story. Influenced, in all likeliness,[7] by Abraham and Torok's 'phantom' (1994) – defined as an inherited gap or secret that cannot be met with an 'aha-experience' because it does not originate in the subject[8] – Derrida's *Specters* develops a social critique of the post-Communist Bloc world. It proposes that such a critique must include a consideration of Marx, who, as Postone argues, has questionably 'been declared dead' by Derrida (Postone 1998: 370). Derrida therefore argues that the critique must be able to come to terms with death as a present entity, with that which goes beyond the 'existential opposition of being and non-being' (Postone 1998: 370) – it must be able to come to terms, or 'learn to live with', ghosts or spectres (Derrida 2006: xxvi). Central to *Specters* is the concept of the 'spectral', which can succinctly be circumscribed as 'what makes the present waver' (Jameson 1995: 85). A second central concept is that of 'hauntology', coined in opposition to 'ontology' to indicate that which undermines the certain,

---

7 According to some (Royle 1995, 2000; Davis 2007), although others question this assumption (Berthin 2010).

8 This also informed Lyotard's account of the ghost (Lyotard 1991: 2); for him, the figure of the ghost always haunts a totalizing system. Rabaté argues in a similar vein when he writes: 'We might say that "modern" philosophy has always attempted to bury [its] irrational Other in some neat crypt, forgetting that it would thereby lead to further ghostly reapparitions' (1996: xviii). For Derrida, too, the ghost is an unknown entity that always haunts hegemony (2006: 46).

known or knowable, and thus, that 'on which conceptuality can be build' (Jameson 1995: 86). In brief, according to Derrida, one must learn to live with this spectrality, this unknowability, because its exorcism would equate to the violent expulsion of that which is 'Other' (the spectral).

Specters is important in the context of this book because it influenced ghost-story scholarship in two main ways. First, Davis has argued that *Specters* 'spawned a minor academic industry' (2007: 10). As a part of this, the production of ghost-story scholarship appears to have increased significantly post-*Specters*,[9] even though it had been declared dead when Briggs claimed '[t]he ghost story [...] no longer has any capacity for growth or adaption' (1977: 44) and when Auerbach observed that 'serious scholarship' on the genre was 'surprisingly sparse' (2004: 278).

Second, *Specters* influenced the scholarly reception of the ghost story because the genre came to be read through the lens of *Specters*. 'Ghost' was increasingly used as a metaphor for any type of (what was considered to be) ghostly, haunting or absent presence, including traces of history in the present and even the non-totalizability of language, and was understood as inherently political in line with *Specters*. Further, the figure of the 'ghost, post-Derrida, [...] seemed to be transformed into a critically mobile figure whose presence helped to illuminate the complex origins and discrete political visions of a variety of intellectual contexts' (Smith 2010: 4–5). As a consequence, the modern ghost-story genre came to be understood as 'political' (which is to say, progressive), and a shift in focus occurred away from genre conventions and towards the 'ghostly', drastically opening up the genre. Illustratively, Siskind defines the ghost story as any text with a ghostly presence, which for him includes *The Bible*, *Hamlet* and *The Communist Manifesto* (not incidentally Derrida's case studies; Siskind 2012: 348). Warwick contends that the ghost story 'form escapes anything but the loosest definitions' (Warwick 2007: 29). Smith and Hughes affirm that 'an essential aspect of the [Victorian] Gothic form' is 'undecidability [...] the most Derridean of terms' (Smith and Hughes 2012: 1). Bergland even writes that '[a]ll stories are ghost stories, if only because each word [...] is

---

9   E.g. Brogan (1998); Smith (2010); Boyd and Thrush (2011); Bergland (2000); Rabaté (1996) and so on.

Thesis and terms

intended [...] to embody and to animate a strange imaginary entity that is both there and not there' (2000: 6). Wolfreys, driving this to its extreme, argues that 'all stories are, more or less, ghost stories' (Wolfreys 2001: 3).

Specters poses a number of problems for ghost-story scholarship as understood in this book (as is also illustrated in the section on the 'traditional field', below). First, objections were raised in line with the 'consensus' in the Derrida community on the 'thesis about radical atheism underlying Jacques Derrida's entire oeuvre' (Habjan 129). Although Derrida's 'spectral' emerges from a social critique aiming to 're-politicize' reading practices (Derrida 2006 [1993]: 94), '[a]ccording to this [radical atheism] thesis, Derrida's 1993 *Spectres de Marx* does not mark any ethical turn in late Derrida but remains faithful to early Derrida's deconstruction of presence' (Habjan 129). Similarly, the political charge ascribed to ghost stories (which now potentially include all stories, if Wolfreys is to be believed) is of dubitable nature. Particularly, if the figure of the ghost is equated with the so-called 'Other' – as *Specters* appears to allow, or even suggest – this does not have to signify, have consequences for and speak to (or about) the genre of the modern ghost story. On the one hand, as Jameson indicates, the spectre and the ghost are not the same figure. He writes that Derrida's ghosts and spectres

> are not the truly malevolent ghosts of the modern tradition [...] the archetypal spectres of sheer class *ressentiment* who are out to subvert the lineage of the masters and bind their children to the land of the dead, of those not merely deprived of wealth and power (or of their own labour-power), but even of life itself. [...] *Ressentiment* is the primal class passion, and [...] begins to govern the relations between the living and the dead. (Jameson 1995: 86)

In fact, if that which 'cannot [be] exorcize[d]' is the 'opposing class', as Jameson suggests (1995: 95), it could even be argued that reading it through a philosophy of 'learning to live with' ghosts equals or approaches reading it through a philosophy of the preservation, acceptance and smoothing out of the conflicts inherent to bourgeois class relations. To reformulate this in Lenin's terms, learning to live with ghosts might then be considered an attempt to 'reconcile' the 'irreconcilable' – which is to say, class antagonism (Lenin 2011: 10–11). To make this even more explicit, the unity of opposites of hauntee and haunter – which is central to the ghost story – may be understood in parallel to the unity of opposites of capital and labour – the central contradiction of the capitalist system of production. To abolish the power to haunt, which generates the need for exorcism, is to harmonize the revolutionary, to extinguish the incendiary. If it constitutes a political act then, far from being a so-called radical politics, it could be understood as the facilitation of class oppression. Understandably, then, Roger Luckhurst argues, in opposition to Derrida's notion of 'learning to live with' ghosts, that 'we *should* risk the violence of reading the ghost, of cracking open its absent presence to answer the demand of its specific symptomatology and its specific locale' (Luckhurst 542).

Luckhurst, on the other hand, hints at a second problem *Specters* poses in the context of this book. Nineteenth- and twentieth-century scholarship, despite the prominence of the omnipresence thesis, have convincingly demonstrated how the modern ghost story is distinct from its premodern predecessors, how it is determined predominantly by a set of formal characteristics and even that, due to this, it does not rely on a ghost figure. However, for *Specters*, any story with a ghostly figure is a ghost story. This trend, which Luckhurst even called the 'spectral turn', in effect escalates the omnipresence thesis (Luckhurst 527). Yet it also opens such studies up to the same critique of ahistoricism. Not incidentally, Jay argues that, 'in celebrating spectral returns as such, the precise content of *what* is repeated may get lost', and that hauntology, 'like ontology, is all but a unified phenomenon, meaning that one should distinguish within this spectral itself' (Jay 1998: 162). Bown, Burdett and Thurschwell also argued that *Specters*-influenced readings are 'evocative and generalizing' (2004: 12), and Luckhurst added that reading ghost stories through the lens of the spectral and hauntology disconnects 'ghosts' from their 'phantasmogenetic centres' – the places, causes and contexts that produce them, and of which they are a 'symptom' – which thus undermines their possible political potential (2002: 542). It could be added that 'spectral turn' readings of the ghost story not only erase the importance of form but also, at times, even deny there is such a thing as the form of the modern ghost story. They thus erase the genre tradition of the modern ghost story and the essential fact that it *signifies as a genre*. Derridean readings of the modern ghost story, hence, are trivial to this book at best.[10]

A travelling genre

The claim of this book is that there is a Mozambican modern ghost story, which participates in the tradition of the modern ghost story and thus in the way that tradition signifies, albeit in a manner deeply inflected by its specific position in the world-system. With Hay, this study argues that Scott's 'Highland Widow' constitutes the beginning of the modern ghost story – or rather *a* beginning; the search for absolute beginnings may be a useless endeavour, if only because, as Miles has shown, 'Scott manifestly has his precursors, including, if not beginning with, Walpole' (Miles 2002: 44). This, then, raises the question of how the form ended up in Mozambique.

---

10   This is not to say that analyses of the ghost-as-metaphor – and, by extension, the rhetorical or metaphorical use of a Gothic idiom – cannot be beneficial. Marx's *Capital* is a case in point, as are sections from Moretti's *Signs Taken for Wonders* (1983: 91), Andrew Smith's *The Ghost Story* (2013: 17) and David McNally's *Monsters of the Market* (2011: 23). Moreover, such usage of the figure of the ghost has also been important for anticolonial works, including that of Aimé Césaire, whose *Notebook of a Return to the Native Land* (1939) posits colonial subjects as ghosts: 'And you ghosts rise blue from alchemy from a forest of hunted beasts' (2000: 12). In *Discourse on Colonialism*, he describes those who were murdered by General Gérard in the city of 'Ambike' as ghosts: 'At the end of the afternoon, the heat caused a light mist to arise: it was the blood of the five thousand victims, the ghost of the city, evaporating in the setting sun' (1972: 40). Similarly, Fanon spoke of the colonial subject as ghost or half-alive subject: 'More dead than alive the colonized subject crouches for ever in the same old dream' (14). Possibly, this is where Mbembe gets his inspiration for describing the colonial world as a 'phantom-like world' in which 'relations between life and death are blurred' (2003: 202). In the context of so-called Lusophone studies, De Medeiros has emphasized the centrality of the 'ghostly figure of the past as a guarantee for the vitality of the nation' (2010: 6–7), and so on.

24   CHAPTER I

The brief answer to this question is circulation. Scott was one of the more institutionalized writers of his time and was admired greatly in many places, specifically after the invention and publication of his historical novels. His elite position in the British Empire certainly did not impede circulation of his work; nor did the fact he wrote in a language that increased in dominance throughout the world-system. His work also circulated in translation. Of 'The Highland Widow', the French translation came out in the same year as the English (in 1827, by Auguste-Jean-Baptiste Defauconpret), the German (by J. V. Theobald) and Italian (by Vincenzo Ferrario) in 1828 and the Castellan (by Rafael Mesa López) in 1831. Although no Portuguese translation seems to have appeared in the nineteenth century, the Portuguese Romanticist Alexandre Herculano wrote about the collection in the journal *O Panorama* in the 1830s, demonstrating the collection was known and being discussed in Portugal, too. Of course, many of Scott's works had already been translated to Portuguese in the years preceding the publication of his ghost stories (Lopes 2010). Domínguez, showing the remarkable circulation of Scott's work throughout what could already be called a world-literary system, traces how, due to its presence in the literary hubs of Paris, Barcelona and Madrid, it reached large parts of the world. Even before 1850, this included 'present day Colombia, Venezuela, Ecuador, Panama, Peru, Guyana, Brazil, [...] Argentina, Bolivia, Paraguay, and Uruguay', as well as Mexico and Cuba (2018: 82). Similarly, Scott circulated in Dutch, Russian, Swedish, Polish, Danish and so on.

Domínguez not only offers an impressive overview of the circulation of Scott's work in translation but also indicates how much more about this circulation is unknown. That this is the case becomes even clearer when focusing on the dynamics of (not unproblematic) concepts such as 'influence'. For instance, the importance of the Latin American writers of the 1950s–70s to Mozambican authors in the 1980s is well known and, as shown in Chapter 4, Rulfo's 1955 *Pedro Páramo* and García Márquez's 1967 [1971] historical novel *Cien Años de Soledad* (which *Páramo* inspired) may arguably be considered predecessors of the Mozambican modern ghost story. Hay convincingly links *Páramo* to Scott's work, but did Rulfo read Scott? Did Márquez? Such questions are difficult to answer in general, and increasingly so when they concern authors who, for whatever reason, gained

Thesis and terms

less fame than Scott in their (after)lifetimes. Thus, while the content of the library of the German author Goethe (who plays a role in Chapters 2 and 5) is largely known, and while he had the habit of writing about the books he read, it is much more difficult to find out what the Mozambican author Mendes (who is central to Chapter 3) read during his studies in Coimbra.

This is complicated further by the fact that ghost-story conventions, which in some way started in Scott's work, do not always circulate directly. The importance of Scott (and British literature in general, even if the Francophone literary ecology was more important still) for Portuguese literature is well known. Machado de Sousa (see also Lisboa and Macedo 1994; Ribeiro de Mello 2003) writes how horror genres were only 'descoberto' [discovered] in Portugal in the late nineteenth century. She indicates they were shaped by poetry 'de origem inglesa' [of English origin] (2013: 16), by translations of British, French and German works (19–23), by the (mostly French) 'journais literários do Romantismo' [Romanticist literary journals] (25)[11] and by the work of Walter Scott (25, 27, 29). A direct influence, however minimal, may thus be assumed. Further, the two most influential Portuguese Romanticists, Garrett and Herculano, who were important for supernatural literature in Portugal, were both 'grande leitor[es] de Scott' [big readers of Walter Scott]. Because the Gothic (horror) is a Romantic form, it may be suggested that Scott also influenced that genre indirectly (Maia Gouveia 1986: 375; cf. Machado de Sousa, 50–5). More indirectly still, Machado de Sousa shows how Poe was read by, and influenced the work of, Pessoa and De Sá-Carneiro, a claim more recently made by Soares (2019). Poe, in turn, had read Scott and was particularly enthused by the 1827 *Chronicles of the Canongate*, in which 'Widow' appeared (cf. Williams

---

11 The French tradition is often understood from the perspective of the fantastic, as analysed by Todorov. For Todorov, the fantastic is a moment of indecision – or, rather, before decision – relative to an event that cannot be explained by the laws of characters' empirical world. Either the 'laws of their world remain the same or [...] reality is controlled by laws unknown to' them. 'The fantastic occupies the duration of this uncertainty' (Todorov 1970: 25). For him, this includes the ghost story (Todorov 41), and the modern ghost story may thus be considered a form of the fantastic. Not incidentally, Todorov relies on Penzoldt's study of the modern ghost story, which was also cited above (Todorov 1970: 141).

2019; Savoye 2007). Similarly indirect, M. R. James's work, which was important for Portuguese authors even before Rocha translated it for the newspaper *Diário Popular* in 1967 (cf. Rocha 1969), was familiar with and influenced by Scott's work (James 2007: 578). Moreover, James's favourite author was Le Fanu (who is important to Chapter 2), who read Scott ferociously and built his modern ghost stories on the structure described in Scott's 'Supernatural' (cf. Cox 1999; Chapman 2007: 11).[12]

Hence, even if Mozambican authors/readers did not have direct access to Scott's work, it is not unlikely they had access to it indirectly via sources from France, Portugal, Columbia, Mexico and so on. They may, in other words, have had access to mediations of Scott's work – to what, with Ann Rigney (2012), can be called the *afterlives* of Walter Scott, not to mention those of other modern ghost-story authors (see, e.g., Gagnier 2013). To formulate this more generally, if Hall wonders in the 1990s whether there are 'any musics left that have not heard some other music?' (Hall 1997: 31), it may be wondered how far this question applies to literatures, including the modern ghost story, from the nineteenth century onwards.

It should be specified, hopefully superfluously, that this book argues that the Mozambican modern ghost story (as discussed from Chapters 3 to 5) participates in a larger modern ghost-story tradition in a complex way, but that the genre is not a copy of the work of Scott or any other author – which does not mean the influence of imperialism and colonialism can be completely ruled out as a factor. Robert H. Moser addresses a similar issue in his book on the Brazilian ghost story, and he cites Jeronimo Monteiro, who argues:

> The fantastic literature read in this country [Brazil] is, on the whole, translated, especially from English. It is the English who adore haunted houses, and their

12 Hay's remark that empire forms the backdrop of the modern ghost story is also evident in some Portuguese modern ghost stories. One example is Mário de Sá-Carneiro *Lucio's Confession*, in which: 'One day a mulatto prisoner – doubtless a fantasist – told me they had beaten him mercilessly with terrible scourges – cold like ice water, he had added in his pidgin tongue. Besides, I mixed with few with of the other prisoners. They clearly had little to recommend the, being creatures without learning or culture, coming no doubt from the lower depths of vice and crime' (1993: 119).

Thesis and terms

> authors who, through literature, provide what is not frequently found in real life. Among Brazilians the opposite seems to be true: there are countless legends, superstitions, and hauntings in these parts and few who make use of these themes in their writing. (Moser 2008: 51)

Monteiro 'overstate[s]' his case, according to Moser, yet the latter, incidentally inflected by the omnipresence thesis, finds the comments of the former 'nonetheless revealing' (Moser 2008: 51). He specifies that, for him, the

> fact that more universal references may appear, either explicitly or implicitly, in the selected texts at different times does not, in any way, undermine the relevance of specific Brazilian traditions and narratives, [but rather] reinforce the interconnectedness of Brazilian death culture to a much broader spectrum of Western (and non-Western) religious and cultural traditions. (43)

This book is sympathetic to the sentiment of Moser's comment that literary traditions may involve circulation beyond the nation state and language of production, yet it takes issue with the terms used (not least the quasi-specifiers of 'Western' and 'non-Western'), and it should be stressed that circulation in the world-literary system does not occur on equal terms. In this book, the preferred understanding of such circulation – and, to use that term, although reluctantly, *influence* – are those put forth by Moretti (2000). He suggests literary circulation occurs in a world-literary system in which literary texts circulate, on unequal terms, based in part on the position of the author/work within that system (core, periphery and semi-periphery). Thus, the form of the modern ghost story circulated in the world-literary system at different points in time, or at least in parts of it, and authors could draw on this form depending where and when they were – and they sometimes did. Once it arrived – in our case, in Mozambique, an arrival that may have (and likely has) occurred many times, mediated in different ways, via many different routes, during which it underwent many different adaptations – it mixed and adapted in the context of its arrival. Specifically, following Moretti's suggestion, the (and let it be emphasized that this often concerns already mediated) 'foreign' forms that circulate in the world-literary system mix with the raw material of 'local' social experience *and* 'local form' (Moretti 2000: 65).

28   CHAPTER I

Despite the unequal nature of literary circulation, it could thus be imagined how Moretti would agree with Bakhtin, who argues genres are discursive traditions that are 'transmitted' through different authors, each expression of which is 'unique and unrepeatable' (2008: 72). Put more simply, in Sahlins's words, '[s]omething happens to [in this case a genre] when people get a hold of it' (2002: 55). Considering this, and the complexity of 'influence', the main method in this book is not 'contract tracing' but rather the analysis of the genre conventions expressed in the different works.

The traditional field

It has been established that the modern ghost story in this book is not understood as an omnipresent form, a postmodern metaphor or even a British form but instead as a set of conventions, which are fixed but also change as participants, their locations in the modern world-system and the genre's itineraries – and the local materials and forms added to and mixed with it – mediate it. To specify further the understanding of the Mozambican modern ghost story in this book, it is necessary to make a final distinction: between the modern ghost story on the one hand and the *traditional field* on the other.

A prominent way in which discourses on ghost stories from the African continent have taken shape is, for lack of a better term, as a form of African supernatural exceptionalism, here referred to as the *African ghost thesis,* according to which people on the vast African continent are closer to forms that may be called 'the supernatural' than others. However, while there may be truth in this thesis in general, its relevance for the modern ghost story is limited. The African ghost thesis can be exemplified by Peeren (2004, henceforth 'Everyday'). 'Everyday' – which is used here as a type – follows Derrida's suggestion to see 'immigrants, foreigners, victims of historical injustices like colonialism and slavery' as the 'metaphorical ghosts of our society', in the context of his dictum 'learn to live with ghosts' (Peeren 107). It attempts to demonstrate and unpack this using Amos Tutuola's (1954) *My Life in the Bush of Ghost* and Ben Okri's (1991) *The Famished Road*, and seemingly to all other expressions of what it calls, in terms typical of the

Thesis and terms 29

spectral turn, the 'ghostly' (Peeren 107). Its justification hereof, and a summary of the African ghost thesis, is the assumption that, on the one hand, in 'many Western *ghost stories* the appearance of a ghost causes surprise, shock, and fear, and represents a rupture in the everyday – an interruption by the unfamiliar and frightening of the familiar, the comfortable, and the routine' (106, emphasis added). On the other hand, there are 'many non-Western (and marginal Western) *traditions of the ghost* where its status as part of the everyday is not seen as something extraordinary or problematic' (109). These traditions, it argues, come from 'folklore or myth' but also play 'an active role in everyday Nigerian life' (109), and 'unlike in Western cultures it is not generally their [i.e. the ghosts'] presence in itself that shocks and surprises, but rather their specific actions' (109). According to 'Everyday', the category of 'non-Western' is therefore closer to the Derridean paradigm in its treatment of the ghost(ly), and it therefore argues that the notion of the ghost that causes shock or surprise is 'reduct[ive]' and 'leaves little room for agency and resistance' (115). 'Everyday' therefore advocates also 'reconfigur[ing]' (115) the relationship between the ghost and the everyday in the 'Western Imagination', so that it becomes a 'harmoniously shared everyday realm' (106).

'Everyday' thus offers a comparison: there are 'many non-Western (and marginal Western) traditions' on the one hand and 'Western cultures' on the other hand, and the latter is 'unlike' the former (109)[13] because the vast African continent supposedly has a stronger relationship with knowledge systems that may be labelled supernatural than, for example, Western European countries.

That some African communities have strong relations to forms of the supernatural has been demonstrated on several occasions and illustrated richly with examples (e.g. Fanon 2007; Petrus and Bogopa 2007; Mawere 2011; Beinart and Brown 2013; Pavanello 2017; Rio et al. 2017). In the case of Mozambique, scholars have shown the importance and ubiquity of supernaturalisms in the everyday life of rural as well as urban Mozambicans.

---

13   '[N]on-Western (and marginal Western)' seemingly refers to homogenous masses that exist only in opposition to the equally mythical unity of the 'West'. As Lazarus (2002) has argued definitively, the term 'West' – not to say 'non-West' – is mystifying.

Bertelsen (2016) references the commonality of *curandeiros* (medicine people), *mhondoro* (spirit mediums) and the importance of the world of spirits in everyday life and politics. Alcinda Honwana, in her work on spirit possession in the south of Mozambique, similarly shows the immense importance of supernatural traditions to Mozambicans and even encourages her readers to consider 'spirits not only as external agents controlling and changing people's identities, but as the very essence of human identity' (1996: i). For her, 'spirit possession constitutes an immediate reality as spirits are the very essence of human identity. Humans and spirits belong to the same agency and share a combined and integrated existence' (1996: 377). Similarly, Bagnol demonstrates how some Mozambicans consider the *lovolo/ lobolo* (bride price) an enabler of communication between the living and the dead (2008: 251). Wilson examines how a rise in supernatural beliefs was registered at the end of the civil war and how there was a competition between 'progressive, traditional, and reactionary actors [during the civil war] for "spiritually empowered agency"' (1992: 529). Nordstrom analyses how the supernatural forces would sometimes prevent Renamo rebels from terrorizing certain villages (1997: 151). And so on.

There can be little doubt that these 'raw materials' – which demonstrably influence lived experience and even constitute or shape social relations – directly and indirectly affect literary production, and a focus on these elements thus appears both expected and legitimate. Yet 'Everyday' appears to compare different types of objects and analyses them on different grounds. In the case of 'the West', 'Everyday' relies on Freud and Derrida and speaks of products of the 'Western imagination' and 'ghost stories'; that is, this category seemingly requires a literary, philosophical and analytical approach (115). In the case of the 'non-Western', the article looks at 'specific ghostly traditions represented in the novels of Tutuola and Okri', which come from 'folklore or myth' but also play 'an active role in everyday Nigerian life' (109). To analyse this case of the 'non-Western', it relies on a comparative theological study, an anthropological study and a statistical study showing 'belief' in ghosts is 'widespread' in Nigeria. 'Everyday' thus appears to have an unbalanced *tertium comparationis*, raising the question 'why?': why does 'Everyday' not compare ghost stories with ghost stories, ghostly traditions that are related to folklore and myth and play a role in

Thesis and terms 31

everyday life with ghostly traditions that are related to folklore and myth and play a role in everyday life?

To answer this question, and to determine whether such a comparison is at all possible on the same terms, or if a difference between the (very problematic categories of the) 'Western' and 'non-Western' realm is so fundamental that this is excluded, four possible justifications will be addressed.

A first possibility would be that the unbalanced comparative frame is justified because 'Western' ghost stories have also been analysed based on their relation to myth, folklore and the everyday. This, however, has not been the case. Scholarship on the modern and predominantly British ghost story has long argued that ghosts and ghost encounters outside of artistic production are *not* identical to those in the modern ghost story. Briggs writes: '[i]nvented ghost stories differ from first-hand accounts in that they share with all fiction an artificially imposed pattern. They have some point to them, whereas only too often genuine experiences and ghostly apparitions in life have no discoverable meaning or application' (1977: 15).[14] A brief comparison of Finucane's social history of ghosts and Scott's 'Tapestried Chamber' also demonstrates this rift between the first-hand account and the literary ghost story. Finucane indicates, about sighted ghosts, that the

> Victorian ghosts […] can […] be summed up in a few words. Most apparitions [i.e. sighted ghosts] involved figures […] of humans whose identity was unknown to the percipients. The forms tended to be insubstantial, vague, often in neutral tones of grey and black, or associated with some random luminescence. […] The best description for the majority of perceptions is 'neutral'. (Finucane 211)

Ghost figures in Victorian ghost stories, however, are narrated in great detail and not at all 'vague'. In Scott's the 'The Tapestried Chamber', the haunted general describes the ghost as

> a little woman […]. The back of this form was turned to me, and I could observe, from the shoulders and neck, it was that of an old woman, whose dress was an old-fashioned gown […] a sort of robe completely loose in the body, but gathered into

---

14 Although Victorian and Mozambican real-life encounters with the supernatural differ significantly, Briggs may be generalized to the extent that there is an irreducible difference between the literary and empirical domains.

broad plaits upon the neck and shoulders, which fall down to the ground, and terminate in a species of train. (Scott 1900: 45)

Moreover, the ghost figure is not 'neutral' in 'Tapestried' but appears as a horrific entity. Finally, Finucane indicates the sighted ghosts are unknown, but in 'Tapestried' the ghost is 'a wretched ancestress' of the protagonist (Scott 1900: 63). Thus, although there is no doubt that extraliterary supernatural traditions influence the literary supernatural of British works, there remains an irreducible difference between the literary on the one hand and social reality on the other.

A second possible justification for the unbalanced comparative frame is that only the (problematic) category of 'non-Western' has 'ghostly traditions' in the 'everyday'. Yet demonstrating the supernatural also plays an important role in the problematic category of the 'Western' is uncomplicated as Finucane demonstrates above. An additional example: when the Major of London instituted a tax for empty rooms in 2014, a woman refused to pay because she said a ghost lived in her spare chamber (Young 2014). British tabloids like *The Sun* and *The Mirror* have dedicated sections in their online publications about news involving ghosts, which include news about haunted houses and towns and possessed dolls, as does *The New York Times*. There is also a large amount of mostly real-life television series about the supernatural. Naming a fraction of these may give an idea of the phenomenon's importance: *Ghost Hunters* (2004–16), *Haunted Lives* (1991–5), *Sightings* (1991–7), *Haunted History* (2013), *My Haunted House* (2013–16), *Paranormal Witness* (2011–present), *A Haunting* (2005–17), *The Haunted* (2009–10), *When Ghosts Attack* (2013–present), *The Ghosts Prophecies* (2010) and so on. The so-called 'West' thus also has a plethora of 'everyday' 'ghostly traditions'.

A third possible justification were if there are only ghostly figures that are subject to exorcism in the category of 'Western', or if exorcism were not part of the 'non-Western' (115). But here, too, examples are plentiful. The London tax incident above shows this, as does the example of *Casper the Friendly Ghost* franchise, to a degree.[15] In addition, if we were to take

---

15 Incidentally, the example of *The Others* that 'Everyday' uses is not one of those works. It may appear to be the case, because the works is focalized through the ghost figures, but the structure of the ghost story – the haunter–hauntee

Thesis and terms   33

Aleluia seriously, Christianity is also a supernatural belief system that exists inside the realm of the social and cultural production; a 'ghostly tradition' in which good and bad spirits play a role. The Pew Research Center demonstrated that 65 per cent of US Americans, to give just one example, describe themselves as part of this tradition (so-called Christians); that is, as believing in an almighty, all-knowing supernatural entity and its intelligent design. The supernatural, ghostly tradition of Christianity includes so-called faith healings performed by medicine (mostly) men, sometimes referred to as pastors, ministers or priests. Christians often believe in what is termed *prayer*, a form of telepathic communication with supernatural entities and even with the dead; *angels*, powerful supernatural spirit beings who are not generally subject to exorcism; and *the Eucharist*, a form of repeated imagined cannibalism in which the cannibalized body is somehow never exhausted (cf. Baylor University 2007).

Conversely, the category of the 'non-Western' contains plenty of ghostly figures that do *not* 'harmoniously' share the 'everyday realm' with humans. Bertelsen indicates that what he calls the *traditional field* – a term to which we shall return below – is complex, ambiguous and continuously in motion and contradictory, and a focus on Mozambique alone reveals a large variety of supernatural beings and practices with different origins and influences.[16] Nordstrom's study describes how a *curandeiro* speaks 'of an attack' that occurred near his village (1997: 159) and how he could, at the location of the attack, feel

> the spirits of the people killed swarming around there, angry and full of vengeance. These people killed, they were not soldiers, they did not battle, they were simple unarmed villagers. They died for no reason, they died unnaturally, in violence. Now they stay with the blood, they seek revenge on those who spilled it. They will follow

---

relation – is no less than archetypal; the hauntees remain in their house after they have exorcized the haunters. That the haunters are the living and the haunted are the dead is irrelevant from the perspective of the modern ghost story, which is determined by a set of genre conventions and not by the figure of the ghost – a perspective screened out by the (in this case Derridean) focus on the figure of the ghost.

16 'Everyday' does not include Mozambique, but considering its inconsistent and problematic category of non-Western, and the slippage therein, it appears not unsuitable to take Mozambique as a case here.

those who killed them – inflicting harm, madness, and death. These Renamo, they should fear these dead, they cannot escape them. I walk by that place now, and still I sense those spirits, restless with anger. The ground is hot with their blood. They will not rest until they have had their revenge. (159)

Nordstrom thus describes an 'everyday' case of haunting and disharmony with the spirits, resulting from improper burial and violent death, creating hauntings by violent and angry ghosts. Bertelsen describes a similar phenomenon. A young man explains to him:

We have lot of these tchiphoko here. A lot. Many of them are Zimbabweans. Those are much more dangerous than Mozambican ones, stronger. Haven't you seen them at the mountain of …? At night tchiphoko come out from there. There was an entire troop of Zimbabweans who were killed there by Renamo. Just like that. It is very dangerous there. You cannot go there, and especially not at night! (2016: 100)

Bertelsen continues to describe how knowledge of 'haunted and perilous places' is 'widely distributed' in his research area, and how places in which violence occurred in the past are often avoided (101). Both scholars, then, describe ghosts who are subject to exorcism. Moreover, it is not the actions but the very presence of the ghosts that is disturbing. A final example: Alcinda Honwana describes how the Mozambican supernatural includes vengeful, evil or malevolent spirits who do not harmoniously coexist in the everyday, some of which 'needed to be exorcised' (1996: 139). Specifically, the *Ndau*, Honwana writes, whose 'religious system is believed to be very powerful' and was exported to several parts of Mozambique through conquest, were supposed to have knowledge of 'mvhuko', a plant that facilitates a deceased's spirits to come back to the world of the living and 'seek revenge' (74). They also have knowledge of '*ku femba* (exorcism)' (74). Describing a *ku femba* ritual, Honwana recalls how 'three initiates […] in trance […] sniffed around until they grabbed the "thing" that afflicted the patient by sneezing three times. The sneezing indicated the capture of the sinister "thing" that was then sent away' (278).

Finally, a possible justification for the unhinged comparative frame in 'Everyday' is that ghost figures subject to exorcism exist in the empirical, but not in the literary, realm of the 'non-Western'. However, this is also demonstrably false; ghosts in 'non-Western' literature who are considered

Thesis and terms   35

not to belong to the realm of the living, and who are considered terrifying simply through their presence, *do* exist. Couto's short story 'A História dos Aparecidos' [The Tale of two Apparitions], central to Chapter 4, is a case in point. It starts with the narrator indicating how the realm of the dead and the living 'devem' [should] be separated: 'É uma verdade: os mortos não devem aparecer, saltar a fronteira do mundo deles' (Couto 2012: 129) [It is a truth: the dead ought not to return, to cross the frontier of their world] (Couto 1989: 10).[17] For the narrator, it is a fact that the dead are *not* supposed to be in the realm of the living. However, the narrator continues, 'há desses mortos que morreram e teimam em aparecer' (Couto 2012: 129) [there are those dead who, having died, persist in coming back] (Couto 1989: 10). These include the protagonists of the 'História', Luís Fernando and Aníbal Mucavel, who 'uma tarde apareceram mais uma outra vez' (Couto 2012: 129) [one afternoon, [...] reappeared yet again] (Couto 1989: 10). Like the narrator, the villagers are amazed and shocked by the reappearance of the men. They are '[a]ssustados [and] chamaram os milícias' (Couto 2012: 129) [alarmed, they called the militia] (Couto 1989: 10), but even the armed forces are scared and 'a tremer' (Couto 2012: 130) [trembling] (Couto 1989: 10) in the presence of the ghosts. When the militias finally gain the courage to speak, they attempt to exorcize them: 'Vão donde vieram' (Couto 2012: 129–30) [Go back from where you came] (Couto 1989: 10).

Hence, if the (problematic) categories of 'Western' and 'non-Western' both have spirit beings in the everyday and in the literary domain, some of which are welcome and some of which must be exorcized, it follows that 'Everyday' compares two related but different categories while presenting them as the same. It follows that its conclusion – the 'West' and 'non-West' are 'unlike' – can hardly be called surprising. This is not without its consequences. The article 'argue[s] for the need to culturally specify the ghost'. However, on the one hand it is questionable whether terms such as 'non-Western' – which is later specified as 'Nigerian', then as 'Yoruba and Igbo' (109), but then slips back into 'African' (115) – are very culturally specific; on the other hand, its purported aim – which it bases on *Specters* – is 'reconfigur[ing] the relation between ghostly and the everyday' so it may

---

17   The translation used for 'História' is by Brookshaw (1989).

36   CHAPTER I

become harmonious. Yet if the 'non-Western' ghosts/spirits are not always a harmonious part of the everyday (as shown above), the ambition to 're-configure' equates to imposing a Derridean way (which, in the terms of 'Everyday', would likely be termed 'Western') of viewing these domains on a 'non-Western' way.

While the largest problems of 'Everyday' emanate from the Derridean approach, they originate in the too-ready application of the African ghost thesis. Problems with such an approach have been highlighted before, both in the Mozambican context and outside it. On the one hand, they should arguably be understood in the context of the 'hypercommodified status of [...] literary categories such as magical realism' (Huggan 2001: 20). On the other, as Kwasi Wiredu writes, the notion that 'Africans see the world as being full of spiritual entities' has 'colonial origins' (Wiredu xiii). Similarly, Redding shows there is a vast and influential colonial archive through which views of the 'African' supernatural are 'filtered or, perhaps more accurately, distorted' (9). Aleluia also notes this distortion. He claims the Mozambican supernatural of his home place is universal in some sense – that there is ultimately no difference between the different supernatural traditions – and his characters comment on the incongruência' [incongruence] and the 'mera hipocrisia' [mere hypocrisy] of distinguishing between different supernaturals (2011: 18–19). Similarly, Couto is asked about the presence of the dead and the half-alive in his work, about those who passed away have 'dificuldade de transitação, encravado na fronteira entre os mundos e em "fantasmas mal morridos". Como é essa relação entre vivos e mortos nesse mundo que descreve?' ['difficulty transitioning, stuck between worlds, and un-dead ghosts'. How is this relationship between the living and the dead of the world you describe?] (Hebmüller 2017). Appearing to reproduce the African ghost thesis, he answers that it is 'uma relação marcada pela ideia de um tempo circular, em que os mortos não chegam nunca a morrer' [a relationship marked by the idea of circular time, in which the dead never really get to die] (Hebmüller 2017). However, he hastens to add, he be-lieves that in 'nenhuma cultura e em nenhuma religião os mortos morrem completamente, portanto isso não é uma coisa exclusiva da África' [in no culture and in no religion do the dead die completely, therefore this is not a thing exclusive to Africa] (Hebmüller 2017). In a different interview,

Couto, implicitly addressing the notion of what Huggan would perhaps call the 'exoticist production of otherness' (2001: 13), says: 'Mozambique is a very young country trying to find and affirm its unique identity in a world that often does not accept alternative narratives unless they conform to a certain folkloric exoticism' (Jin 2013).

The aim of this somewhat extended discussion of 'Everyday' is to demonstrate not only that a certain caution is warranted – if not necessary – when dealing with the African ghost thesis but also that there *are* in fact different categories of the supernatural, which may be confused with the ghost story, as 'Everyday' does. The first category is evident, is named as such in 'Everyday' and is illustrated with archetypal examples, such as Alejandro Amenábar's (2001) *The Others*: the modern ghost story. The second category is more elusive, in part because it is not clarified in 'Everyday'. In this book, that category will be referred to as what Bertelsen calls the *traditional field*.

Bertelsen uses the term *traditional field* to speak of the highly complex, multiple and contradictory Mozambican supernatural domains. He specifies that this traditional field, as he understand it, is diverse and ambiguous, includes what is referred to as *tradição, tsika* and *tchianhu wo atwe*, contains destructive and constructive energies, has powers that appropriate and are appropriated, is disintegrating in contemporary society while also being reinvented 'constantly' and informs 'perceptions of contemporary and past state dynamics' (2016: 6–7). Further, in his definition, *traditional field* does not mean a 'redeploy[ing of] what one might broadly call non-Western perspectives'; nor does it 'resurrect or reformulate the colonial category of "tradition"', refer to notions of '(supposedly) premodern social orders or cosmologies' or 'reactualize' oppositions between 'tradition' and 'modern' (6–8). Rather, with his concept he aims to 'grasp experiential dimensions and broad historical trends that crucially shape contemporary and past dynamics of statehood, sociality, and power as these unfold' (7). This *traditional field* is not a closed entity for Bertelsen but a 'non-entity' – a field; not a 'constituent of an ontologically consistent and stable reality, but as a term that captures the cosmogenetic force of the social or, better, sociality's constitutive ontogenetic thrust' (7).

38   CHAPTER I

It should be clarified that the modern ghost story and the *traditional field* operate on different levels because the former is a literary genre and the latter is an empirical concept. It is possible and even likely that there is a genre centring on aspects of the *traditional field* but (e.g. Rofino Roque's *Tschanaze, O Donzela de Sena*) but this lies beyond the scope of this book. However, elements of the *traditional field* will inevitably be expressed in literary production and can also be an essential part of Mozambican modern ghost stories – as Moretti's mixing of foreign forms with local forms and materials implies. Moreover, there may be an overlap between (elements of) the *traditional field* and the modern ghost story. So, the trope of the (vengeful) dead, who return to deal with an unresolved issue in the past, is central to the modern ghost story and the *traditional field*, as demonstrated above. It would be difficult, perhaps impossible, to entangle all those cases definitively. Nevertheless – and most importantly – to speak with Hay, 'the truth of any story lies in its structure' and the 'truth of any structure is its history' (21).[18] In the case of the (Mozambican) modern ghost story, this means (as implied in the discussion above) that even if a work is dotted with 'ghostly' elements of the *traditional field*, it may not be a ghost story if it does not participate in the narrative tradition that is the modern ghost story. Conversely, it is possible that a (possible) *traditional field* element is a pivotal element in a Mozambican modern ghost story.

Finally, a point that could be raised is that it is possible – maybe even likely – that *traditional field* elements are more common than Mozambican modern ghost stories in Mozambican literature. The only response this book has is that, to speak with Cooppan (2004: 20), 'if we look only for [the ghosts'] most familiar apparitions, we may well miss their transformations'.

18   '[Any] given story can be explained in primarily formalist terms: […] tropes and figures, the construction and role of the narrator, the shape and function of introductory frames, and the completeness of the narrative' (Hay 21).

Thesis and terms 39

The modern ghost story: A definition

A preliminary definition of the modern ghost story, as understood in this book, can now be formulated. The ghost story is understood here as a modern narrative tradition that consists of a set of genre conventions. These conventions include sparsely present, frightening supernatural figures, which are not necessarily ghosts; a climactic structure, rather than a plot (not unlike Freytag's pyramid, although with its climax about 75 per cent of the way through the story); the refusal to narrative closure; and issues with the law, empire and class identity. In the modern ghost story, something (traumatic) returns from an otherwise inaccessible past, a past that it negotiates somehow. The modern ghost story is not any text with a loosely defined ghostly figure, although it can contain them; nor is it any text that involves the *traditional field*, although the *traditional field* may play a role in, and even overlap with, the (Mozambican) modern ghost story aspects. The modern ghost story form is, paradoxically, fixed; but it also changes as it moves through the world-literary system and across time and space, and as it is combined with local forms and contents repeatedly. It narrates transition – specifically, the transition from feudalism to capitalism – and it emerges with primitive accumulation.[19]

As this book shall argue, the modern ghost story not only occurs relative to, thematizes and emerges with primitive accumulation, but also registers it, even in moments when debates about it take place or when the seizures it caused reverberate through the world-system.

---

19   Hay writes that the 'ghost story is in all sorts of ways a sub-genre of the gothic', and he even suggests that, with 'its central concern with both the trauma of the transition from feudalism to capitalism and with the repetition of that trauma through processes of imperialism, the ghost story is a paradigmatic gothic narrative' (23).

CHAPTER 2

The modern ghost story

In his monograph on the modern ghost story, Hay argues that to read an

> anthology of ghost stories is to watch the several traumas of each story accumulate, like the history that Benjamin's angel watches piling up, to the point where history figures only as a single repeated trauma, the traumatic transition [...] from feudalism to capitalism lived out over and over again. (2011: 2)

For Hay, every modern ghost story restages, relives or is an expression of this 'traumatic' and 'bloody transition into modernity' (15), and can usefully be understood against the historical novel because the 'historical novel and the ghost story both stage history for us by bringing the dead before us as a spectacle' (29). Yet 'the ghost story is, unlike the historical novel, a failed modernity narrative' because, 'as narratives, ghost stories typically fail to account for modernity; and what they are struggling in vain to account for is a failed (or at least, endangered) transition to modernity' (15).

Scott's ghost stories are, for Hay, a beginning of this modern ghost story genre because, while earlier literary works with ghost figures existed, those 'earlier narratives become comprehensible as precursors to the ghost story only in the light of Scott's work' (29). 'The Highland Widow' (2003 [1827]) is arguably Scott's first modern ghost story and, expectedly, Hay focuses on transition in his analysis of that work. In 'Widow', protagonist Mrs Bethune Baliol takes a Highland tour with her guide Donald MacLeish. They encounter a widow living in poverty and misery at a large oak as the result of her preventing her son, Hamish, from fulfilling his sworn duties to the English army, for which his superiors eventually execute him. Elspat (the widow) wanted her son Hamish to follow the example of his father and become a Highland cattle thief. Her character, understandably, represents the feudal past for Hay. Hamish sensed times were changing for Scotland and that a new economic system was becoming dominant. He considers signing up for the army the honourable thing to do, and the ghost of his father convinces him this is the right choice. Hay therefore takes these characters to represent the shift to the (modern) capitalist present, in which the widow exists despite her attempt to stop a transition, while her son and husband have died (Hay 2011: 30).

With Hay, this book considers Scott and his ghost stories an important starting point of the modern ghost story – a *founder of discursivity*, in Foucauldian terms – and there is little doubt here that 'Widow' indeed concerns the transition from feudalism to capitalism. Yet the question that remains unanswered in Hay is why a work such as 'Widow', arguably Scott's first modern ghost story, would be published in 1827; on what raw materials does it draw? This question is particularly pressing taking into account Shapiro's comment that the Gothic correlates to primitive accumulation, while the British transition into capitalism occurred in the eighteenth century (cf. Saville 1969; Callinicos 1994). More important still, this question is paramount for the claim of this book that the modern ghost story registers primitive accumulation.

This chapter therefore unpacks how Scott's 'Widow' registers transition, and what transition it registers, and demonstrates that it does so in a different – and much more explicit – way than Hay suggests. In brief, this chapter claims 'Widow' registers the financial crisis of 1825 through the formal aspects of: (1) (more) terrifying ghost figures (2) the *structure of debt*; and (3) the use of what this chapter calls the haunted *cosmopolitan space*. Before discussing these three, however, this chapter must first address what the cosmopolitan space is at some length. It does so by establishing a connection between Scott's modern ghost story and Goethe's world-literature. The chapter ends with a discussion of two modern ghost stories, which were published after 'Widow', to demonstrate that – and how – the form continued.

The cosmopolitan space

Goethe's modern concept of world-literature and Scott's modern ghost story, both the first of their kind, emerged only months apart: in January

The modern ghost story

and October 1827 respectively.[1] A connection between the concept and the literary form, or between the two authors, seems cursory at first glance. Certainly, Goethe and Scott were contemporaries; they died thirteen days apart in 1832, were described by Carlyle as the 'two kings of poetry' and were continuously familiar with each other's work (in Scott 1891: 379n1). Yet Scott never mentioned world-literature in his journal or letters, and even seemingly opposed the ideal of world-literature in practice. As he wrote in his journal, he made it 'a rule seldom to read, and never to answer, foreign letters from literary folks' – with the exception of letters from Goethe, 'a wonderful fellow, the Ariosto at once, and almost the Voltaire of Germany' (Scott 1891: 234). Goethe admired Scott for his essays on the supernatural as well as for his novels, and said Scott was 'a great genius; he has not his equal, [his] art [is] wholly [...] new, with laws of its own' and 'so high that it is hard to give a public opinion about it' (Goethe 1901: 358, 360). However, there appears to be no evidence that Goethe read Scott's ghost stories, much less that they had influenced his world-literature. As Eppers has argued, the Goethe–Scott relationship remained a 'Berührung [...] aus der Ferne' [encounter from afar] (2006: 166).

The connection, however, is historical rather than personal, which is to say that both Goethe and Scott draw on the same raw material in the form of the cosmopolitan space. This book proposes the cosmopolitan space as an instance of an 'ideologeme', a concept first used prominently by Bakhtin and Medvedev (1981) and developed by Kristeva as a way to analyse ideology intertextually, at 'the different structural levels of the text' (1980: 36). Jameson, building on those accounts, specified *ideologemes* as the 'smallest intelligible' (1983: 61) units or building blocks of ideology – the 'ultimate raw material' (73) of cultural products. For him, they are 'amphibious formation[s]', because they can manifest themselves conceptually and as a 'protonarrative' or 'collective class fantasy' (73). The

---

[1] Wieland coined the term 'world-literature', according to Weitz (1987), who says it is unclear when Wieland used it first. Günther (1990) argues it was in 1790. For Wieland, world-literature referred exclusively to the literature of Horace's time and that of the Roman Empire; that is, to classical masterpieces (Weitz 208). Berczik (1967) argues it was first coined by August Ludwig Schlözer.

cosmopolitan space, then, is an (ideological) unit of meaning, which can be expressed on various textual levels and in various media – in this case, Goethe's concept of modern world-literature and Scott's literary form of the modern ghost story.

The ideological content of the cosmopolitan space is necessarily imprecise due to its 'amphibious' nature. Its defining ideological quality, this book argues, is relatively unobstructed mobility (of commodities and individuals alike). This *ideologeme* is productive, and connotes predominantly positively, in different class contexts; relatively unobstructed mobility may be considered a realm of potentials – a realm to be excluded from, to desire inclusion in or access to, and so on. This cosmopolitan space is ideological because, to different extents, it is severed from its conditions of possibility – the system of production of which it is a function. In the *Grundrisse*, Marx shows that, because the creation of surplus value ('the self-realization of capital') is prioritized in the capitalist system of production, '[c]apital by its nature drives beyond every spatial barrier' to open new markets after its current ones are saturated (1973: 524–5) – the process of primitive accumulation. This constitutes a problem from the perspective of the physical conditions of exchange; that is, communication and transport. Creating new markets implies an increase in the necessary distance to cover for circulation and exchange and an increase in (socially) necessary labour time. Thus, the necessary expansion of the capitalist world-system for capital's self-realization also increases the cost of circulation and exchange, impeding that self-realization. To resolve this contradiction, Marx argues, the 'annihilation of space by time [...] becomes an extraordinary necessity', and '*for that reason*' the production of cheap means of communication and transport is promoted by capital (Marx 1973: 525; original emphasis). He summarizes that

> while capital must on one side strive to tear down every spatial barrier to intercourse, i.e. to exchange, and conquer the whole earth for its market, it strives on the other side to annihilate this space with time, i.e. to reduce to a minimum the time spent in motion from one place to another. The more developed the capital [...], the more extensive the market over which it circulates [...], the more does it strive [...] for greater annihilation of space by time. (Marx 1973: 539)

Relatively unobstructed mobility is thus a function of the capitalist world-system, and specifically of its expansion: of primitive accumulation.[2] However, the cosmopolitan space is severed from the system of production and appears as autonomous – not unlike the way in which the theme of 'technology and invention' is often separated from the ' "ugliness" of the factory and industrial work' (Jameson 2005: 153) – which constitutes that space as ideological.

Goethe's world-literature and Scott's modern ghost story share the cosmopolitan space as their fundamental ideological unit, although it functions drastically differently in the works of these two authors – a difference that is clarifying for this aims of this book. In Goethe's account, relatively unobstructed mobility is not considered a function of capitalism but rather results from post-Napoleonic cosmopolitan humanism. And because mobility constitutes the condition of world-literature, the developments that a fuller integration into the capitalist world-system may bring – particularly the annihilation of space by time – is anticipated. By contrast, Scott writes from post-1825 Britain, where the consequences of such an integration – Harvey's 'continuing force' – have just materialized as a financial crisis. And while 'Widow' also separates mobility from its conditions of possibility, it constructs the cosmopolitan space as haunted; while Baliol starts her journey 'fearless[ly]' (Scott 2003: 68), mobility is negated and praise is replaced by 'dreadful terror' as the narrative progresses (121). To demonstrate this more clearly, a closer look at Goethe's world-literature and Scott's 'Widow' is necessary.

---

2   Even if the 'annihilation of space by time' is ultimately a function of a system of production, its potential extends far beyond the self-realization of capital. Marx's own work demonstrates this on more than one occasion; in 'On Imperialism in India' he shows how the means of transportation formed the possibility of the nation state, while in *The Communist Manifesto* he and Engels argue that a world-literature arises from the network of circulation and exchange.

46   CHAPTER 2

The cosmopolitan space in Goethe's world-literature

Writer and critic Theodor Mundt complained in 1838 that Goethe's notion of world-literature was so vague he would rather not engage with
it at all. That proved impossible because the term followed him around
'like the Marlborough-tune' (in Lawall 2010: 20). Mundt might well have
been writing in the first two decades of the 2000s. As discussed at more
length in Chapter 5, after the publication of Casanova's *World Republic
of Letters* (2007 [1999]) and Moretti's 'Conjectures on World Literature'
(2000), 'world-literature' rapidly became one of the most important terms
for the (comparative) study of literature, arguably only rivalled by the related terms 'translation' and 'globalization'. As Beecroft noted (disapprovingly), most studies on the topic 'necessarily and automatically begin with
Goethe's use of the term Weltliteratur in conversation with the young
Johann Peter Eckermann' (2008: 87).[3] It seems redundant, then, to once
again discuss at length the twenty-some fragments in which Goethe elab-
orated his concept (or rather 'proto-concept') of international exchange,
announced that world-literature 'is at hand' and urged: 'Everyone must
strive to hasten its approach' (1901: 175). Instead, this section provides
a characterization of that proto-concept, based on a brief outline of its
political and economic context, to highlight the centrality of the cosmopolitan space to it.

   Paramount to Goethe's conception of modern world-literature is the
peculiar, pre-nation-state, quasi-feudal political unity of Germany at the
time. After the Napoleonic Wars, during the 1815 Congress of Vienna,
an association of German-speaking states was formed under the name
German Federation. Its formation had been discussed before and met
with resistance, but Napoleon's escape from Elba (during the Congress),
and the clear economic and defensive advantage it would offer, led thirty-
nine 'sovereign princes and free cities of Germany' to sign the agreement

---

3   For overviews of the world-literature debate, see: Brandt Corstius (1957); D'haen,
     Domínguez and Thomsen (2012); Bender and Melzer (1958); Berczik (1967); and
     Pizer (2006).

(Dorn Brose 1997: 81). Paradoxically, Germany was both exceptional in and characteristic of the post-Napoleonic European political landscape. On the one hand, nationalism and the nation state had become dominant in Europe; but on the other hand, a supranational sociopolitical philosophy had arisen on the continent in the form of cosmopolitanism. As Fillafer and Osterhammel (2011) show, this specifically modern form of cosmopolitanism initially emerged in the Dutch Republic during its so-called golden age, where it was a function of religious tolerance and the transnational expansion of business interests. After the decline of the Dutch Empire, cosmopolitanism disappeared and re-emerged several times in Europe, in the process of which it 'transcended mercantile egoism' and took on a more humanist content (Fillafer and Osterhammel 2011: 121). The Napoleonic Wars catalysed this modern cosmopolitan sentiment in Europe. It functioned as a tool to avoid future conflict and support trade; but the wars had also generated, as Conway maintained, a humanist 'belief in the essential unity of humankind and in the values and sympathies that underpin that unity' (2018: 30). Post-Napoleonic cosmopolitanism, then, had a specific economic and cultural dimension.

Goethe, whose 'keen sense of history' even Georg Lukács admired (Vazsonyi 1997: 136), was explicitly aware of Germany's position in Europe and of post-Napoleonic cosmopolitanism, and suggested both as conditions for his world-literature. While cosmopolitanism and nationalism were not contradictory per se, the absence of a German nation state and the newly established, semi-cosmopolitan formation of the Federation were a comfortable position from which to claim, as Goethe did, that '[n]ational literature is now rather an unmeaning term' (1901: 175). Not accidentally, he emphasized the 'honorable role [...] reserved for us Germans' in the development of world-literature, and stressed that the 'German nation can and should be more involved' in that process than other nations (Goethe, in Strich 1946: 397; my translation).

In his foreword to the German translation of Carlyle's *The Life of Schiller*, Goethe further elaborates on world-literature and says the 'reason' it could emerge is that

> all the [European] nations that had been unsettled in the most horrible [Napoleonic] wars and afterwards had fallen back into isolation came to realize that they

48   CHAPTER 2

> had become aware of a number of foreign things, had adopted some, and had, on
> occasion, felt intellectual, spiritual/mental needs that had hitherto been unknown.
> This recognition had given them a sense of being neighbors; and instead of closing
> in on itself, as had been the habit in the past, the mind eventually developed a desire
> to have a share in a more or less free trade in matters of the mind and spirit [freien
> geistigen Handelsverkehr]. (Goethe, in Frank 2007: 1515)

Two aspects of Goethe's foreword merit highlighting in the context of this discussion of the cosmopolitan space. First, Goethe suggests post-Napoleonic cosmopolitanism as the main condition of world-literature and, importantly, he foregrounds the cultural – and specifically the humanist – dimension of that sociopolitical philosophy. He would do so consistently, and he specified on a different occasion that world-literature meant authors found a 'common spirit' in each other's works and, as a result, started working as a 'community' (Goethe 1960: 392–3). This is not to say the economic dimension of cosmopolitanism was absent from Goethe's work on world-literature. He addressed what Marx would later call the 'annihilation of space by time' on several occasions. He even cited the 'ever-increasing speed' of 'intercourse [Verkehr]' and the 'efficiency of today's book trade' (in Strich 1946: 400; my translation) as essential to the formation of such a world-literature – leading Birus to praise him for his 'great pragmatic rationality' (1995: 16; my translation). Yet that dimension is not identified as such. Rather, as in the case of 'free trade' in the citation above, which is framed explicitly and solely as an intellectual and humanist project ('freie[r] geistige[r] Handelsverkehr'), the humanist scope severs or substitutes the relation to the system of production.

This ambiguous shape of cosmopolitanism's economic dimension in Goethe's writing on world-literature does not contradict his 'keen sense of history' or 'pragmatic rationality'. Rather, as Goethe's conversations on economic exchange illustrate, it is symptomatic of the way in which he perceived certain historical developments. For example, when Goethe and Eckermann discuss the possibility of a Panama Canal, the former expresses his hopes that the 'young Nation' of the 'United States' will take an active role in that project (Goethe 1901: 179–80). He goes on to predict the US will soon populate the vast area 'beyond the Rocky Mountains' (Goethe 1901: 179–80). Together, he continues, these 'great works' – which

The modern ghost story
49

he wishes he would 'live to see – but [realizes he] shall not' – will allow the opening up of new and 'important commercial towns' and the 'furtherance of a great intercourse between China and the East Indies and the United States' (1901: 180). Remarkably, even in this discussion about the primitive accumulation (and colonization) of parts of the (now-) United States of America, in which culture does not play a primary role, Goethe frames the annihilation of space by time as a humanist project; he goes as far as to argue it will have 'innumerable benefits' for the 'whole human race, civilized and uncivilized' (179–80). In Goethe's writing on both cultural and economic exchange, then, capitalism collapses into humanism and the latter mystifies the former, as well as the (physical) conditions associated with it.[4]

To formulate this more explicitly, Goethe's world-literature relies on the cosmopolitan space as its main ideological building block because his elaborations on the proto-concept did not connect its physical conditions of possibility to the emerging and expanding capitalist system of production of which they are a function.

The second aspect of Goethe's foreword to Carlyle's *The Life of Schiller* to be highlighted here – the novelty it assigns to world-literature – illustrates why this may be the case. In line with Birus (2000), who emphasized the ambiguity of Goethe's language, it has become commonplace to argue that world-literature for Goethe was either arriving or had just arrived, usually based on his comment that world-literature 'is at hand [an der Zeit]', which signifies both (Goethe 1901: 175). While this may be true, it is important to stress that world-literature, for Goethe, was more of the future than of the present. His relation to the international magazine *Le Globe*, which he saw as an early example of what world-literature could be (just as the Italian *Eco* and the British *Edinburgh Review*), illustrates this. Having read in *Le Globe* a review of his own work that he particularly liked, Goethe

---

4   The contrast with Marx and Engels's account of world-literature twenty years later highlights this once again. Like Goethe, they also relate world-literature to 'the discovery of America' and the 'immense development [given] to commerce, to navigation, to communication by land [...] industry, commerce, navigation, railways'. However, they make clear, the condition thereof is the development of 'the world market' (Marx and Engels 221–4).

invited the reviewer, J. J. Ampère, to a meeting and a dinner. When Ampère arrived, Goethe and Eckermann were 'extremely surprised' he was only 'some twenty years old', and even more so when they learned 'the whole of the contributors to the 'Globe' [...] were only young people like [Ampère] himself' (Goethe 1901: 205). After their guest left, Goethe told Eckermann this phenomenon of *Le Globe* was 'entirely new' and praised Ampère as a 'citizen of the world', contrasting him to the national 'narrow-mindedness of many of his countrymen' (209).

Goethe thus seems to suggest a generational shift relative to world-literature, which is already present in his comment that he will not live to see the Panama Canal. This shift is further elucidated by the specific context of the German Federation. As Ogilvie points out, even though some regions of the Federation – predominantly the Rhineland and Saxony – had forms of 'pre-industrialization', the majority of the German states 'failed to industrialize' at the same pace as other countries (most notably Britain and France) (1996: 122). This included the undeveloped modes of exchange necessary for world-literature, and was a direct consequence of the different principalities – a transitioning, fragmented feudal system with 'different legac[ies] of social institutions, and thus different framework[s] for economic activity' (122). Goethe formulated this as a problem to be overcome, and expressed his faith in 'our good high roads and future railroads [which] will of themselves do their part'; that is, establish a more solid German unification and free exchange (1901: 287). His prediction was not far from the truth, although he typically failed to recognize capitalism as the main catalyst of the creation of the physical conditions of exchange. Thus, the elimination of the Federation's tariff barriers with the introduction of the *Zollverein* (a customs union) in 1834 would be a catalyst for the German unification of 1871, as would the start of the development of a more extended railway system one year later (in 1835). Nevertheless, even though Germany would become the largest European industrialized capitalist economy in the twentieth century, through much of the nineteenth century – as Ogilvie has shown – and certainly during Goethe's lifetime Germany remained proto-industrial (Ogilvie 1996: 122).

Goethe's inability to consider relatively unobstructed mobility in relation to the expanding capitalist system of production may be considered

The modern ghost story 51

symptomatic of his position in Germany, and his world-literature may thus be characterized as a proto-conceptual expression of post-Napoleonic, European, modern cosmopolitanism, from a proto-industrial, proto-capitalist, non-nation-state Federation. Paradoxically, the constellation that provided fruitful ground for the conceptualization of world-literature also formed an obstacle to its realization. Hence, Goethe advocated the hastening of the approach of world-literature, which includes not only the transnational collaboration between literati but also the physical conditions of exchange and primitive accumulation of new territories. It may have been precisely this anticipation that made world-literature particularly susceptible to the fantasy of the cosmopolitan space.

As will now become clear, the particular historical conjunction that determined the last years of Scott's life, and that was registered in 'Widow', did not leave that fantasy intact in the same way.

The cosmopolitan space in Scott's 'The Highland Widow'

The cosmopolitan space in Scott's 'The Highland Widow' is expressed in several ways, which resonate immediately with Goethe's world-literature. These include the notion of transnational poetry, mid-sentence leaps from one geographical region to another (what shall be called *spatial jumps* in this book, and which will figure more prominently in Chapter 5) and protagonist Baliol's cosmopolitanism. These shall be returned to briefly below; presently, the focus is the most noticeable expression of the cosmopolitan space in 'Widow': the roads, and Baliol's commentary on them.

In her first sentence, Baliol indicates that, 'fearless[ly]', she 'undertook [a] Highland tour [which] had become in some degree fashionable' (Scott 2003: 68). Baliol is a travelling enthusiast, a tourist, who aims to appreciate 'the most beautiful districts' (69), 'romantic retreat[s]' (71) and 'traditional stories of the country' (72). Yet the greatest commendation is reserved for the roads themselves. She praises them as 'excellent' (68) and speaks of the 'substantial excellence of these great works' (72). She says she appreciates the 'legends by which the road, and the objects which occurred in traveling it, had been distinguished' (69), indicating she enjoys the legends for their effect on the road rather than for themselves. Similarly, she praises a mountain as 'majestic', only to praise the (anthropomorphized) road indirectly for conquering that mountain ('[the] military road, which never or rarely condescends to turn aside from the steepest ascent, but proceeds right up and down hill', 72). She admires her guide, Donald, for his knowledge of legends – but, above all, for being 'acquainted with the road every mile' (68). She is unbothered by Donald's drinking because it makes him drive 'slower', allowing her to enjoy the road more (70).

The roads, it may be evident, allow a relatively unobstructed mobility in what was before an impenetrable 'wilderness', and Baliol's praise for these structures reaches its climax in the following passage (72). The roads, she exclaims passionately, deserve

> the compliment of the poet, who, whether he came from our sister kingdom, and spoke in his own dialect, or whether he supposed those whom he addressed might have some national pretension to the second sight, produced the celebrated couplet – 'Had you but seen these roads before they were made / You would hold up your hands, and bless General Wade'.

> Nothing indeed, can be more wonderful than to see these wildernesses penetrated and pervious in every quarter by broad accesses of the best possible construction, and so superior to what the country could have demanded for many centuries for any pacific purpose of commercial intercourse. Thus the traces of war are sometimes happily accommodated to the purposes of peace. The victories of Bonaparte have been without results; but his road over the Simplon will long be the communication betwixt peaceful countries, who will apply to the ends of commerce and friendly intercourse that gigantic work, which was formed for the ambitious purpose of warlike invasion. (Scott 2003: 72)

Commentators have foregrounded this passage to emphasize the way in which it symbolizes the transition to modernity. Sabiron argues that these 'new constructions crisscross the Scottish body and replace the Antique body' (2015: 10), and Hay understands the section as Baliol's 'approval of the modernization of Scotland' (2011: 32). Hay, who does not read the section in conjunction with Baliol's earlier celebration of the roads, adds that her praise is ambiguous because it is phrased 'in terms of a military rape' (32). However, there is little ambiguity in Baliol's opinion

The modern ghost story 53

of the roads. Certainly, she identifies the destruction of the past as a condition of the roads' existence, and uses the signifier 'penetrated', which Hay understandably considers a marker for rape. But the erasure of the past does not pose a problem for Baliol, who claims '[n]othing [...] can be more wonderful'. For Baliol, the roads are to be 'celebrated'; they are 'wonderful', 'excellent', of the 'best possible construction' and so forth.

As in Goethe, Baliol's excessive and lyrical praise of the roads, and the relatively unobstructed mobility they provide, are separated from the system of production of which they are (or have become) a function. At most, Baliol considers them as modernization, a notion that itself insufficiently accounts for the development of capitalism, as addressed in Chapter 1. Worth highlighting in this context, too, are the post-Napoleonic cosmopolitan climate and its humanist dimension in the form of the reference to Napoleon; the universalization of the 'poet', whose 'dialect' and 'kingdom' (i.e. particular location) are deemed irrelevant; and the 'communication betwixt peaceful countries', which all resonate with Goethe's account of world-literature. Attention could even be drawn to the spatial jump in which the narrator shifts seamlessly from the Highlands to the Simplon and back, as if space itself was (to use Marx's term) annihilated.

'Widow', this is to say, relies on the *ideologeme* of the cosmopolitan space. Nevertheless, it is shaped fundamentally differently to Goethe's world-literature. To demonstrate this, it is necessary to look more closely at the short story's form and context of production.

The context of production of 'Widow'

Scott started writing 'Widow' on the evening of 27 May 1826, he writes in his journal, during a sleepless night just thirteen days after his wife died. Her death affected him greatly, and he repeatedly addressed his distressed condition in his journal. A break from writing, however, was no option: 'I must not fail myself and my family – and the necessity of exertion becomes apparent' (Scott 1891: 129).

This necessity to write resulted from the financial crisis of 1825, initially known as 'The Panic'. Some commentators, such as Dick, consider The Panic (somewhat tautologically) as the 'first modern financial crisis', because it 'came about not because of exogenous circumstances, like war, but through the normal course of financial circulation and diversification' (2013: 146). Indeed, although the crisis was in many ways connected to the Napoleonic Wars – that is, to the debt created during that period and to the flow of capital out of Britain ending after it – debt had started rising with the development of the banking system during the Industrial Revolution. To reduce debt, the British government took measures including the implementation of a gold standard. This resulted in a panic, a (brief) crash of the English (not the British) financial sector and the failure of over sixty banks (Neal 1998).

The crisis severely affected Scott, and left him indebted for the rest of his life, due to two mechanisms. First, in the period leading up to the crisis, Scott was granted credit by his publishers (Archibald Constable and Co. and Ballantyne and Co.) based on a promise to deliver work at a later date; Scott was to write nine works by 1824, for which he received a £10,000 advance, and he spent part of this on his Abbotsford estate, which served as security for the debt. Second, his publishers plentifully used so-called 'accommodation bills', which were granted by a first party to provide a loan to a second party. A creditor would provide that loan, and the debtors would retire the bill on its due date. If they did not, or could not, the first party would stand guarantee for the second party's debt – if the creditor demanded the money on that date, which was not always the case. When The Panic occurred, as McKinstry and Fletcher explain, those debts were collected and, as a result, the system collapsed:

> The London agents of Constable defaulted on a bill payable to Constables whose own credit dried up and who were linked through indebtedness with James Ballantyne and Company. The latter firm, whose capital had for some time belonged to Scott alone, was obliged to stop payment and thus became bankrupt. (McKinstry and Fletcher 2002: 83–4)

The modern ghost story   55

To Scott, this collapse was 'unintelligible', because Constable made '[g]reat profits on almost all the adventures [and made] no bad speculations' (Scott 1891: 62). Nevertheless, Constable's bankruptcy and Scott's involvement with Ballantyne made him responsible for a total amount of £120,899 (Anderson 1998: xxx). Abbotsford had initially served as a guarantee for the debts, but Scott had transferred ownership of his estate to his son – a precondition for the son to marry the wealthy heiress Jane Jobson – of which Scott's partners in debt had been unaware. With no material security, the best hope of the creditors was, as Anderson points out, 'to trust in Scott's own resolve to write his way out of his difficulties' (1998: xxxi). They constructed a trust fund based on the promise that Scott would produce texts, the profits of which would be directed to the funds. This initiated the most ferocious writing period of Scott's life. In the two-and-a-half years that followed, he wrote 1.5 million words – and, while the quality of his work suffered, his popularity did not. Nevertheless, as Quayle (1968) shows, the debt outlasted the author and was paid off only fifteen years after Scott's death, in 1847, after the sale of the remaining copyrights.

Scott's necessity to write thus resulted from the position The Panic had put him in (and, partly, that he had put himself in) – writing had become the way to pay off his debts. The first work Scott started after financial ruin hit was 'Widow', which formally registers its context in three main and interrelated ways: through monstrosity, the structure of debt and the haunted cosmopolitan space.

Monstrosity

Around the time of The Panic, Scott had been working on his majestic *The Life of Napoleon Bonaparte*; but, as he wrote in his journal, before being able to finish 'Nap' he now 'must try a hors d'œuvre' (Scott 1891: 129) – 'Widow'. Scott wrote that he wanted to base 'Widow' on 'Mrs. M. K.'s [Murray Keith's] Tale of the Deserter', which required expansion because it was too short (1891: 129). He therefore chose to add a 'frame-work [that] may be a Highland Tour, under the guardianship of [a] postilion' (129).

A day later, he commented on the structure of the work, which he intended to be 'an olla podrida, into which any species of narrative or discussion may be thrown' (130). This provisional generic specifier, *olla podrida* – referring to a Spanish dish, the name of which translates as 'rotten pot' – is symptomatic of the novelty of 'Widow' on the levels of both species and genre. 'Widow' can retrospectively be labelled a short story, but that term did not signify as clearly then as it does now. It may be an exaggeration to claim, as Allen did, that the short story was absent before Scott's *Chronicles of the Canongate*, the collection in which 'Widow' was published (1981: 5–16). Nonetheless, in 1826 Britain, it was certainly not the dominant form. Scott thus gave an impulse to the short story but also, and more importantly for this book, reinvented the genre of supernatural fiction through 'Widow'.

The best account of what this reinvention entailed is arguably his own 1827 'On the Supernatural in Fictitious Composition', published the same year as 'Widow'. In 'Supernatural', Scott redefines the supernatural genre using German supernatural fiction and the Gothic novel/Romance as negative examples. In the former, Scott argues, everything, 'however ludicrous', is possible (Scott 1827: 72). In the latter, the supernatural is plentiful and talkative. For Scott, however, the excess of the German genre would not work in Britain, not even 'in translations' (73). Scott viewed the excess of the Gothic novel/Romance as counterproductive; while he does not explicate this, he evidently means it was counterproductive for the construction of the monstrosity of the supernatural entity, and for the associated terror experienced by the reader. To increase monstrosity, he questions whether supernatural creatures (he uses the generalizer 'goblin' (63)) should be 'permitt[ed] to speak at all' (63). He continues that the supernatural is 'of a character which is extremely difficult to sustain' (62); it loses its 'effect by being brought much into view', and a 'small proportion may [therefore] be said to be better than the whole' (62). '[I]f possible', he says, the 'imagination of the reader' should even be excited – 'without being gratified' (62). Scott sums up

The modern ghost story   57

> the exhibition of the supernatural appearances in fictitious narrative ought to be
> rare, brief, indistinct, and such as may become a being to us so incomprehensible,
> and so different from ourselves, of whom we cannot justly conjecture whence he
> comes, or for what purpose, and of whose attributes we can have no regular or dis-
> tinct perception. (Scott 1827: 63)

Importantly, then, Scott redefines the genre of the supernatural through 'Widow' by replacing excess with scarcity and comprehensibility with incomprehensibility. In different terms, and identifying the first way in which the historical moment that shaped 'Widow' is registered in it, Scott uses the effects of the crisis as he experienced them to intensify the monstrosity of the supernatural in fiction.

The structure of debt

The second way in which 'Widow' registers its historical conjunction is in its structure. 'Widow' is opened by the extradiegetic narrator, Croftangry, who writes: 'Mrs. Bethune Baliol's memorandum begins thus:' (Scott 2003: 68). After the first sentence, 'Widow' switches to a second level of narration, that of Baliol, who is the intradiegetic narrator and tells of her Highland tour. The tour leads Baliol and her guide Donald to the widow, and Donald tells Baliol the widow's story in a conversation that is hidden from the reader who is instead told that, 'in a few hurried words, [Donald] made [Baliol] acquainted with the story which I [Baliol] am now to tell in more detail' (74–5). It is never clarified where Donald heard the story. Rather than a third level of narration, then, in which the events of Elspat and Hamish are told by Donald, those events are seemingly mediated by Baliol, keeping the story within her narrative level, although shifting from internal to zero focalization. Remarkably, however, the story is concluded by not Baliol but Croftangry, who says that, while he (not Baliol) told the reader the story of the widow's life, of the story of her 'death, I can tell [the reader] nothing. It is supposed to have happened several years after [the widow] had attracted the attention of my excellent friend Mrs. Bethune Baliol' (120).

'Widow', then, has a *mise-en-abyme*-like narrative structure; it is a frame narrative, which is characteristic of the modern ghost story (cf. Brewster and Thurston 2018). This structure was already seen in Gothic works, such as Walpole's (1764) *The Castle of Otranto*, and has been much debated. It is therefore clarifying to pause briefly and address that it has been understood, inter alia, to induce suspense, as a mediation between the historical and the literary, and as a way to distance the empirical author from the supernatural and reduce supernatural scepticism in the reader (e.g. Wood 2017: 92).

Smajić shows how, in the nineteenth century, 'representations of the spectral are directly informed by contemporary philosophical and scientific debates' (Smajić 2003: 1108). At that time, a great number of studies on the supernatural appeared. They include 'A Memoir on the Appearance of Specters or Phantoms Occasioned by Disease, With Psychological Remarks' (Nicolai 1803), *An Essay Towards a Theory of Apparition* (Ferriar 1813), and *The Philosophy of Apparitions* (Hibbert 2011 [1825]). These studies argued, with greater insistence than before (Plato and Aristotle already believed the mind could produce images outward, and a not-uncommon theme of Renaissance philosophy was the production of phantoms by the *mind's eye*), that ghosts are 'figments or phantasmata produced by a disordered or overwrought brain' (Castle 1995: 170). This discourse may largely be understood relative to Weber's concept of *disenchantment*. Nevertheless, popular belief still supported the existence of ghosts; the detachment the frame narrative provides, and the overcoming of scepticism such a frame facilitates, may register those developments.

It is useful here to touch briefly on the example of Scott's 'The Tapestried Chamber'. That short story was written shortly after 'Widow' but published only in 1829, and is a more paradigmatic example of the modern ghost story than 'Widow' – probably because, at that point, Scott had had more time to streamline the specific narrative structure he envisioned. 'Tapestried' starts with an 'introduction' in which the narrator says 'the late Miss Anna Seward' told him the story, reducing his responsibility for that story, which he will now tell the reader (Scott 1900: 33). Seward's death is necessary so the information cannot be verified (as in 'Widow'). Moreover, as a respected person (in the 1829 version this is implied; in the

The modern ghost story   59

earlier, 1818 predecessor of the story, she is characterized as 'much celebrated
in the literary world, but now deceased' (Scott 1818: 708)), she cannot be
doubted in death, and history cannot be accessed differently. The narrator
spreads responsibility for and reduces scepticism of these stories further
by saying that 'there are hours and moods when most people are not dis-
pleased to listen to such things [ghost stories]', and that he 'heard some of
the greatest and wisest of [his] contemporaries take their share in telling
them' (Scott 1900: 33). The undoing of ghost scepticism even extends to the
main thrust of the plot (or rather, climax). Protagonist General Browne
sleeps in the haunted tapestried chamber by way of 'experiment' because
the host, Lord Woodville, does not believe rumours of a ghost haunting
the room. To test this, he needs a 'fitting subject' whose 'courage was in-
dubitable' and whose 'mind [was] free of any preoccupation on the subject',
which he finds in his friend the general. When Browne reports that he saw
the ghost, Woodville, who was a 'complete skeptic' the night before, now
says there 'can remain no longer any doubt of the horrible reality of your
apparition' (1900: 52) – and, by extension, of apparitions in general. The
'credibility function' of opening by narrative displacement, then, supports
the suspension of disbelief necessary (perhaps in particular) for its contemporary sceptical readers.

It would be thoughtless to reject the earlier interpretations and ex-
planations of the frame narrative; this chapter rather suggests an additional
reason for the narrative displacement, and particularly (although not exclusively) for the messy variation thereof, as found in 'Widow'. Specifically, the claim put forward here is that the narrative structure registers the
structure of the 'accommodation bills' – and, by extension, the structure
of the 1825 financial crash. Similar to the accommodation bills, the reader
of 'Widow' is confronted with an event that maybe or that allegedly has
a real source (Anne Murray Keith), but the responsibility for which is de-
ferred from one narrative level to another. And while there appear to be
several narrative levels, each supposedly guaranteeing the veracity of the
other, certain transfers of knowledge – such as those between Donald and
Baliol, and between Donald and an unknown interlocutor – are missing.
Unclear, too, is how Baliol hears the story from Donald in a 'few hurried
words' and subsequently spends forty-five pages retelling it to the reader – an

60   CHAPTER 2

unintelligible increase in value. Moreover, in the case of the widow's story, it is unclear who is responsible for the narration because the two narrators flow over into each other – the threshold between them is erased; it is unclear where the one stops and the other starts. Finally, the ultimate guarantor of 'Widow' is Anne Murray Keith, the empirical person who told the empirical Scott the 'tale of the Deserter', of which it is uncertain whether it was fictional. But Keith died in 1818, almost a decade before the story was published.

To reformulate, as with the accommodation bills, the frame narrative creates a narrative system that at first sight appears to be firmly grounded in an identifiable source, but which on closer inspection appears to be, to adopt Scott's term, an 'incomprehensible' system of narratives – a narrative bubble, *the structure of debt*. This book suggest understanding this structure of debt – which, in its incomprehensibility, echoes the monstrosity envisioned in Scott's revision of the supernatural – as foundational of the narrative form of Scott's modern ghost story. The third and final way in which the historical moment is registered in 'Widow' can now be addressed.

The haunted cosmopolitan space

The *ideologeme* of the cosmopolitan space in 'Widow' consists of several aspects. The most important, as addressed above, are the (celebration of the) roads, which facilitate the mobility central to the *ideologeme*, and – inseparable from the roads – Baliol's cosmopolitanism, which leads her to take to and celebrate the roads and commence her tour. It is relevant to note that Hay, commenting on Baliol's cosmopolitanism, argues Baliol is 'too English, too cosmopolitan, not agrarian or provincial enough to be haunted' (2011: 32), yet it is questionable whether this is the case. The protagonist starts her journey 'fearless[ly]' and, arriving at the tree, is told it involves a 'mystery' (Scott 2003: 68). Using concepts of monsters known to her, she attempts to grasp the situation, asking Donald if '[t]here is a bogle or a brownie, a witch of a gyre-carlin, a bodach or a fairy, in the case?' Donald replies that she is 'clean aff the road [sic]' – that she is wrong (73). He tells her the story of the widow, to which Baliol listens with 'horror

The modern ghost story 61

and sympathy' and which makes her want to help the widow, while also being 'afraid to do so' (75).

Croftangry (now narrator) conveys how the widow does not leave Baliol's mind after hearing the story, and how she attempts to understand Elspat better and to 'alleviate the condition of this most wretched woman' (120). She tries to give the widow more money and succeeds in making her 'means of subsistence less precarious' (120). Croftangry notes this would be appreciated even by the 'most wretched outcast', but the widow reciprocates only 'total indifference' and 'resentment', and Baliol's efforts are 'never satisfied' (120). Baliol subsequently disappears from the narrative completely, although it is uncertain at precisely what point (120). Croftangry, meanwhile, proceeds to tell the widow's story and increases the uncertainty about her existence, as well as her monstrosity. He narrates that, even during the widow's life, the villagers were 'frightened at her looks' because she resembled a 'lifeless corpse' who did not have a 'mode of life [but] rather of existence' (120). One night, Croftangry says, the widow disappeared without trace; ever since, the villagers rise 'in terror', in 'dreadful terror', thinking they 'sometimes hear her voice' (121). When a 'latch rattle[s]' at night, they still expect the 'entrance of their terrible patient, animated by supernatural strength, and in the company, perhaps, of some being more dreadful than herself' (121), and 'many are still unwilling, at untimely hours, to pass the oak-tree, [because] beneath [it], as they allege, [the widow] may still be seen seated' (122).

Contrary to Hay's claims, then, Baliol appears to be haunted by the widow *because* she is cosmopolitan – her cosmopolitanism is the very condition for haunting, because her beloved roads lead her to become haunted. Although 'Widow' starts as a fearless journey and a celebration of the roads that facilitate it, it ends in dreadful terror, and although it starts with the appreciation of 'romantic retreat[s]' and 'traditional stories of the country', it ends in the unknowability of the widow and her story (71–2). To be sure, Baliol's mobility terminates with the monstrosity that haunts the tree, and she is indeed 'clean aff the road' – and not just in the way her guide intends with that remark (73). 'Widow' thus starts with cosmopolitan mobility and ends in monstrous petrification.

It is helpful for the understanding of 'Widow' to discuss briefly how Hay comes to his conclusion. For him, seemingly, Baliol is not haunted because his focus is the apparition of the widow's husband, who is the only character in 'Widow' explicitly identified as a ghost. Based on this chapter, however, it can be argued that the husband-ghost is irrelevant in the context of 'Widow' as a modern ghost story. It was argued in Chapter 1 that the modern ghost story is, above all, a set of formal conventions, to which ghostly figures are not as relevant as the way the haunter/hauntee relationship is formally constructed. Particularly, as Scott describes, the modern ghost story involves a transition from talkative to unintelligible, silent and therefore monstrous supernatural figures – an intensification of the monstrosity through scarcity and incomprehensibility. Yet the husband-ghost is a friendly and talkative adviser to Hamish – and, paradoxically, because he has been identified above as a marker for modernity, belongs to the feudal realm. The widow, on the other hand, is incomprehensible and silent, and becomes increasingly monstrous as the narrative progresses. Paradoxically, then, she belongs to the realm of the modern (ghost story). To reformulate this once more, the widow is a modern ghost figure, even though she is never identified as ghost explicitly.

Importantly, the widow also echoes – and can even be seen as sedimentation of – the *structure of debt*, which is organized along the same principle of incomprehensibility; that is, the financial crisis of 1825. The monstrosity of the structure of debt thus cuts through *and* is located at the heart of the fantasy of the cosmopolitan space in 'Widow', establishing it as haunted.

'Widow': The form of The Panic

'Widow' was thus the first instance of a new, literary (or para-literary) form – the modern ghost story – the raw materials of which may be said to have been extracted directly from Scott's personal experience. This seems to be even more the case in terms of relating the haunted cosmopolitan space to his biography. The Panic severely affected Scott's ability to travel, as illustrated by his journal. On the very first page, Scott looks back at how he was 'in Ireland last summer and had a most delightful tour' (1891: 3); yet his delight is directly followed by an overview of the

The modern ghost story

expenses, which were 'upwards of £500 [...] for we travelld a large party and in stile [sic]' (3). He proceeds to describe the 'poverty' of the Irish, who live in 'cottages [that] would scarce serve for pigsties even in Scotland', and who are dressed in

> rags that seem the very refuse of a ragshop and are disposed on their bodies with such ingenious variety of wretchedness that you would think nothing but some sort of perverted taste could have assembled so many shreds together. (Scott 1891: 3)

The memory of the tour is fresh, fond and dear, but recollecting the fantastic splendour of the cosmopolitan space also leads to the remembrance of the burden of travel expense, and of primitive accumulation in the form of colonialism (and colonial poverty), of which the cosmopolitan space is a function (and which was invisible as such in Goethe). Not accidentally, Scott uses the descriptor 'wretched' for both the widow and the Irish.

The Ireland tour, addressed directly and indirectly (as is often specified in Anderson's footnotes), returns throughout Scott's journal as a form of mirage; an image of a desirable, yet now inaccessible and unrecoverable, past. Journeys, for Scott, become a burden; his desire to travel is 'corrupted' (404) and he has a 'great unwillingness' to do so. He even describes travel as 'ominous' (239) and as doing 'penance' (130, 580) because going on trips had become labour for Scott, in the form of promoting and discussing his work. Travel for leisure, on the other hand, was greatly restricted compared to pre-1825 due to a lack of money, and the theme of travel expenses that starts on the first page returns throughout the journal (e.g. 173, 198, 206, 213, 244, 347, 350, 372, 573, 741, 841). For non-work-related travel he had to borrow money repeatedly, which bothered him greatly, and again creates nostalgia for the pre-*Journal* period:

> The expense of my journey will be some thing considerable which I can fence against by borrowing £500 from Mr. Gibson. To Mr. Cadell I owe already about £200 and must run it up to £500 more at least [...] Yet this heavy burthens would easily be borne if I were the to be the Walter Scott I once was. (741)[5]

---

5 Incidentally, as Anderson points out, he owed Cadell £2,630 (Anderson 741f1).

64   CHAPTER 2

Ironically, then, while Goethe's historical conjuncture provided fruitful ground for the conceptualization and idealization/mystification of the cosmopolitan space but formed an obstacle to its realization, Scott's historical conjuncture provided fruitful ground for its realization but formed an obstacle to its (continued) idealization.

However, the focus on Scott's biography may distract from the way in which the raw materials of 'Widow' were also historical. Millgate showed that Scott's financial situation was exemplary for 'the problem of London' at that time (Millgate 1996: 110), and Checkland (1975) pointed out that the two mechanisms that left Scott indebted had become standard in publishing in 1825. Erickson (1996) and Mason (2005) showed this caused bankruptcies among all the dominant publishers in Britain and led to a paradigm shift in literary production. Before the crash, dominant publishers mainly printed romantic novels, for which their authors were paid (large sums) in advance. After the crash, the emphasis was on serials and low-priced reprints instead. This catalysed the popularity of the short story and the rise of the literary magazine, in which the modern ghost story was a protagonist. Thus, as Mason put it, The Panic – fittingly occurring shortly after the death of Shelley, Keats and Byron – meant the death of Romanticism in Britain (2005: 4); a turn of the screw that enhanced the grip of the capitalist system of production on nineteenth-century Britain, not least on publishing. It is these events that 'Widow' registers, and Scott's modern ghost story may, in a way, be considered the literary form of The Panic.

The modern ghost story after 'Widow'

Goethe's modern world-literature and Scott's modern ghost story both rely on the *ideologeme* of the cosmopolitan space, but their specific location of production, and the uneven capitalist development of early nineteenth-century Europe, drastically affected the way in which this *ideologeme* took shape in their work. In Goethe, the cosmopolitan space

The modern ghost story   65

is in line with an anticipation of the establishment of the conditions of exchange connected to the emerging and expanding capitalist world-system. Yet, rather than connecting those conditions of exchange to the system of production of which they are a function, they were severed from it and collapsed into a humanist project. Scott's modern ghost story is shaped in a Britain where an already dominant capitalism tightens its grip, and in direct response to the first modern financial crisis. The cosmopolitan space in 'Widow', consequently, is reconnected to the system of production via a second sign system – the structure of debt and monstrous supernaturalism, modelled after the crisis. While not demystifying the fantasy of the cosmopolitan space, this juxtaposition frames the *ideologeme* in the structure of debt and positions monstrosity at its centre, constituting it as haunted.

As said, Germany's peculiar situation in Europe made it both a fruitful place for world-literature to be conceptualized and a complicated place for world-literature to be realized. The materialization of the conditions Goethe anticipated was therefore accompanied by the rise of what Pizer called a 'virulent nationalism' (2006: 13–14). It culminated in German unification in 1871 and the decline of Goethe's cosmopolitan ideal of world-literature – which would come to connote, as Pizer shows, 'canonicity and commerce' until after the First World War (2006: 14). Chapter 5 shall return to this topic. Scott's modern ghost story, on the other hand, would become the template of ghost stories to come, and is still relevant if not dominant. Even in the film *An American Haunting* (2005), Scott's modern ghost story form can still be recognized – its frame narrative; its climax; its silent, unintelligible ghosts; and so on – although, expectedly, several other forms have been mixed into that film, too. This, of course, is what this book also shows in its next chapters.

Less obviously (arguably), but certainly no less importantly, haunted mobility became a recurring characteristic of the modern ghost story genre. The tropes of the ghost ship, haunted mail coaches, ghost trains and so on are seen from Scott onwards. Examples are Dickens's 'The Ghost of the Mail' (1836), the hit film *Ghostbusters* II (1989), the *Are You Afraid of the Dark?* episode 'The Tale of Train Magic' (Series 4 Episode 13, 1995), the film *Ghost Ship* (2002) and Swayne's *Haunted Rails* (2019). To show a further

66

CHAPTER 2

glimpse of the afterlife of 'Widow', and the way in which similar issues keep playing a role in the modern ghost story, and before we turn to the Mozambican modern ghost story, two more examples are discussed: Scott's own 'The Tapestried Chamber' and Le Fanu's 'Green Tea'.

'The Tapestried Chamber'

Scott's short story 'Tapestried' is a useful example because, while written shortly after 'Widow', it has a similar but more polished modern ghost story narrative structure. Unsurprisingly, it also plays a bigger role in modern ghost story scholarship. A frame narrative with different narrators, the narrator in the outermost frame says the story of Tapestried 'was told to me many years ago by the late Miss Anna Seward' (Scott 1900: 33). The narrator continues to establish his own reliability, as well as the veracity of the story, and writes that the 'following narrative is given from the pen, so far as memory permits, in the same character in which it was presented to the author's ear' (33), and that 'he has studiously avoided any attempt at ornament which might interfere with the simplicity of the tale' (33). He then undermines his freshly established reliability, and specifies that he did commit to 'selecting his materials' (33) and that his version cannot be fully truthful because this type of 'marvelous' story is better spoken out loud than read on paper, which is how 'the present writer heard the following events related' by Seward (33). The narrator continues to undermine his own reliability and writes that he heard the original story 'more than twenty years since' (34) and even draws Seward's reliability into question; she 'always affirmed that she had derived her information from an authentic source, although she suppressed the names of the two persons chiefly concerned' (34). Moreover, Seward's story is about a 'general officer' whom she 'gave the name of Browne', not because this was his name but 'merely, as I understood, to save the inconvenience of introducing a nameless agent in the narrative' (34). Even though the narrator supposedly learned some of the actual facts about the story as it had occurred, he tells the readers he will not 'avail' himself of 'any particulars I may have since received concerning the localities of the detail' (34). As in the case of 'Widow', then, 'Tapestried' is constructed as an

The modern ghost story 67

incomprehensible system of narratives – a narrative bubble, the structure of debt.

Protagonist Browne, not unlike Baliol, is narrated as cosmopolitan and it is his cosmopolitanism that leads him to be haunted. He returned from 'Yorktown' after the 'American war' to his own 'country' and, while it is not specified where this is, it may be assumed that it is in Britain (34). He then sets out on a 'tour', this time through not the Highlands but the 'western counties', when he finds himself in the 'vicinity of a small country town' (34). It is not specified where this is, although the narrator indicates the scene is 'of uncommon beauty' and a 'peculiarly English' character (34). Browne travels further into that landscape and finally encounters an 'ancient feudal fortress', where he hopes to find some 'family pictures or other objects of curiosity worthy of a stranger's visit' (35). Before 'ordering horses, to proceed on his journey', Browne asks around to find out who lives in the castle; when he finds out it is his old friend, Frank Woodville, he decides to visit. With 'fresh horses', he continues in his 'carriage' (35) to the castle, where he arrives in a 'modern Gothic [!] lodge' (36).

As in the case of 'Widow', Browne interrupts his tour for what are supposed to be pleasantries. Woodville receives his old friend and encourages him to stay a week; yet, when the host wakes up the next morning, he finds his guest already awake and ready to leave. Browne explains: 'I am sorry I cannot have the opportunity of spending another day with your lordship; my post horses are ordered, and will be here directly' (39). When Woodville asks the general how he slept, he answers: 'Most wretchedly indeed, my lord' (40). Woodville is unable to convince Browne to stay for the week, yet the latter fails to regain his mobility directly, even after noting his 'post horses are arrived' (45). His host urges him to stay at least 'half an hour more' to see the family portraits (45) and, upon seeing one of them, the general breaks down. In it, he recognizes the ghost of an ancestor of Woodville, who haunted his room the night before – an appearance that excluded 'any thought of her being a living being. Upon a face which wore the fixed features of a corpse were imprinted the traces of the vilest and most hideous passions which had animated her while she lived' (42). Woodville then admits that in 'yon fatal apartment incest and unnatural murder were committed', and that the tapestried chamber has been haunted ever since (45).

68   CHAPTER 2

As in Baliol's case, then, the tour leads to haunting, and when Browne
leaves the castle it is not to continue traveling but to 'seek in some less
beautiful country, and with some less dignified friend, forgetfulness of
the painful night which he had passed in Woodville Castle' (46). It is illu-
minating to add here that the 1818 version of this story does not contain
this aspect. That version starts after a short note by the author (who calls
himself A.B.) with the arrival of the general (now a colonel called 'D.') in
a friend's 'house' in 'the north of England' in 'October' (Scott 1818: 705).
Thus, in contrast to the vagueness in 'Tapestried', the 1818 version is precise
about its location and no travel is mentioned. Even the colonel's departure,
which must involve travel, is not narrated. For Scott, then, his obsession
with the haunted tour was a post-1825 issue.

'Green Tea'

Fanu's 'Green Tea' (1999 [1872]) emphasizes the psychological realm
more strongly than Scott's work, conforming to the adaptations in the
genre that Hay outlines, as discussed in the introduction. Nevertheless,
Sullivan considers it an 'archetypal' and 'thoroughly modern' ghost story
(1978: 11–12), and M. R. James deems it 'of paramount excellence' to the
modern ghost story genre (1911: 347). Indeed, 'Green' has the convoluted
narrative frame structure and silent, incomprehensible ghost figures, and
is structured by a climax. It is concerned with the transition to capitalism
in the form of primitive accumulation and colonialism/Empire, and has
a cosmopolitan space that is haunted.

The narrative frame of 'Green' is constructed in a now recognizable
way; with its final source no longer determinable. 'Green' narrates the
encounter between the bourgeois character Dr Martin Hesselius and the
feudal character Rev. Robert Lynder Jennings, the troubled demise of the
latter and the former's supposed attempt to help. The story starts with a
heterodiegetic narrator, who explains how he knows of Jennings's story.
Subsequently, a main narrator (possibly but not certainly the same as the
narrator in the previous part) – who is likely an English student of medicine, although he 'seldom[ly spent] twelve months together in the same
place' (1999: 5) – writes how he met a 'German physician' by the name of

The modern ghost story

Martin Hesselius during his 'wanderings', who turns out to be a 'wanderer' too (5). The narrator becomes an admirer of the doctor, and comments that in 'Dr. Hesselius I found my master. His knowledge was immense. [...] My admiration has stood the test of time and survived the separation of death. I am sure it was well founded' (5).

While Hesselius has died (like Seward in 'Tapestried' and Keith in 'Widow'), the narrator has his notes, which were originally letters Hesselius wrote 'during a tour of England' to his 'friend Professor Van Loo of Leyden' (6). The notes were written in English, French and German, and 'appear to have been returned' to Hesselius after Van Loo died (6). The narrator gives himself the task of organizing the notes so he can convey the story to the reader and, already hinting at a next level in the frame narrative as well as establishing reliability, he says 'the narrator [of that next level] is Dr. Martin Hesselius' (6). Nevertheless, he adds, characteristically undermining the reliability he just established, he has made 'slight modifications' to the 'language' and 'names' (6). Moreover, he claims, 'I am a faithful, though I am conscious, by no means a graceful translator, and although here and there I omit some passages, and shorten others, and disguise names, I have interpolated nothing' (6). He thus also makes the voices of different narrators flow into each other, making it impossible in what is about to follow to tell where one narrator stops and the other starts. This narrative confusion is enhanced later in the story with the addition of another narrative level, the one in which Jennings tells his story to Hesselius, which is mediated by the latter and told, edited, translated and modified by the main narrator(s).

The cosmopolitan space is woven through this unintelligible narrative bubble. The story, according to the narrator, results from the interaction between cosmopolitans – (almost-) homeless wanderers – and travelling documents that go back and forth between the sender and receiver, and which are ultimately the result of an England tour. This juxtaposition of documents and travel is continued on the next, diegetic level. Hesselius meets Jennings for the first time during a social event, and he directly realizes (according to the narrator) that Jennings is troubled and that he has a family member who saw a ghost. Hesselius decides to help him and, to open the conversation, he starts with the topic of travel and documents. In his notes, he writes it was an agreeable conversation because, when 'two

70 CHAPTER 2

people, who like reading, and know books and places, having travelled, wish to converse, it is very strange if they can't find topics' (9). Their conversation then transitions to the topic of international publishing.

Books and travel, however, do not maintain their initial splendour. The next meeting of the men takes place in Jennings's study. Hesselius arrives before Jennings, and appears to be impressed. He writes in his notes that this is

> really a study – almost a library. [The room] was much larger than I had expected, and stored with books on either side, from the floor to the ceiling. […] The book-cases standing out, placed the windows, particularly the narrow ones, in deep recesses. The effect of the room was, although extremely comfortable, and even luxurious, decidedly gloomy, and aided by the silence, almost oppressive. […] I stepped into [the] room, with a peculiar foreboding; and its darkness, and solemn clothing of books, for except where two narrow looking-glasses were set in the wall, they were everywhere, helped this sombre feeling. (13)

The books that previously connected the men now create the gloomy setting of a horror story, and again international publishing is highlighted. Hesselius finds a 'complete set of Swedenborg's *"Arcana Caelestia"*, in the original Latin', opens the book and is confronted with some of the passages on 'evil spirits' who are 'from the hells', of which it is said they are sometimes 'with man' (14). He translates the passages for Van Loo, and eventually leaves the room.

Mobility and cosmopolitanism are foregrounded again when, before the next meeting between the men, Hesselius describes a series of journeys to 'Warwickshire', 'Kenlis', 'Piccadilly', 'Shropshire', 'Brighton', 'London', 'Richmond' and 'Blank Street' (18–19). (This narrative strategy will be called *locale enumeration* in Chapter 5.) When the two men finally meet, the room in which they convene is even gloomier than before – 'all was growing dim, and the gloom was insensibly toning [his] mind, already prepared for what was sinister' (20) – and there was just 'light enough to see each other's faces' (20). Without wasting another word, the reverend sits down and 'began his narrative' (20).[6]

---

6 The setting of Jennings's room is the type of ghost story environment prescribed by 'Tapestried'.

The modern ghost story

Jennings's 'narrative' thus starts a new level in the frame narrative, in which Jennings (now mediated by a set of narrators and editors) explains he has been working on the topic of Paganism, during which he drank a 'good deal' of green tea (22). One day, returning home from a meeting with a man who 'had some odd old books, German editions in the medieval Latin', he sees in the 'omnibus' (a horse and carriage) 'a small black monkey' (23). He is interested, and attempts to poke it with his umbrella, yet the umbrella passes through the monkey 'without the slightest resistance' (24). It is a ghost. After Jennings has introduced the creature and implied it has haunted him ever since, a new section of the short story starts, titled 'The Journey' (24), which Sullivan characterizes as the narration of Jennings's 'extraordinary obsession, chronicled in graded steps: three "stages" in a hellish "journey"' (Sullivan 1978: 16). Jennings tells how the monkey follows him, disappearing at times but becoming more aggressive over time (Le Fanu 1999: 30). Explaining the type of moments when the monkey appears, he gives the example of '[o]n lifting my eyes from a book' (28). Over the course of two years, Jennings explains, the situation reached the 'extremity' that 'while I was reading to the congregation, it would spring upon the book and squat there, so that I was unable to see the page' (29).

When Jennings finishes speaking, Hesselius tells a servant that, if the monkey returns, he 'should be sent for immediately' (33). However, he returns to his inn and installs himself 'without the possibility of intrusion or distraction' (34). The next morning, he finds a note from Jennings saying the monkey has begun speaking, and he rushes to see the reverend. When he arrives, he finds the servant with his hands covered in blood and Jennings dead, 'his throat cut with a razor', lying in an 'immense pool of blood' (35). 'Green' ends with Hesselius explaining the situation to Van Loo. The doctor determines Jennings's 'spectral illusions' were caused by 'abuses [like] the habitual use of such agents as green tea' (39). Green tea, according to Hesselius, affects a 'fluid' that runs through the 'nerves' and is 'spiritual though not immaterial' (39). This 'fluid being that which we have in common with spirits [...] forms a surface unduly exposed, on which disembodied spirits may operate: communication is thus more or less effectually established' (39).

While earlier studies of 'Green' interpret the ghost as sin, neurosis or chaos (Sullivan 1978: 17), later ones connect it to colonialism. Nally (2009), for example, shows how the monkey stands in for colonial subjects, and Hay (2011) specifies it concerns Irish colonial subjects specifically. The colonial commodity of tea, for Hay, is the trigger of the ghost and lays bare the social system in its (Lukácsian) totality. The 'anxiety' of empire, he thus argues, 'structures the story' (11).

The tea/ghost connection can even be shown to be stronger than Hay claims and, for the argument of the book, it is relevant to do so. First, Schivelbusch (1992) has shown the historical connection between tea and the Protestant work ethic – tea, unlike alcohol, kept one awake, thus improving work output – and Jennings indeed drinks tea to be able to work long hours. Further, Luxemburg described in her account on primitive accumulation that

> European civilization, that is to say, commodity exchange with European capital, made its first impact on China with the Opium Wars when she was compelled to buy the drug from Indian plantations in order to make money for British capitalists. In the seventeenth century, the East India Company had introduced the cultivation of poppies in Bengal; the use of the drug was disseminated in China by its Canton branch. (1951: 387)

The British thus destroyed the Indian textile market and started poppy cultivation to force China to trade with them. Yet as Liu (2020) demonstrates, tea played at least an equally important role in this process. A desired commodity by the British, the Chinese had a monopoly on tea. To break that monopoly, the British started cultivating tea in India, which was not a tea producer, even though the Assam region had a native tea plant. The British aim was successful; from 1837 onwards, the tea industry rapidly grew, eventually displacing the Chinese monopoly. The tea in 'Green' thus registers not only colonialism but also – and arguably equally, if not primarily – primitive accumulation.

Yet the reliability of the ghost/tea connection is also questionable. It is made on three occasions; namely, when Hesselius speaks to the hostess of the party after he first meets Jennings, in Jennings's room and, in Hesselius's diagnosis, his explanation to Van Loo. The first is, at most, a suggestion that

The modern ghost story 73

tea and ghosts are somehow linked to 'books' and 'places'. The second gains importance through a combination of its position, length and formulation. That section is positioned at the beginning of Jennings's explanation of his problems, suggesting it is the foundation for them. With 313 words and 23 lines, the section is almost twice as long as the average paragraph – it is the longest paragraph of the entire story in words, and the second longest in lines (the longest being the horror descriptions of the demon monkey in its final stages, with twenty-four lines). It is formulated with a bias: tea is presented as a drug because, when one is working, one needs to be 'on something' (22). The third ghost/tea connection is Hesselius's analysis of Jennings's problems for Van Loo.

The ghost/tea link is suspect, then, because the reader is set up to support Hesselius's findings. The first two times it is made, it encourages the reader to establish a link between tea and the ghost so that when they arrive at the third time – Hesselius's conclusion – they will be inclined to agree with him. However, Hesselius is not to be trusted as a physician. He is bad at his job – he makes himself unavailable upon realizing Jennings is in a fragile state, and cannot be reached for help – and is chiefly concerned with, as Sullivan puts it, 'validat[ing] his theories' (Sullivan 1978: 28). The narrator organizing Hesselius's papers is a fan, who aims to keep a legacy alive and is overtly unreliable.

Rather than discard Hay's reading, I suggest adding the importance of the connection between books/places/ghosts. It is less obvious than the ghost/tea connection, because Hesselius does not highlight it, but – as the above demonstrates – the story provides evidence of its importance. Indeed, the monkey first appears in an omnibus (another haunted mode of mobility) on the way back from a library; it reappears when Jennings is reading and eventually prevents him from reading, and the story climaxes during the 'hellish journey'. It is, in other words – and recalling Goethe's world-literature and the circulation of literary works that it anticipates – books, travel and the cosmopolitans involved who are haunted, not (just) green tea (consumption). As in Scott's work, the cosmopolitan space initially celebrated is constructed as haunted.

Before continuing to the next chapter, a final aspect of 'Green' – namely, the way in which it registers the transition from feudalism to capitalism – deserves attention. After Jennings's death, labour materializes in the figure of the servant (an important figure in the ghost story; see, for instance, Robbins 2010). The servant appears throughout the narrative but may never speak for himself; his voice is instead rendered in indirect discourse ('the servant told me', 'the servant begged my pardon', 'asking me', 13), or he is spoken to ('I told the servant', 33). After Jennings dies, Hesselius writes that he and the servant went 'downstairs together' (36). Subsequently, Hesselius 'heard all the servant had to tell', adding that it 'was not a great deal' (36). Contrary to that claim, however, the servant says a great deal: he says 583 words, says 'I' thirty-nine times, gets a name ('Jones', 39) and can use verbs like 'attend' and 'assist' (belonging to his profession as a servant); but he can also 'think' (six times, 39–40) and go 'up' and down the stairs on his own accord, signifying social mobility and the narrative recognition of his ability to act (twice, 39–40). In fact, this part of the narrative is focalized through the servant; the reader sees with the servant's eyes, gazing not from master to servant but from servant to master, and it is the servant who is asking the master (Jennings) questions ('I asked him [...] and he said' 39).

Of course, the servant disappears as suddenly as he appeared. Hesselius takes over the narrative again, and says: 'Jones had no more to tell. Poor Mr. Jennings was very gentle, and very kind. All his people were fond of him. I could see that the servant was very much moved' (40). Hesselius, it will be clear, may be wrong, and the servant may have killed Jennings – the reader does not have enough information to prove or disprove this. Either way, in this sentence, the servant shifts back from 'Jones' to 'servant' in Hesselius's gaze. And, while Jennings's death in an 'immense pool of blood' may stand in for the 'bloody transition into modernity' referenced by Hay at the beginning of this chapter, the servant is reintegrated into the dialectics of oppression by the bourgeois doctor Hesselius (Hay 2011: 15).

It is this form of the modern ghost story as established by 'Widow', and reproduced in varying shapes afterwards, that would also come to be used by Mozambican authors.

CHAPTER 3

Emergence of the Mozambican modern ghost story

The modern ghost story has not been associated hitherto with Mozambican literature written in Portuguese (MlwP). Yet this chapter demonstrates that Mozambican authors did draw on its genre characteristics during the period 1866–1982. The chapter discusses the 1866 Gothic ghost poem, 'Uma Visão' [An Apparition], by Campos de Oliveira, which it considers an early – if not the earliest – node of emergence for the Mozambican modern ghost story. It continues to show that the genre is absent in the following decades, although what can be considered modern ghost figures do appear in MlwP. The core of the chapter is an analysis of Orlando Mendes's 1965 *Portagem* [Toll], which arguably contains the first example of a Mozambican modern ghost story. The chapter proposes that, while the *Portagem* explicitly thematizes racial relations, the modern ghost story that forms a part of the novel draws attention to, and registers, the 1926 formal and legal sedimentation of Mozambique's nineteenth-century primitive accumulation into colonial capitalism. The chapter ends with a discussion of a transition period in MlwP's use of the supernatural, which it suggests is a response to official political party Frelimo's attitudes towards the supernatural, and again contributed to the genre's absence.

Importantly, while none of the works discussed in this chapter immediately appear to be archetypal modern ghost stories from the perspective of the British modern ghost story as discussed in the previous chapter, they do illustrate how (literary) form circulated in the world-literary system, could be and was used, and was combined with local forms and content – predominantly what is called here *Mozambican Neorealism*. Chapters 4 and 5 will show how subsequent authors could then draw on the building blocks from both national and international literary ecologies, to use Beecroft's term (2015).

76   CHAPTER 3

Before turning to the literary works, it is beneficial for the understanding of the role of the modern ghost story in Mozambique to address some general questions that this chapter anticipates because it struggled with them itself. Indeed, the Portuguese anchored off the coast of contemporary Mozambique in 1498, so why does this chapter start in 1866? How can this chapter span almost an entire century, and why were there so few ghost stories during this period? To answer these questions, this chapter starts with an overview of a history of Portuguese settler colonialism and literature in the territory now known as Mozambique.

Colonization, Mozambique, literature: A brief history

One 'of the most striking features of Portuguese colonialism', writes Darwin, 'was the lateness [compared to other colonizers] of its settler migration, especially to Africa' (2013: 322). Portugal's late colonization of Mozambique had consequences for the production of MlwP because it meant the late spread of the Portuguese language, the late creation of Mozambique as a unit and the late emergence of a Mozambican consciousness – and, thus, of a Mozambican literature. In 1498, Vasco da Gama moored his ships off Ilha de Moçambique, an island off the East African coast then ruled by Mussa Al Bique, on whom the name Mozambique is based. While the Portuguese established a permanent settlement there in 1506, their goal was not to colonize the Mozambican territory, as Newitt shows, but rather to establish a foothold 'in the Indian Ocean' to monopolize the gold trade from the Eastern African and Indian coasts. They 'declared the sea, rather than any land, to be the sovereign realm of the Portuguese Crown', and built coastal settlements along the East African and Indian coast to control and defend the area, repair and replenish ships, and tax foreign merchants who wanted to make use of this 'Estado da India' [State of India] (Newitt 2017: 23–4).

Although the Portuguese presence in the East African region increased in the following years, this did not have significant structural consequences. Settlers travelling inland established trading communities   •

Emergence of the Mozambican modern ghost story   77

and large *prazos* (a form of *latifundia* based on monopolies granted by the Portuguese Crown). As Bertelsen points out, this would have consequences for the way the 'traditional' was 'molded', namely by continuous influences from both Africa and Europe (48). However, many *prazeiros* – the *prazos*' owners – integrated into the local population, took on local customs and married local women (Newitt 27). Moreover, Maravi kingdoms 'effectively blocked any attempts by the Portuguese to expand north of Zambesi and controlled the main trade routes to the coast' (32). By the seventeenth century, Portugal had thus become 'just one of a number of merchant communities adhering to the age old patterns of monsoon trade' (28–9).

During 'the three hundred years from the fifteenth to the eighteenth centuries', Newitt says, there was 'certain stability' in the region (53). This changed in the nineteenth century due to three main developments. After 'the end of the Napoleonic wars, eastern Africa was drawn increasingly into the world dominated by global capitalism' (53) and the associated European need for labour and raw materials – the roughly 2.5 million slaves shipped to Brazil between 1800 and 1850 mostly went through East African Portuguese ports (53–4). Second, severe droughts and famines disturbed and destroyed African communities as well as *prazos*, leaving trade networks paralyzed and creating a power vacuum. This eventually resulted in the consolidation of most Zambesi *prazos* in the hands of five families, who established themselves as de facto warlords or kings, later forming a new obstacle to Portuguese expansion (51, 61). Droughts also led to invasions by the Ngoni, who united the area between the Zambesi and Limpopo under one ruler. Coalitions were created in the north to protect against the invaders (58–9). Third, the droughts facilitated slavery. Displaced families were 'rounded up and sold into slavery', and the new *prazeiros* and Ngoni acted as slave traders (52).

Yet even in the nineteenth century, Portuguese control of the Mozambican interior remained minimal; new attempts to conquer the territory failed, in part due to the new power blocks. Only when the British interest in Eastern Africa increased, and propaganda from organizations such as the Lisbon Geographical Society hailed Africa to be the new Brazil – at least to the extent that it had similar riches in the offing – did the acuteness of Portuguese settler colonialist efforts also increase. The Portuguese Crown

78   CHAPTER 3

gave out mining concessions in the hope of claiming territory, even with the limitations of its material means, and organized military campaigns. These clashed with overlapping British ambitions and campaigns resulting from the end of the so-called British 'informal Empire' (Wallerstein 2011: 125), notably those of Cecil Rhodes, and eventually formed the incentive to hold the Berlin Conference (1884–5). The tour de force ended with the 1890 British Ultimatum, forcing Portugal to secede areas in contemporary Zimbabwe and Malawi. In 1891, a treaty was signed that (largely) established Mozambican borders as they are now known (Newitt 2017: 84–94).

Considering this brief history, it would be premature to speak of a category such as Mozambican literature before 1891. Certainly, De Albuquerque and Ferraz Motta, in their periodization of Mozambican literature, do take the literary production from the fifteenth century onwards into account and suggest a first period labelled 'período da expansão portuguesa' (1498–1864) [period of Portuguese expansion] (8). During this period, they argue, writers 'na generalidade, não residiam em Moçambique' [generally, did not reside in Mozambique] and were generally Portuguese (1998: 8). Laranjeira adds that the works of these authors were 'não necessariamente literários nem africanos' [not necessarily literary, nor African] (2001: 185). Thus, although the approach of De Albuquerque and Motta has the advantage of highlighting that a part of the proto-history of MlwP is rooted in Portuguese colonial literature, and thus of establishing Mozambican literature as rooted in an international literary system from its very conception, it would be an exaggeration to suggest that Mozambican literature – and, by extension, Mozambican ghost stories – could have been produced during these first centuries.

Even after the 1891 agreement, Portugal was 'faced with the problem of turning paper claims into some kind of effective government' (Newitt 2017: 95), and it failed to shape coherence for some time. Perhaps unsurprisingly, then, the formation of Mozambique on paper did not coincide with the formation of a literature that in some way – in its production, function, theme, style, aesthetic or consciousness – was Mozambican. According to Mendonça, Mozambican literature only begins with the literature published in newspapers such as *O Africano* (1908–18) and *O Brado Africano* (1918–74), and with the poetry of Rui de Noronha – a first phase that she labels

Emergence of the Mozambican modern ghost story

'Protonacionalismo' [proto-nationalism] and that, for her, lasts from 1908 to the 1930s (2008: 22). The start of Mendonça's proto-nationalist period coincides with the newspaper efforts of the Albasini brothers – efforts preceded by publications such as *Illustração Goana* (1864–6, published in Goa), in which De Campos's 'Visão' was published. Laranjeira instead takes 1849, the year of 'o primeiro livro impresso' [the first printed book], as the starting point of African literature written in Portuguese (2001: 185), and De Albuquerque and Motta speak of a 'colonial period' in between their 'expansion-' and Mendonça's 'protonationalism' phase (Albuquerque and Motta 1998: 27). With Mendonça, this chapter maintains the Albasinis did indeed create a literary infrastructure in the form of newspapers *in* Mozambique run *by* Mozambicans. Nevertheless, some of the writers from the 'colonial period', such as De Oliveira, did express a (proto-)Mozambican national consciousness and may thus be considered Mozambican, even in the absence of a Mozambican literature.

Despite the literary developments at the beginning of the twentieth century, MlwP remains sparse during its first decades. The Albasini infrastructure was consistent – it started in 1908 and outlasted the brothers João (who died in 1922) and José (who died in 1932) by forty-two years (1974) – but it was also modest in size and reach, and necessarily so. Newitt writes that, due to the 'extreme weakness of Portugal's position' (95) – politically, militarily and economically – 'Portugal's effective presence in Mozambique was very limited and in practice did not extend far beyond the coastal port towns and the historic settlements in the Zambesi valley', even after the treaty (98). The 'whole country' would come under 'a single administration' only in 1942 (Newitt 2017: 147). Portugal did attempt to increase the number of settlers across the territory by administering concessions to companies for the exploitation of large parts of Mozambique and by sending labourers overseas (99). This had some effect and, according to Darwin, in 1900 the 'white population of Angola and Mozambique was perhaps 15,000 to 20,000 – less than two per cent of that of South Africa's at the same period' (2013: 322). Hedges and Rocha suggest this grew to 17,842 in 1930, 27,438 in 1940, 48,213 in 1950 and 97,245 in 1960 (1999: 165; see also Penvenne 2005: 86). However, Penvenne points out that the projected number of settler families was never reached (1979: 9). This was, in part, because Portuguese workers considered Mozambique a space for short-term labour. João Albasini even complained that they arrive for 'a short stay in the land of the blacks to gather enough savings; and then escape it all to return to Portugal' (in Penvenne 1979: 10). Additionally, as Darwin writes, the 'Portuguese state controlled out-migration much more rigorously than the British, partly because it feared the creation of new "Brazils"'; that is, a state establishing its own independence (2013: 322). Hence, the Portuguese were only 'allowed to move freely into any part of the "Portuguese economic space"' in 1962 (2013: 323). This, finally, led to a significant settler increase, and by 1973 'the white population of Angola and Mozambique had surged up to 500,000, although this figure includes the military personnel that were sent there' (2013: 323).

The low number of Portuguese settlers also affected the number of MlwP publications, for the simple reason that the Portuguese language did not spread as widely and as quickly as it would have otherwise among the African population in the form of *assimilados*. Duffy shows the professed goal of the Portuguese colonizer was to assimilate the entire African population into so-called 'Portuguese values' (including language) through education (1961: 299) – a policy that, as Alexander Keese (2007) argues, is an 'immediate effect of the "civilizing mission" as perceived by the Portuguese colonizer' (47). The first step in that education system was the *ensino rudimentar/ensino de adaptação* [rudimentary education/adaptive education], a three-year programme with a focus on speaking and reading Portuguese (Duffy 1961: 299). Duffy demonstrates that, if the aim was assimilating the entire African population, this effort was characterized by 'inadequacy' (1961: 299). The number of African students was over twenty times lower in Mozambique than in the neighbouring colony of Rhodesia, and few of the students who started also finished the *ensino rudimentar*. Even in 1955, 98 per cent of the African population could not read or write in Portuguese (Duffy 1961: 299) due to a lack of 'teachers for Africa, not enough money, not enough interest' (Duffy 1961: 301). Mendonça explicates that assimilation in Portuguese colonies was really the process of educating a small African elite to homogenize the culture of the colonizer with what was considered the 'inferior' culture of the colonized (Mendonça 1988: 87). Duffy, too, specifies that, specifically during the Salazar era, 'the design'

Emergence of the Mozambican modern ghost story

of the assimilation policy was 'to see to it that the African majority does not become any more politically conscious than is metropolitan Portugal's rural majority' (1961: 301). He continues: 'Salazarian sociology envisages the formation of a devout, semi-literate, hard-working and conservative African population. For them the *ensino de adaptação* is sufficient' (301). As a result, and as a 1950 census illustrates, at that point only 4,353 Mozambicans had the assimilated status (Spencer 1974: 169).

The idiosyncrasies of the formation of the Mozambican literary system, including the 'lateness' of Portuguese settler colonialism and the attempts to minimize the number of Africans who could read and write, have direct consequences for this chapter. It does not discuss the period before 1866 because it is doubtful that Mozambican literature existed at that time; although, even if only the Albasinis established a literary *system* of production, Mozambican writers could still exist before that, in relative isolation. Indeed, this chapter considers De Oliveira to be Mozambique's first poet (Albuquerque and Motta 8; Ferreira 1985).[1] The timespan of this chapter

1   This issue is not without debate. According to Raul Calane da Silva, the printing press first came to Ilha de Moçambique in 1845 (2011: 150). De Oliveira was among the first persons whose works were printed on that press, having been born in Mozambique, writing in Portuguese and voicing a specifically Mozambican nationalist sentiment in his work (Ferreira 1987: 19). The poem 'O Pescador de Moçambique' [The Fisherman of Mozambique] shows this well. The poetic voice claims to have been born in Mozambique, identifies with the island life of Ilha de Moçambique and with Mozambican geography, and invokes several place names, such as Sancul and Mossuril. It also identifies with the people and their 'cor negra' [Black colour], thus contrasting the Portuguese with Mozambicans (in Ferreira 1985: 111). However, Ana Mafalda Leite highlights that most of De Oliveira's work had no such 'inscrição localista' [markers of localism] or 'consciência de pertença' [consciousness of belonging] to Mozambique (Leite 2008: 63). Francisco Noa adds that, at least as a response to colonialism, De Oliveira's work was 'pouco significativa e pouco consequente' [of little significance and of little consequence] (2008: 36). Ferreira (1985) considers De Oliveira's work a reaction triggered by the exoticist colonial literature that was dominant at the end of the nineteenth century. Nevertheless, because of his involvement with the printing press, his engagement in publishing and his editing of a number of magazines, De Oliveira 'dinamizou a actividade literária da primeira capital moçambicano' [catalyzed the literary activity in Mozambique's first capital] (Leite 2008: 61). This book therefore considers De Oliveira's work as Mozambican.

is long because Mozambican literary production was sparse – even after the official unification of its territory in 1891, the Albasini efforts at the beginning of the twentieth century and the institution of a single administration in 1942. The number of modern ghost stories is small because the genre is a minor part of the total literary production in any literary ecology, and it thus follows that the number of Mozambican modern ghost stories during this initial period is, expectedly, very small.

There are additional reasons why few modern ghost stories are expected during the period discussed in this chapter. Based on the preceding chapter, certain social conditions for the ghost story were arguably absent in Mozambique. There was no Panic in Mozambique, colonialism was part of everyday lived experience (although the metropolis may not have been), the transition away from *latifundios* and feudalism would mean the transition away from one form of colonialism to another, and so on. Further, upper-class writers registering their economic downfall, or their concerns with being modern or the resentful working classes – as well as middle-class authors expressing the invisible totality of colonial capitalism in the colonial metropolis – would predominantly be Portuguese and located in Portugal. The Mozambican *assimilado* class – its highest class under colonial domination – was shaped as a class lower than Portuguese labourers and were, for example, paid significantly less for their labour power (Sumich 2018: 38). Sumich recently demonstrated that, even in contemporary Mozambique, the 'middle class' is small (9). Ghost stories would thus be expected from Portuguese settlers or assimilated writers at best. Another obstacle to the en masse appearance of modern ghost stories in Mozambique was the dominance of poetry, which lasted well into the twentieth century. Dealing with the reality of censorship, authors were drawn mostly to codified (that is, poetry) or seemingly politically neutral genres (as in the example of Rui de Noronha's poetry, below). Moreover, the 'competing' supernatural paradigm of the *traditional field* in Mozambique was arguably dominant with the majority of the population, although not necessarily with Mozambican (*assimilado*) authors.

Although the consequence for the modern ghost story in Mozambican literature is that its numbers are small, a number of other conditions of the ghost story were, in fact, present. Most importantly, the African

Emergence of the Mozambican modern ghost story 83

colonies were increasingly drawn into the capitalist world-system – and this included the primitive accumulation of the (partly) feudal Portuguese colonial system. This, then – as discussed presently – is registered in the early Mozambican modern ghost story.

Predecessors: The Mozambican Gothic of Campos de Oliveira

A Romantic period preceded the modern ghost story in European literary contexts, and a similar development occurred in Mozambique in the form of Campos de Oliveira's poem 'Uma Visão'. Discussing the Gothic form and its social referent briefly is therefore clarifying to the purposes of this chapter.

Romanticism in Europe was considered in contrast to Enlightenment thought, and involved a considerable supernatural component in the form of the Gothic. Miles (2002) summarizes that the Gothic draws on a set of recognizable features, including the geographical features of the ruin, haunted cavern and recess; the locations of the castle, abbey, ancient house and cloister; the generic pointers of the historical romance, tales and memoirs; ghost and related figures of the apparition, ghost-seer and magician; and so on (42). By the 1790s, the 'novel-writing market [was] flooded by the Gothic' (41), a success that has been explained in different ways. The Marquis de Sade famously considered it 'collateral damage of the French Revolution', a bloody history that writers attempted to match and come to terms with in fictional works (Miles 43). Yet, as Miles points out, not only did the Gothic start before the French Revolution but contemporary critics of the form also knew it was derived from 'the Burkean cult of the sublime', which resonated with Gothic terror (43). The reason to suggest otherwise, he argues, was politically motivated. The sublime was associated with the prestigious forms of tragedy and epic and authors of the Gothic thus attempted to pitch their works 'towards the high end of the literary market' (43). By connecting Gothic terror to that of the French Revolution, Miles

84 CHAPTER 3

argues, critics countered those pretensions and characterized authors of the Gothic as dangerous revolutionaries on the one hand and bad authors on the other. The Gothic was also considered a revolutionary form, but this is incongruent with attempts to appease the high end of the literary market. Miles therefore argues:

> The Gothic derived its interest for readers, not because it was the necessary art of a revolutionary age [...], or because it was itself revolutionary [...], but because there was a widespread perception that all old structures were in a tottering condition, such as, for instance, castles, or the constitution, with its feudal, Gothic foundations. (44)

In other words, for Miles, The Gothic resonated with social anxiety about a transition away from feudalism, echoing Shapiro's claim that, during the 'transition' in or to capitalism, 'Gothic tales express the terror of capitalist systematicity, for during these conjunctural moments, capitalism's gruesome nature is most sensationally revealed' (44).

De Oliveira's 1866 poem 'Uma Visão' [An Apparition][2] (in Ferreira 1985: 87–9) is the first example of the Mozambican Gothic that was found in the context of this study. His work was influenced by a number of (mainly) French and Portuguese authors, such as Camilo Castelo Branco, Victor Hugo, Nicolau Tolentino and Manuel du Bocage, and several literary currents, including satire, Neoclassicism and lyricism (Leite 62; Albuquerque and Motta 26). The most important influence on his work was arguably the 'romantismo tardio português' [belated Portuguese Romanticism] (Albuquerque and Motta, 6), which was taught in the Portuguese colonies – including in Goa, where De Oliveira studied (Cabral 1957: 285). Portuguese Romanticism, as in Miles's account, was also associated with sociopolitical transition. It became a dominant trend within Portuguese literature after the Napoleonic Wars, which led to the Liberal Revolution of 1820, the transformation of the absolutist monarchy into a constitutional monarchy in 1822 and the independence of Brazil in that same year.

Despite – or because of – this lateness, it was heavily inflected by international Romantic tendencies. Rodrigues (1983) notes that a significant literary exchange between Britain and Portugal had commenced in

---

2   This could also be translated as 'A Vision'.

Emergence of the Mozambican modern ghost story 85

the eighteenth century (1). Literary texts were increasingly cross read, and the 'reformed teaching at Coimbra', as well as several literary magazines, helped with 'spreading information about British culture' throughout Portugal (Varga 2006: 205). Walter Scott's work made a particularly 'lasting impression' on Portuguese Romanticism, as Varga shows (10), as it influenced the two foundational Portuguese Romanticists: Herculano and Garrett. Both Garrett (a 'grande leitor de Walter Scott' [big reader of Walter Scott], Gouveia 1986: 375) and Herculano (who said Scott is 'o modelo e desesperação de todos os romancistas' [the model and desperation of all romanciers], Gouveia 1986: 374) were forced to seek exile in Britain (and France) after the re-emergence of absolutism in Portugal at the end of the 1820s. There, they encountered Scott's work, as well as the British Romantic aesthetic (Rodrigues 77–9; Varga 211–12). Paradoxically, then, the authors who influenced De Oliveira are not only predominantly associated with Romanticism but also connected to the rise of modern literature in Portugal (cf. Buescu 109; Frier 121).[3]

If De Oliveira's oeuvre can be understood against the backdrop of Portuguese Romanticism, 'Visão' is contextualized more specifically by the third generation of Portuguese Romanticism. Also referred to as Ultraromanticism, the form was thematically closer to the Gothic and is thought to have started with the publication of Soares de Passos's poem, 'O Noivado do Sepulcro' ['Grave Engagement[4]'] (1952), after the Portuguese monarchy had (yet again) overcome popular opposition and established a fragile political balance in the country. Considering the overlap in theme and imagery, 'Noivado' may well have been a main source of inspiration for 'Visão'. It is theatrically melodramatic, has a strong Romantic idealism and has a certain irrationality and excessiveness to it that may be expected from a Romantic/Gothic work.

3   Note that British modern ghost stories in general, not just the work of Walter Scott, circulated widely in Portugal. For instance, as Maria Leonor Machado de Sousa (2013) has shown, Dickens's work had a lasting presence in Portugal. *O Jornal do Porto* published a Portuguese translation of *A Christmas Carol* as early as 1864, and a year later published a volume containing all the Portuguese translations of Dickens. Pessoa spoke lovingly of the author's work, and *Carol* was included in one of the most successful literature collections in Portugal, 'Coleção Azul', published between 1940 and 1960.

4   This translation is by Vera Peixoto, and I am thankful for her inventive suggestion.

86   CHAPTER 3

It is organized in nineteen quatrains and the rhyme associated with that form, draws on a morbid imagination and is set at least partly in a graveyard, where the lyrical voice conveys the loss of a dearly beloved. The poetic voice expresses a fascination with not only the lost virgin woman, who he loves in life and in death, but also with her inanimate body. Death, however, is not (just) considered a negative in the end; it is also the way for the poetic voice to be reunited with his love subject, and the poem ends with the lines: 'Dois esqueletos, um ao outro unido/Foram achados num sepulcro só' [two skeletons, joined together/were found in one single tomb] (in Moisés 1968: 276). While the poem has been understood as a response against the upper class in which De Passos grew up, the morbid imagination is also typical for a *mal du siècle* sentiment, and could be correlated to the resurrected-but-fragile structures of the Portuguese monarchy.

'Visão', like 'Noivado', thematizes idyllic, virginal and passionate love, as well as death, and the Gothic, phantasmagoric scenes of night, ruins and the cemetery. It lacks the strict quatrain structure of 'Noivado'. At the start of 'Visão', the lyrical voice contemplates a woman – a virgin – whom he loves, and who is probably a lover, although she is only 14 years old. Lost in thoughts, he peacefully ('tranquilo', 87) falls asleep in the third verse and, to his shock, finds that in his dream – which he does not realize is a dream – the woman he loves is dead. He sees her body being 'desfigurada, sem vida, já morta!!!' [disfigured, lifeless, already dead!!!] but still admires the corpse – and even eroticizes it (87):

> Vi o seu corpo esbelto, donairoso,
> Imóvel e, como a neve, gelado!
> Aqueles olhos meigos, fascinantes,
> Já despidos do seu fulgor divino!
> Os lábios mudos, sem a cor carmínea!
> Desbotadas de todo, as róseas faces! (De Oliveira 87)

> [I saw your slender, elegant body,
> Still and, like snow, ice cold!
> Those sweet, fascinating eyes,
> Already stripped of their divine radiance!
> The lips mute, without the carmine color!
> Emptied of everything, the rosy cheeks!]

Emergence of the Mozambican modern ghost story 87

The voice continues to describe the body, as well as the other people he sees mourning for his lost love, until he can no longer bear it and turns away. When he turns back for one more look, the atmosphere of the poem changes – it turns out that the body has disappeared ('não achei ninguém' [I did not find anyone], 87). The poetic voice (as well as the reader) suddenly finds himself in a cemetery, where he sees a column of people carrying the body to her grave. The Gothicness of this already Gothic location is amplified by the description of the 'sepulturas, cabisbaixos' [gravestones, heads hanging] (88). The excessive use of hyperbolic language rises to a crescendo in this scene, as perhaps best demonstrated by the following two verses, which are used to describe the singing of the crowd: 'cânticos dolorosas, que echoavam/Majestosos pela amplidão enorme de soturna morada' [grieving chants, that echoed/majestically through the vastness of their gloomy abode] (88). After this crescendo, two dotted lines interrupt the poem, followed by a narrated silence. The protagonist finds himself alone in what appears to be one of the cemetery buildings, away from the crowd, when he exclaims: 'Oh! Que horror me infundiam as caveiras/Alvacentas, mirradas e disformes/que em roda de mim eu via espalhadas' [Oh! The horror that the skulls infused me with/whitish, withered and deformed/that I saw scattered around me] (88). It is at this point, with silence working for suspense, that the narrator is terrified and exclaims: 'que medonhos fantasmas pareciam/quietos divagar ante meus olhos!' [what terrifying ghosts they resembled/quietly, slowly before my eyes!] (88). Horrified, the protagonist attempts to flee the scene, when he finds a 'mocho' [owl] staring at him, adding to his fear with its horror-like screech ['horríssonos'] (89). He then falls back into quiet mourning and kneels at his love's gravestone. The only hope he now entertains is to die so he can join his love. Then, he suddenly hears a voice. It startles him – it appears a ghost is speaking to him from the grave – but then the protagonist wakes up from his 'horrível, pavoroso' [horrible, dreadful] dream (88). Although it might not have been real, it does have real effects, and 'uma lagrima!' [a tear!] drops from his eyes (89).

Lyricism, Romanticism and the Gothic are clearly visible in the poem. The first is best illustrated by the lyrical 'oh!' and excessive use of exclamation marks and ellipses. The second is demonstrated by the theme of love and loss and the excessive use of language. The latter is evident in the imagery of the cemetery, the morbid imagination, the ghosts and the terror the poetic voice experiences. Many of these elements were seen in De Passos's poem, yet there are some clear and relevant differences: 'Visão' starts from a displacement of the narrative frame, common to the modern ghost story, leading the readers to a second level of narration – the dream – from which they emerge at the end of the poem. Additionally, at the beginning of the poem, the protagonist is 'Cismando' [Musing] (88), emphasizing the seriousness of the 'eu' [I] in the very first signifier of the first verse, and his connection to thought and rationality. At the end of the poem, this is reversed. He emerges scared and emotional from his dream and, above all, susceptible to the supernatural elements he might not have believed in without the dream – reminiscent of Woodville's remark, at the end of Scott's 'Tapestried', that there 'can remain no longer any doubt of the horrible reality of your apparition' (Scott 1900: 52).

The function of the narrative displacement may thus, among other things, be a way for the protagonist to approach the supernatural without the possibility of being reproached for superstition. Yet, just like its silent terrifying ghosts, it also aligns 'Visão' with the modern ghost story. Evidently, 'Visão' is a poem, not a short story; it is characterized by verses and the frequent use of common poetic devices, such as rhyme and enjambment. But it is much freer than Passos' strict quatrains, and its rhyme scheme and stanzas are irregular and function more like paragraphs. 'Visão' is, arguably, a narrative poem – especially considering the linearity of the second narrative level, which ends in the climax characteristic of the modern ghost story: the narrative starts from quiet contemplation and proceeds to sadness, to the anxiety of the sudden disappearance of his love and to the horror of the ghosts. When grief briefly cuts short the horror again, the poem explodes in the terror of a possible ghost speaking to him.

'Visão' differs from 'Noivado' in another aspect: it is not a narrative of a corroding and ending system, but rather a narrative of transition – transition is the overarching structure of the poem, the content of the outer frame. This is not unexpected, considering its context of production. While the Portuguese monarchy had been re-established around that time,

Emergence of the Mozambican modern ghost story 89

Mozambique was drawn deeper into the bourgeois system of production, with the growth of export of agricultural products staring in the 1860s and peaking only in the 1880s (Newitt 2017: 69). As a narrative of not only the corrosion of an old system of production but also the transition to a new one – and despite the influence of 'Noivado' – 'Visão' participates in the tradition of the Gothic in general and, arguably, of the modern ghost story. It is for this reason that 'Visão' is suggested here, not as a modern ghost story but as an early possible node of emergence of the modern ghost story in Mozambique. Consequently, De Oliveira's work could be regarded as 'despontar do fenómeno literário moçambicano' [being at the dawn of the phenomenon of Mozambican literature] (Leite 2008: 64), as well as at the dawn of the Mozambican modern ghost story.

Modern ghost figures in twentieth-century Mozambican literature

No modern ghost stories were found in the context of this study until the end of what Mendonça refers to as the *assimilado* period (which, for her ends in 1947), and the genre remains sparse even subsequently (1988: 34–6). This absence even persists in works in which a modern ghost story would fit thematically, stylistically or formally. Dias's *Godido e Outros Contos* [*Godido and Other Tales*] (1952) is one example in which a ghost story is almost expected. The metaphor of 'ghostly', generally resisted in this book, would not be misplaced in a description of that collection because of how it thematizes the oppression of Black Mozambicans and their related exclusion from entire parts of social life – predominantly the city, which, in *Godido*, is associated with wealth and food (Dias 35). With the risk of relating *Godido*'s thematic too directly to its author's biography, it may be recalled that *Godido* was written in Coimbra, where Dias lived isolated as a Black student, and 'where even Mozambicans ignored him' (Sadlier 246f25). The collection, then, discusses issues of absence and presence on the one hand and race/class resentment on the other. Moreover, narrators in *Godido* focalize a colonial belief about spirituality and the supernatural as superstitious (Dias 1952: 36). All of this could provide fruitful ground for modern ghost stories.

Notwithstanding the modern ghost story's absence during this period, the modern figure of the ghost – that frightening, incomprehensible, threateningly silent and largely absent presence, which does not belong, as opposed to some figures from the premodern Gothic and the *traditional field* – does appear. This study found the first significant modern ghost figure, after De Oliveira, in the work of Rui de Noronha. That poet is known for drawing on European forms, such as the sonnet and 'Parnassian-like verse', but also used an 'African thematic' (Hamilton 1975: 168). Albuquerque and Motta therefore argue that he is the first poet in whose work a 'Mozambican consciousness' is clearly expressed, and is, as such, the first 'verdadeira poeta de Moçambique' [true Mozambican poet], as 'certos puristas' [certain purists] would define it (30). Influenced by the socialist poetry of the Portuguese Antero de Quental, De Noronha identified with 'socialismo utópico' [utopian socialism] (Mendonça in M. de S. e Silva 1996: 32). His poetry had, as some say, a 'missão revolucionária' [revolutionary mission] and was '[s]ensivel ao espectáculo da oppressão' [sensitive to the spectacle of oppression] (in M. de S. e Silva 33). Others, however, accuse him of exoticism. Ilídio Rocha states that a poem like 'Quenguelequeze', relying as it does chiefly on Ronga words for exotic effect, shows 'o folklore visto por brancos, turistas de passagem' [folklore as seen by White people, passing tourists] (in Albuquerque and Motta 31). Mendonça makes a similar claim about De Noronha's work more generally (in Silva 1996: 31), and Lisboa argues he is not representative of Mozambique because his 'poetry, is little more than mediocre' (in Hamilton 168). Manoel de Sousa e Silva (1996) recognizes the criticism, but argues that it is, at most, the case for a part of De Noronha's work. It could be suggested, perhaps, that his work is situated between these two poles; that it is an early attempt to create a Mozambican consciousness that, at times, collapses back into a colonial mode of exoticist discursivity.

De Noronha is certainly not reproducing the colonizers' gaze in the sporadic poems in which he uses the figure of the ghost, as they are largely devoid of what Hamilton calls an 'African thematic'. The use of the figure

Emergence of the Mozambican modern ghost story 91

rather follows a modern form. One such example is his sonnet 'Namorados' [Lovers] (2006 [1935]: 26), which is playful and generally light in tone and theme. In the first two stanzas, the poetic voice draws attention to birds and questions if they are clouds instead, and to the sunlight to ask if it may instead be moonlight. After this creation of ontological uncertainty, the tone changes briefly as the 'noite cai. As árvores distantes/São sombras de fantasmas coleantes/Cantando em coro misterióso e triste' [night falls. The distant trees/are shadows of winding ghost/Singing in chorus sad and mysterious] (De Noronha 26). Trees becoming ghosts can be reformulated as the reversal of the known into the unknown, caused in this case by nightfall. Yet it is not an unknown for the focalizer, who is able to see the trees in the ghosts and is (therefore) not scared of them, even though they are presented as gloomy creatures. These ghosts can thus be identified as a variant of the shadow on the wall that, at night, transforms into a monster in the mind of a child – especially because, after the reassurance of the poetic voice and the return of the day in the last stanza, the ghosts become trees once more. Thus, even if the ghosts are associated with fear and uncertainty, it is not near the level of terror experienced by the poetic voice of 'Visão'.

Genuine horror, as in 'Visão', is absent from De Noronha's work – even from his poem 'Horror', which, at most, conveys the poetic voice fearing death in the face of a grave, but does not produce any affect to support that dread (45). De Noronha's 'A Poesia Morreu' [The Poetry Died] also demonstrates this. The poem has, as its premise, the death of poetry by the hands of poets. However, poetry has not been granted proper burial rites: 'A poesia morreu. E não a sepultaram/Ficou ambalsamada em artes mentirosas' [Poetry died. And they did not bury her/She remained embalmed in lying arts] (90). It is from this situation that ghosts emerge: 'E no museu da Vida aqueles que a acharam/julgaram-nas um fantasma em noites pavorosas' [And those who found her in the museum of Life/judged her to be a ghost in dreadful nights] (90). In his use of the figure of the ghost, then, De Noronha employs a number of modern ghost story conventions, including that of haunted (albeit metaphoric) real estate and the concept of the frightening ghost. The ghost creatures for the poetic voice do not belong in the earthly realm.

After De Noronha, the figure of the ghost was absent from MlwP for some time, and only resurfaced in the work of Rui Knopfli in the 1950s. For Mendonça, this concerns the next period in Mozambican literature (1947–64), which is characterized by a higher literary quality and more idiosyncratic style. This is certainly visible in Knopfli's work; his oeuvre is especially interesting, in the context of this study, because it follows a similar development as Mozambican literature more generally – the peak in modern ghost-story use in Mozambique, which took place halfway through the 1980s and is discussed in the next chapter, is also present in Knopfli's oeuvre. Although he consistently uses the signifier 'fantasma' or 'espectro' to refer to supernatural beings, in his later work he uses typically Mozambican supernatural figures – like the '[p]assanoute', 'xipocúe' and 'shiguêvengo' – which, for him, are different names for the same supernatural creature (Knopfli 2003: 498, 529). Incidentally, the term 'xipocúe' is assumed to be a Mozambicanification of the English 'spooky' (Knopfli 529).[5]

Knopfli first uses the figure of the ghost in the poem 'Diagnóstico' [Diagnostics] in his first collection, *O País dos Outros* [*The Land of the Others*] (1959) (2003: 62). The tone of the poem is dark – much darker than the work of De Noronha – and, although not Romantic in style or form, it resonates with the Romantic desire for death. The poetic 'eu' [I] appears to be lying in a (hospital) bed, where he contemplates his own death as well as the withering away of his body. In the opening verses he addresses the rotting away of his past, and in the later verses he highlights the total decomposition of his being – in which, paradoxically, the poetic voice is fully realized ('Na decomposição,/total, complete, sou vivo' [In decomposition,/total, complete, I am alive]). It is also in this state of decomposition that he sees '[f]antasmas de vivos – não gnomos, não duendes – sentamse à minha/beira como aparelhos de raios X' [ghosts of the living – not gnomes, not goblins – sit down at my/side like X-ray machines]. The ghosts are modern presences, which most clearly results from the fact that the voice slowly loses his grip on life. But there is an additional reason to suggest this. In *País*, death is consistently posited as an irreversible end with

---

5   In Chapter 5, a second peak is described in around 2006. This does not show in Knopfli's work because he died in 1997.

Emergence of the Mozambican modern ghost story 93

no afterlife, no possibility of returning. There is even an instance of what could be called an anti-ghost in the poem 'Testamento' [Testament], in which a first-person poetic voice tells his lover that, if he dies, 'me não repito' [I will not repeat myself] (2003: 46), indicating he will not come back to haunt.[6] The realms of the living and dead are thus strictly separated, as is common to the modern understanding of the ghost. In affirmation thereof, the speaker even specifies these ghosts are not 'duendes' but 'fantasmas' – ghosts.

After Knopfli, ghost figures that are convincingly modern in their structure would be used a number of times during the period central to this chapter. João Fonseca Amaral (arguably a Portuguese poet) uses ghosts in his 1960 poem ('vaga um vago fantasma sorridente' [a vague smiling ghost wanders], Amaral 55). In Bermudes's 1962 poem, 'Cancão do País de Cecília' [Song of Cecília's Country], ghosts are connected to an upcoming war, which the speaker associates with a procession of ghosts and fears ('Guerra inevitável que não quero,/com o seu cortejo de fantasmas e de medos' [Inevitable war that I don't want,/with its procession of ghosts and fears], 91). José Craveirinha uses the figure metaphorically in the Negritude poem 'Manifesto' to indicate an element that does not belong. There, 'fantasmas estranhos motorizados' [strange motorized ghosts] are described to refer to the colonialist machinery of oppression (Craveirinha 1995: 33). In the same volume, Craveirinha uses a 'xipocúe' who appears to be a 'negrinho' [small Black child] and is 'quase vestido quase morto' [almost dressed almost dead] (40–1). The *xipocúe*, in other words, is used as figure to indicate, as Jameson described in the introduction, 'those not merely deprived of wealth and power (or of their own labor-power), but even of life itself', not unlike the characters in *Godido* addressed above (Jameson 1995: 86). The most convincing ghost story of this period, however, is Orlando Mendes's *Portagem* (1981 [1965]).

---

6   The attitude towards death as irreversible would slowly change, with a turning point in his 1972 poetry collection, *A Ilha do Prospero* [The Island of Prospero].

A modern ghost story in Mozambique: Orlando Mendes' *Portagem*

The first Mozambican work combining several conventions of the modern ghost story is Orlando Mendes's *Portagem*, a novel written in 1950 and published in 1965. Mendes moved to Portugal in 1944, where he studied biology (he moved back to Lourenço Marques in 1951); had he not encountered the modern ghost story in Mozambique he may have encountered it in Coimbra, where he studied, either in English, in translation or in one of its various Portuguese ghost story shapes. Mendes played with the modern figure of the ghost in his poetry before *Portagem*, as illustrated by the poem 'Manha de Natal' [Christmas Morning]:

> Lembro-me agora que é dia de Natal
> E talvez as sombras aguardassem esta visão
> Mas é ainda cedo demais, muito cedo
> Para as sombras que estendem suas mãos em festa
> Quando aparece no espaço um avião a jacto. (Mendes 1963: 64)

> [I remember now that it is Christmas day
> And perhaps the shadows had awaited that vision
> But it is too early still, very early
> For the shadows which extend their hands festively
> As in space a jet plane appears.]

The poem – while not operating according to the conventions of the modern ghost story, or even to those of the Gothic – plays with the ghostly presence typical of the modern ghost figure. Shadows in the poem are more than just an area of darkness resulting from the partial or complete blockage of light; they are anthropomorphized, made to appear acting subjects and appear to have hands that are extended in expectation or anticipation. The possibility that they are just shadows is never completely excluded, but it is precisely this uncertainty that makes their presence waver and establishes them as ghostly figures. That these ghosts are connected to the modern is shown not only in their uncertainty – the general feeling, which the poem establishes, of the ghost not

Emergence of the Mozambican modern ghost story 95

belonging – but also by the figure of the jet plane (or the modernization view of modernity), which is itself a quasi-ghostly presence through its abrupt appearance. The connection of the shadows to Christmas arguably correlates the poem with the British modern ghost story tradition, as it took shape under Dickens's editorship of the periodical *All Year Round*.

Where 'Manha de Natal' at most plays with the figure of the ghost, *Portagem* more explicitly draws on its generic conventions. More precisely, the claim of this chapter is that, using the conventions of the modern ghost story, *Portagem* registers – and establishes a criticism of – the primitive accumulation of the Mozambican labour market in the nineteenth century and, more specifically, of the formal and legal sedimentation of that primitive accumulation in the colonial capitalism of the 1926–62 period.

It is important to highlight that this does not necessarily mean the entire novel should be understood as a modern ghost story. *Portagem* was influenced by Portuguese Neorealism (PNR): a cultural response to the Salazarist state that had started with the publication of Alves Redol's *Gaibéus* (1992 [1939]). Departing from a Marxist view of society, Portuguese Neorealists considered humans 'como entidade condicionada por circunstâncias económicas e sociais' [as an entity conditioned by economic and social circumstances] (Reis 1983: 39). And, as Reis – paraphrasing Marx's eleventh thesis on Feuerbach – argues, neorealism does not simply want to describe reality, but transform it. Hence, it highlights those who are the means or motor of that transformation, which is to say the worker (Reis 29).

PNR thus considers literature a tool for intervention in the social realm. Thematically, this takes on the form of a conflict between an oppressor and an oppressed; formally, it is focalized from the latter's perspective. While PNR influenced authors in Mozambique, Mozambican Neorealism (MNR) differed from its Portuguese counterpart, as *Portagem* demonstrates. The novel narrates the life of an oppressed protagonist, João Xilim, who is the son of a White father and a Black mother. He suffers from colonial oppression in the form of racism, and tries to gain social mobility, but his class struggle is ultimately unsuccessful. *Portagem* ends with João's inability to feed and protect his family, with him abusing his wife and with the death of their newborn baby. This type of tragic narrative arc is not uncommon in Mozambican works related to Neorealism

96   CHAPTER 3

(Geoffrey Mitchell 2003: 83); to give just one other example, Aleluia's short story 'Ma-Bhato' narrates the story of how a protagonist's baby dies – in this case, of a relatively innocent disease – because the taxi driver does not accept a poor Black man into his cab (Aleluia 1987: 193–201). Bernardo Honwana therefore speaks of 'narraç[ões] de sofrimento' [narratives of suffering] (Honwana 1988: 2).

Unlike in the case of PNR, then, MNR stories do not create hopeful visions of the (colonial) class struggle, and *Portagem*'s main generic kinship is thus not to the ghost story but to MNR – or, using Honwana's term, to the *narrações de sofrimento*. This may be one of the reasons why *Portagem* was not considered politically controversial, at the time, and was not censored by the colonial administration. Yet as will be claimed here, a part of *Portagem* does stage a successful class struggle from the perspective of the colonized, namely by drawing on the conventions of the modern ghost story. To show this, it is necessary to contextualize the novel thematically and historically.

Portagem starts in the quasi-ghost town of Ridjalembe, in which an old Black woman ('a velha negra', 5) named Alima lives a mostly isolated life. Three times per week, her daughter Kati visits, brings food and tries to convince her mother to come and live in Marandal. All former inhabitants of Ridjalembe moved to Marandal in the 'ano longínquo da grande emigração' [the distant year of the great emigration], during the drought of that year, and their descendants live there still (6). Alima, however, refused to go then and refuses to go now. Her grandfather, 'o escravo Mafanissane' [Mafanissane the slave], settled in Ridjalembe and, on the day of his liberation, planted a cashew tree 'simbólico' [symbolic] that still stands there today (6). Alima, she knows, is the only person alive to remember this, and to have heard that history from 'da boca dos escravos' [from the slaves' mouths] (6). Moreover, only she appears to remember how, later, 'os brancos' [the Whites] came with their 'máquinas para abrirem os grandes buracos na terra e tirar o carvão quo os negros carregam para as vagonetas' [machines to open large holes in the ground and extract coal that Blacks folks carried to carts]. That situation has now become the status quo (6).

The first chapter has three functions that are important for the purposes of this section: it makes history inaccessible, creates a contrast for

Emergence of the Mozambican modern ghost story

João's narrative to signal historical transition and allows for locating João's narrative historically.

First, the Alima character is associated with a historical period that the first chapter connects to a specific type of social organization, the cultural production of which is associated with orality and the use of an (unidentified) native language. The connection to orality is established stylistically using the mnemonic device of repetition, which is common to Mozambican oral literature and, later, to Mozambican work songs and poetry. The opening phrase, 'a velha negra sai' [the old Black woman exits] (5), illustrates this; it is repeated throughout the first chapter with small variations.[7] Of course, the association of Alima and the historical period she represents with orality is also manifest in that Alima herself is an oral historian. Ribeiro Cruz writes that she is not an archetypal *griot* but 'uma contentora da história de sua pátria' [container of the history of her homeland] (129). Alima even embodies the history she retells, because she is the last person to remember it. As for the language spoken between daughter and mother, this is a topic of explicit debate between them. Alima blames Kati for 'falar língua do branco' [speaking the language of the White man] and for trying to make it the language in which they converse (8). For Alima, this is part of a larger attempt to bring her into the 'mundo de pretos e brancos' [world of Blacks and Whites] of which she refuses to become a part (9). Because she realizes there is no stopping that world, she tells Kati in her 'língua nativa' [native language] that 'Já ninguém tem a mim e eu não tenho ninguém. [...] Deixa a mim só, até eu ter morrido e os pássaros da terra Ridjalembe terem comido os meus olhos' [No one has me anymore and I don't have anyone. [...] Leave me alone, until I have died and the birds of the land of Ridjalembe have eaten my eyes] (9). Alima then enters her hut and (as the reader later learns) dies, and birds eat her eyes. This ends the first chapter, as well as the use of the mnemonic device of repetition and the life of the oral historian in *Portagem*. It constitutes the history Alima embodied as no longer accessible or even visible (with her eyes

---

7   '[A] velha ainda' [the old woman still] (6), 'a velha Alima' [the old woman Alima] (7), 'a velha afasta' [the old woman distances herself] (8), 'a velha estica' [the old woman stretches] (8), 'a negra sente' [the Black woman sits] (9) and so on.

eaten) – as history – and thus establishes a condition for the modern ghost story in which, as Hay indicated, nothing should return, although it does.

Second, the form of social organization Alima is associated with is connected to a period of (at least imagined) relative stability, of rootedness – even in the face of large-scale emigration and the hardship of drought – and of freedom, as symbolized by the liberated slave Mafanissane and the tree he planted. The period has a relative absence of 'brancos' and their language, and is thus contrasted with the narration of João's life, which is characterized in opposition to Alima's period, namely by continuous precarity, displacement and oppression.

Third, through this contrast, the novel signals a historical transition to a different form of social organization. Based on Alima's remarks about the end of slavery and the arrival of 'os brancos', it can be suggested that this concerns the transition from – to use Cahen's periodization – the period after 'the end of the slave trade' to 'colonial capitalism' (2012: 151). For Cahen, this period starts in 1926 with the introduction of forced-labour legislation, discussed further below. João's narrative thus takes place during colonial capitalism.

João's life is characterized by and ends with misfortune, which his character considers the result of being mulatto. The child of Kati (Alima's daughter) and of the patriarch and owner of the Marandal mines, Patrão Campos, the boy leads a stable life. When Campos dies, João is forced to migrate in search of a way to earn his subsistence. That search fails repeatedly, forcing him to move from one location to the next and starting his hardship. That the novel posits João's situation as the result of the colour of his skin is clear from the comments characters and narrator make throughout the novel. Introducing the João character to the reader, the narrator says the Black mine workers consider the boy to be 'diferente' [different] from themselves (10). On a later occasion, João explains to his friend that he cannot find work because 'os brancos ficam desconfiados de mim' [the Whites are distrustful of me] (51). He continues that if he had been a 'negro' [Black person] he would not have had the same problem, because Whites always consider that a 'mulato é filho dum crime' [mulatto is the child of a crime] and 'preto tem vergonha' [Black folks are ashamed] of

Emergence of the Mozambican modern ghost story 99

mulattos (51). He himself also feels this disgrace and, on one of the many occasions on which he laments his fate, he attributes it to 'daquela desgraça de naser mulato' [that disgrace of being born mulatto] (67). Later again, João complains that the 'brancos fazem o que querem com a gente. [...] E com os mulatos ainda é pior com os pretos' [Whites do to us whatever they want. [...] And it is even worse for mulattos than for Blacks] (127). A character, Izidro, feeds this fire by arguing that João cannot be trusted because 'Mulato não é gente de confiança. Tem sangue de branco' [Mulattos aren't people you can trust. They have the blood of Whites], a phrase he repeats word for word later in the novel (70, 93). In line with this, João contemplates at the end of the novel:

> O erro fundamental que comprometeu a paz da sua vida, foi o abraço da mãe Kati e de patrão Campos [...] que fez dele um ser duma [...] raça infamada. Tudo que se passou depois [resultou] desse erro [;] rejeitada pelos brancos e pelos negros. Deserdada pelas duas raças puras. (169–70)
>
> [The fundamental mistake that compromised his life's peace, was the embrace of his mother Kati and of boss Campos [...] which made him into a being of an [...] infamous race. Everything that happened since [resulted from] this mistake [;] rejected by whites and blacks. Disinherited by both pure races.]

Evidently, considering the historical period in which *Portagem* is located and the importance of MNR to the novel, in which discrimination is a pivotal theme, the issue of race is highly relevant to João's experiences. By the time the novel was written (1950) and published (1965), Portugal had labelled the social organization it forced upon its colonies ('provinces', in the colonial terminology) non-racist, according to the ideological paradigm of Lusotropicalism. Keese described that, like the French, the Portuguese colonial system 'depended ideologically' on the understanding that their empire

> did not only exist as a sign of the nation's greatness. The national elite interested in the colonial project mostly assumed that their motherland was accomplishing a special civilizing mission. French and Portuguese presence was a means to advance 'primitive peoples', to bring them knowledge and some kind of protection and welfare. (47)

Of course, Penvenne highlights the 'bankruptcy of idealized Portuguese racial toleration' and asserts that the 'facts simply do not corroborate the propaganda' (1979: 1). Cahen also asserts that Portuguese colonialism was a 'racist system and produced a highly racialized society' (Cahen 2012: 170). Penvenne shows how between '1877 and 1962 the colonial construction of inequality in Mozambique developed piece by piece' (1995: 156), largely through the implementation of an *indigenato/cidadão* [native/citizen] division, corresponding to those the Portuguese considered, respectively, non-civilized and civilized. The latter group of White Portuguese were subject to Portuguese law, while the former of non-White Mozambican born subjects was subject to a different set of laws (including forced-labour laws). Specifically, this former group concerned: 'Individuals of black race or being descended from them, who, by the way of their instruction and customs, do not distinguish themselves from the common people of this race' (in Cahen 2012: 160). The integration of this system was successful, according to Penvenne, to the extent that 'the colonial administration had deflected virtually all direct confrontations by warriors, workers, and intellectuals' by the 1920s (1995: 156–7).

These structurally racist Portuguese colonial laws thus targeted all non-White subjects and could be avoided officially only by becoming *assimilado*, for which being mulatto was – at least officially – not an advantage. Nevertheless, racial prejudice specific to mulatto subjects did exist in colonial Mozambique. Interracial unions were forbidden, discouraged and considered a problem to be solved by the Portuguese, which may also inform the understanding of the mulatto as the product of a crime, as voiced in *Portagem*. Portuguese authors would expound on how the 'mestiço' was racially inferior (e.g. Alberto 1947), and Isaacman recalls some of the friction between Black Africans and mulattos relative to the (elite) social and civic organization Grêmio Africano. 'Africans' in that organization, he writes, resented the 'arrogance of the more established mulatto families' because they 'claimed privileged [a] leadership position' and because of the refusal of 'mulatto women to dance with black men' (76). Eventually, this led to the breakup of Grêmio and the foundation of Instituto Négrofilo, which Isaacman suspects was, in part, a colonial attempt to 'undercut [a] non-white alliance' that could form a possible threat to the colonizer (1988: 76).

Emergence of the Mozambican modern ghost story

Yet he also believes many of the 'older mulatto families had internalized the colonial racial and class stereotypes which set them apart from all Africans and protected some vestiges of their power and prestige' (1988: 77). (João Xilim, it may be noticed in passing, reproduces such notions; for example, when speaking of 'raças puras' [pure races] – and the 'non-pure races' that remark implies.) In addition, while Grêmio Africano and Instituto Négrofilo may be considered a response to colonial racism, *mestiços* (as well as *assimilados*) were also employed by the colonial administration as comprador class, providing them with access to a more comfortable social status than the vast majority of the population. Following the First World War, the position of comprador classes in Mozambique declined, which intensified after the fall of the Portuguese monarchy in 1926 and the establishment and consolidation of its republic. The First World War caused economic hardship in Portugal, and the institution of the republic would increase migration to Mozambique, causing a conflict in the labour market that was decided in favour of the (White) Portuguese. The colonizer, then, used the comprador class until it was no longer necessary and then decreased its class status (Funada-Classen 2012: 155). As Penvenne summarizes, these groups were thus 'vulnerable to white tolerance, due in part to their own aspirations for equal treatment, and their historical role as comprador group', leading them to be 'harassed and humiliated by whites and tolerated, distrusted or despised by other blacks' (1979: 18).

Taking this into account, it would be tempting to understand João's experience as a translation of the actual lived experience of mulatto subjects in colonial Mozambique into a fictional narrative and, with him, to see his 'race' as the primary reason for his misfortunes. Understandably, this is one of the positions Calane da Silva takes, arguing that *Portagem* is about the 'mundo dos assimilados, dos mulatos e negros rejeitados socialmente pelos colonos' [world of the assimilated, of mulattos and Blacks, rejected socially by the colonialists] (in Kahn, 141; see also Mitchel 2004). Yet, while there can be no doubt that some of João's hardship is due to his race, it is questionable whether this offers a full explanation. To show this, it is necessary to return to a dominant aspect in the narrative: labour.

João lives at the Marandal mines until his father, Patrão Campos, dies. After the death of the owner, João and his (White) half-sister, Maria

Helena, briefly try to run the mine. They succeed until Maria Helena interrupts João's day report one evening and asks him about his travels and relationships. Subsequently, erotic tension occurs between them, and she tells him one 'de nós tem que ir embora do Marandal' [of us has to leave Marandal], after which João leaves the mine (Mendes 1981: 44). João thus loses his job, which displaces him from 'o mato' [the bush] of Marandal and forces him to sell his labour power to secure his own subsistence, setting in motion a series of further displacements that inevitably mean travel (44). João looks for 'emprego por toda a cidade. Ofereceu os braços fortes, apregoou a boa vontade para trabalhar' [work throughout the city. Offered his strong arms, proclaimed his desire to work] (50). However, he quickly 'perdeu as esperanças de arranjar emprego' [loses hope of arranging a job] and concludes he has to 'emigrar. Ele nasceu para andar de terra em terra, sem poder parar muito tempo no mesmo lugar' [emigrate. He was born to roam from land to land, without being able to stop in one place for a long time] (50). With no other options, he finds himself having to go to South Africa to work in the mines, 'que tinham sido o refúgio desesperado dos negros do Marandal' [which had been the desperate refuge for the Blacks of Marandal] (52). When he returns from South Africa, he is imprisoned, after which he travels to look for a job (78). He finds a position in a bar, which needs someone who can speak with the 'negros na língua deles' [Blacks in their language] (80), and stays there until the place burns down (109). He then moves on again in search of a job, and ends up working for and living at Juza's, who owns a fish stand. When Juza murders his wife and kills himself, João inherits the fish stand. However, after a brief period of successful subsistence, their competitor Coxo lowers his prices and thus destroys João's business.

Arguably, then, although João's race is certainly integral to the story of *Portagem*, the driving force behind his repeated displacement – the forced journeys he has to undertake – is his search for employment. It is therefore useful to look closer at the organization of labour during the historical period in which the narrative is set.

Cahen explains how the Portuguese prohibition of slave trade was instituted in 1836, came into partial effect in 1850 and was set to be in effect fully in 1878. The government planned this slow transition period

Emergence of the Mozambican modern ghost story   103

so that *latifundios, prazeiros* and other slave owners had time to switch from slavery to so-called 'free labor', from a slave economy to a 'new, capitalist economy' and wage labour (2012: 154). Part of the prohibition was a 'prohibition of "forced labor" – referring to the former slavery – [that] was enacted alongside the vagrancy clause' under which the 'non-productive African could be judged a vagrant and made to contract for his services' (154). Importantly, Cahen argues, this 'amounted to the creation of modern forced labour' (2012: 154). And it is clarifying to recall how Marx describes primitive accumulation not simply as the incorporation of precapitalist modes of production into the capitalist system but also of the *'en masse'* production of 'beggars, robbers, [and] vagabonds' and the 'hurl[ing]' of people into wage labour (Marx 2008a: 372). However, unlike what was planned, there was no smooth transition in Mozambique but rather a 'break' and change in 'production modes' (Cahen 2012: 155). Former slave owners resisted transition for such a long period it left them with insufficient time to transfer into a new system of production and, as a result, new plantations and mines were owned by new owners and funded by 'foreign or metropolitan capital, and in any case, external capital' (153). Another important difference, according to Cahen, was that the modern forced labour of this new age of colonial capitalism concerned 'the whole of the African population', while slavery had concerned 'only a minority' (155). It was, he suggests, 'developmentalist' in nature and aimed to make Mozambique (and Angola) into 'a general work camp for Africans' (159).

Keese demonstrates how, during the 1926–62 period – the labour legislation came into effect in 1926 (Cahen 2012: 151) and was replaced in 1962 by the *Código do trabalho rural* [Rural Labor Code] (Cahen 2012: 159) – this system became increasingly exploitative; a 'mere profit machine at the expense of local rural producers' (Keese 153). Cahen shows how all non-Portuguese who were not *assimilado* could be forced to work. To become *assimilado*, three conditions had to be met: the African had to have abandoned indigenous habits and customs, speak Portuguese and practise a profession as understood by the Europeans (Cahen 2012: 160). Perhaps unsurprisingly, considering these rules and the room they allow for interpretation, in the 1950s only '4,353 out of 5,733,000 black inhabitants' were *assimilado* (162). It is for this reason Cahen argues that, in Mozambique,

104   CHAPTER 3

the meaning of this legislation was very clearly that '*any (black) person not directly integrated into the capitalist economy*' could be forced to labour (160, emphasis in the original). In practice, according to Cahen, this meant '*all* males [the labour system was strongly separated on the basis of sex] who could be recruited for forced labour [...] had in fact been recruited' for a shorter or longer period (161, emphasis in the original).

In their organization of labour in Mozambique, the Portuguese government explicitly attempted to prevent a proletarianization, 'for the fear of a proletarian mass' and because it was more profitable not to have to pay proletarians the cost of their 'social reproduction' (Cahen 2012: 164). That these fears were justified is clear from Keese's work, which demonstrates how, during the 1950s, army officers called for the liberalization of the labour system because 'rural discontent [resulting from] extreme exploitation by settlers and concession companies in some parts of the territories' acutely raised the risk of a 'potential for peasant rebellion' (172). Before such liberalizations were instituted, however, the Portuguese colonizer took several measures to prevent the creation of a proletariat. Cahen writes: 'Contracts were never permanent ones, because Africans had to "rest" and return home' – a rest that was a de facto prohibition from staying at the location of seasonal/contract labour, as this would create the possibility of forming a proletarian class. In practice, because payment was so low, the male workers who worked abroad (often in the notoriously dangerous mines of the South Africa, cf. Newitt 2017: 106) or outside of their home regions had to go back home to help in the local economy – which women kept running in their absence – when the contracts ran out. This policy of 'rest' was also enforced institutionally in three other ways, as Cahen shows. The Portuguese collaborated with traditional chiefs, used the promise of violence (*cipaios*, or native police, armed with guns) and implemented *pagamento diferido* [deferred payment], in which part of the wages were only paid after the workers had returned home (this also simplified the collection of 'taxes') (Cahen 2012: 165).[8] This 'capitalist *domination*' of

---

8   Césaire (1972: 43, 45) already noted 'old tyrants get on very well with the new ones' and 'Europe has gotten on very well indeed with all the local feudal lords who agreed to serve, woven a villainous complicity with them, rendered their tyranny

Emergence of the Mozambican modern ghost story   105

the natives through 'a combination of colonial constraint and maintenance of the domestic economy' was necessary in 'order to be globally profitable for the colonial institution' (Cahen 2012: 165). Seasonal migratory labour was at the heart of this dynamic.

By design, then, Portuguese colonial capitalism organized Mozambique's colonial labour market, with the labour of the natives as the main resource to be exploited, as a patchwork in which non-proletarianized workers were forced to have multiple short-term jobs – and which, by definition, involved migration and displacement. This was particularly the case during the 1926–62 period.

This patchwork, this chapter claims, also structures *Portagem*. Manuel Ferreira has claimed that *Portagem* is 'o primeiro romance moçambicano' [the first Mozambican novel] (1977: 103); Maurits, however, noted that *Portagem* is not a hard break with the short story – which was the dominant prose form at the time – but rather resembles a collection of short stories (2015: 182). Gerald Moser (1982) similarly observed that *Portagem*'s 'dramatic episodes, which could stand by themselves as short stories, are piled upon each other without much background information or character development. The work retains some value since it marks a stage in the short history of Mozambican literature' (1982: 395). Moser may be correct in saying the episodic nature of the work results from the novelistic skills of the author, yet it also results from the way in which the narrative is organized. João migrates from one place to another in search of work to ensure his subsistence, leading to a shifting character cast, different spaces and an altogether patchwork-like structure. Incidentally, this also prevents the use of the cosmopolitan space: when João does reflect on his fate of having to 'andar de terra em terra, sem poder parar muito tempo no mesmo lugar' [roam from land to land without being able to spend much time in the same place], this is an expression of misfortune. Indeed, his mobility is unmistakably connected to the labour market of which Mozambique had become part after its primitive accumulation.

---

more effective and more efficient'. For him, it 'actually tended to prolong artificially the survival of local pasts in their most pernicious aspects' (1972: 43, 45).

Portagem, then, is certainly a novel about the life of a mulatto and the racial discrimination he experiences. Notwithstanding, it is also the story about a mulatto who has lost his privileged position at his father's mine and is now continuously displaced by his search for labour. *Portagem*, in short, registers colonial capitalism's organization of labour in Mozambique during the 1926–62 period, in both its inseparably connected patchwork structure and labour theme. Indeed, João is separated from the means of production and is hurled into the wage-labour system, is produced as a wage labourer and becomes one of 'the free laboring poor' (Marx 2008a: 377). He is, in other words, a character of primitive accumulation; his very trajectory is that of primitive accumulation, registers primitive accumulation.

Before continuing to *Portagem*'s ghost story element, it is necessary to address how the characters thematize colonial capitalism's domination through labour – or, rather, it is important to address that criticisms of this structure are all but absent in *Portagem* because they are displaced by the issue of race. Indeed, for João, all his misfortunes result from the 'erro fundamental' that was the embrace of his mother and overseer Campos (Mendes 1981: 169).

Interestingly, the absence of social criticism is not a general feature of the novel. For example, women in *Portagem* are treated exceedingly badly, which culminates in the character of Luísa, João's wife. Early in their relationship, Luísa complains: 'eu não quero viver mais. Para quê?' [I don't want to live anymore. What for?] (117). Her death wish is not fulfilled; João saves her life and the couple manages to find some happiness when they settle in a town with their friends Juza and Beatriz. When Juza finds out Beatriz has been unfaithful to him, he murders Beatriz and kills himself, and João takes over the fish business. When competitor Coxo prices him out of business, Luísa goes to Coxo to negotiate, hoping to allow them to at least 'ganhar, em paz, o suficiente para viverem pobremente' [earn, in peace, sufficiently to survive in poverty] (153). The visit, however, teaches Coxo that Luísa is at home alone during the day – information he abuses by coming over and raping her. She does not tell João, and is eventually comforted that Coxo has not come back, gaining 'uma sensação de segurança, uma nova confiança no futuro' [a sense of safety, a new confidence in the future] (159). Shortly after, however, Coxo again comes over to rape the now

Emergence of the Mozambican modern ghost story 107

nine-month-pregnant woman. When João walks in on them and Luísa screams for help, João beats up Coxo but also insults his wife ('Sua cadela mais ordinária!' [you most ordinary bitch!]) and deserts her (163). When their daughter is born shortly after, Luísa, alone, is unable to walk. After three days of being unable to nourish herself, she has no more resources to feed the baby, who then dies.

Patriarchy in *Portagem*, arguably, is thus subject to explicit critical commentary – however effective or ineffective it may be – in the form of the affect Luísa's raw suffering generates. Yet the novel does not criticize the struggle between capital and labour in the same way. The capitalist oppressor is mostly absent from the novel, the (structurality of the) forced-labour system is next to invisible and João even justifies the rare hints of active oppression. When a dysentery epidemic rages through Marandal and half the workers are too sick to work, women and children are mobilized to work in the mines. João, then still a child, is also forced to work, but does not lament the forced child labour this constitutes. Instead, he celebrates it, and the narrator describes how 'seus músculos de criança responderam com alegria ao esforço violento desegurar firme um espigão para que um mineiro adulto lhe batesse com a marreta' [his youthly muscles responded with joy to the violent effort of firmly securing a pick, so an adult miner could hit it with a sledgehammer] (15). Another example: at the beginning of the novel, the Black workers of the Marandal coalmine fantasize about a better life. In Marandal, they have to spend all their money in the company shop to survive (note that João focalizes these issues; the miners have no voice), and many of them therefore have the ambition to cross the border to South Africa and work in the mines in Kaniamato, where, supposedly, the miners still have money left at the end of a 'contrato' [contract] (29). João intervenes to suppress the miners' utopian impulse. Certainly, he affirms, Campos is the 'dono' [boss/owner] (29) of the miners. They have to work more and more to buy what is necessary; they work night and day, and have to spend all their money 'na cantina' [in the canteen] of the mine (29). However, he continues, they 'têm sempre que comer e que vestir, a sua ração de tabaco e vinho' [always have food and clothes, and your tobacco and wine rations] (29–30). Those 'que partem para as minas de além da fronteira, deixam as mulheres e os filhos e, como são clandestinos, muitas vezes nem mandam dinheiro nenhum. Alguns ficam por lá para sempre e outros voltam tuberculosis ou aleijados' [who leave for the mines across the border, leave their women and children and, because they are illegal, often do not even send any money. Some stay there forever and others return with tuberculosis or crippled] (30). João thus attempts to convince the miners to accept their fate, which, he argues, is not that bad compared to the alternatives. A final example: when Campos dies, João believes the mine should stay in operation and that, in order to do so, it needs 'gente competente' [competent people] to run it – by which he means himself and his half-sister (39). Their discussion about this issue is formulated along the lines of philanthropy; they want to keep the mine going – even if it means 'viver pobremente' [living in poverty] (39) – because, João and Maria Helena argue, if they do not manage the mine, the workers will either 'fugirão' [flee] to Kaniamato or other mine owners will recruit them (39). Hence, João and Maria Helena conclude, together they will 'corajosamente' [courageously] pursue the 'exploração da mina' [exploitation of the mine] (40). They will, in other words, continue the exploitation of the miners through the mine, under the pretence of care for their wellbeing. Needless to say, they do not even consider abandoning former hierarchies in the mine and sharing the means of production.

There is, however, one more or less explicit criticism of the conflict between capital and labour in *Portagem*, and it is found in the modern ghost story part of the novel. The ghost story scene in *Portagem* centres on Patrão Campos, the owner of the Marandal mines and João's biological father. The firm buying the coal Campos produces (Santos & Alves) demands larger quantities, leading Campos to intensify production. With three shifts, the mine becomes operational twenty-four hours a day, giving a 'quasi febril' [almost feverish] character to the work (32). During one of the night shifts, the structure of the mine gives way, trapping a group of twenty-three miners under the surface. Campos panics, and the wives of the trapped miners scream and cry in terror, but no one knows how to free the men, who are thus doomed to die, underground, of asphyxiation.

After the event, Campos locks himself in his office. He stays there for hours and looks back on his life, thus changing focalization and allowing

Emergence of the Mozambican modern ghost story

the reader to learn he is not a former slave owner but a new mine owner. Moreover, in doing so, history becomes a haunting and almost supernatural presence for Campos; looking back, it feels to him as if his entire life was set in motion by 'forças estranhas' [strange forces] (33). Above all, Campos is haunted by the 'fantasmas dos mineiros' [ghosts of the miners], who are buried in the mine because of his policy (33). Attempting to justify his choices, he claims he did the 'negros do Ridjalembe' [Negroes of Ridjalembe] a favour ('gratifico') by employing them (34). Yet he is no longer capable of mystifying the reality of the mines for himself. Because he is haunted inside his office – inside his colonial mansion – he eventually flees outside, where he is confronted with the corpses of the twenty-three miners, who are rotting ('aprodecer') in their collective grave (35). Even nature itself then turns against him as the Marandal landscape takes on the shape of a 'monstro de terra e pedra' [monster of land and stone] (35). In an attempt to distance himself from it all, he climbs a mountain, but the monster of land and stone that brought him wealth no longer supports him. The rocks under his feet give way, and 'o corpo do dono da mina despenha-se pela vertente da serra, para vir cair próximo do cemitério dos mineiros' [the body of the mine owner falls down the slope of the mountain, close to the miners' cemetery] (36).

There are several reasons to argue that *Portagem* draws on modern ghost story conventions. It has already been suggested that the novel constructs history as inaccessible – allowing the past in the present to constitute haunting – and that the novel thematizes a transition to modernity and registers primitive accumulation. It may be added that *Portagem*'s stance towards the supernatural conforms with colonial values rather than those of the *traditional field*. João denigratingly refers to supernatural beliefs as superstition (31), and Maria Helena wants to 'combater e vencer a superstição dos trabalhadores da mina' [combat and overcome the superstition of the miners] (40); she does not 'acredita na comunição com os espíritos' [believe in communication with spirits] – although she does believe she can speak to her dead father (40). The main supernatural figure in the novel is the stereotype of the 'cigana' [gypsy] fortune teller (Mendes 1981: 60), a problematic racial caricature with a long history, which Walter Scott's character Meg Merrilies popularized in modernity. Furthermore, the ghost scene is formally distinct from the rest of the novel. In line with MNR and *narrações de sofrimento*, *Portagem* is narrated from João's perspective and ends tragically. However, the ghost story part switches its focalization from the oppressed to the (haunted) oppressor, which allows the reader to monitor Campos's thoughts, feelings, worries and anxieties – to identify with the haunted Campos himself. This is not the expected perspective for an MNR work or for *narrações de sofrimento*. It is, however, the expected perspective for the modern ghost story, in which a feudal or bourgeois protagonist is haunted and in some cases – as in that of Jennings in 'Green Tea' – killed. During this switch in focalization, the ghost miners – as a community of ghosts – successfully exercise their resentment in the class struggle, at least to the extent that their death creates the condition for the Black workers to haunt their colonial oppressor from within his colonial mansion. They drive Campos to his death and end the Marandal mine, which falls into decay after Maria Helena and João part ways.

It is important to emphasize at this point that, as soon as João leaves the Marandal mines, he and the Marandal miners inhabit the same structural position within the wage-labour system that organizes João's lived experience (and the novel). The journey to South Africa, which the miners fantasize about, is the same journey João is forced to make after he leaves the Marandal mine, and it is not unlikely that the other miners make the same journey after the mine falls into decay when João has left. If this is the case, then the rage of the miners is structurally also the rage of João.

The ghost story scene of *Portagem* offers the resolution to the problem of the miners – at least to the extent that they are

> the truly the malevolent ghosts of the modern tradition [...] the archetypal spectres of sheer class *ressentiment* who are out to subvert the lineage of the masters and bind their children to the land of the dead, of those not merely deprived of wealth and power (or of their own labour-power), but even of life itself. (Jameson 1995: 86)

Importantly, the retribution the ghost miners exact – the death of the colonial capitalist – is towards a shared oppressor position. João's position is thus commented upon *in advance* by the haunting and death of Campos (although the criticism is symbolic at most, because the death of Campos leads to the closing of the Marandal mines, but does not have

Emergence of the Mozambican modern ghost story   III

further structural consequences – it does not eliminate Santos & Alves). From this perspective, although the climax is positioned before its build-up, *Portagem* has a recognizable modern ghost story structure.

In brief, *Portagem* can be understood as modern ghost story, that explicitly thematizes racial relations in colonial Mozambique at the time of its production, but that also registers the formal and legal sedimentation of nineteenth-century primitive accumulation in the 1926 labour legislation in its patchwork, short-story-like structure, in the labour theme, and in the João character.

After *Portagem*: Modern ghost figures, anti-supernaturalism

After *Portagem*, no modern ghost stories would be published in Mozambique until 1986, which is in part explained by poetry remaining the dominant form until the 1980s. However, modern ghost imagery occurs frequently during this period – as metaphor, as wavering presence, as frightening non-belonging entity or as the inaccessible or returning past. In Mendes's 'Comércio' [Commerce] (Mendes 1968: 37), there are 'fantasmas de seu ofício' [ghosts of their craft] (37); in Craveirinha's 'História de Amor' [History of Love], there are 'fantasmas da nossa tristeza' [ghosts of our sadness] (1982: 109); and in Sebastião Alba's 'Palavras de Ponta e Mola' [Switchblade Words[9]], there are 'fantasmas de forasteiros' [ghosts of outsiders] (Alba 23). Eduardo Pita writes about 'o medo de revisitados fantasmas' [fear of the revisited ghosts] (in M. Ferreira 1997: 385–6). Lourenço de Carvalho links the figure of the ghost to fear in his *Minha Ave Africana* (1972) ('receio antigo/ [...] aos fantasmas' [ancient fear/ [...] of ghosts] (3)) and even equates fear and ghosts ('os teus medos se anoitece/os teus fantasmas' [your fears become night/your ghosts] (14)). Mendes's 'Flores Para os Vivos' [Flowers for the Living] (1980) uses the haunting imagery of 'corpos e fantasmas' [bodies and ghosts] (66). Knopfli draws on modern ghost imagery several times.

9   For this translation I have Vera Peixoto to thank.

Most importantly, for this study, he describes the city of São Paulo as a haunted house (2003: 356). A miniature modern ghost story, the poetic voice finds itself in a mansion 'Povoado de sombras e fantasmas' [inhabited by shadows and ghosts], and creates suspense by asking whether the creaks he hears are footsteps or history itself burnt into the mansion's dried-out wood ['arde na madeira ressequida dos sobrados']. The voice continues to narrate the history of the house, which has been pillaged in service of the greed of despots, clerks and soldiers. What remains are empty buildings, 'portas e muros' [gates and walls] – and, the poetic voice adds, '[t]ambém as sombras. E os fantasmas' [also the shadows. And the ghosts] (356).

Another reason the modern ghost story was absent for roughly twenty years after *Portagem* lies in the rising influence of Frelimo. Particularly after the start of the anticolonial struggle, as Bertelsen (2016) writes, the Portuguese Empire attempted to use 'elements of the traditional field against the Frelimo guerrillas' (70). Local chiefs (*régulos*) and their 'ritual, social, and political organization' were used to enforce taxation and forced labour, and to create allegiances between colonizer and colonized, by 'showing acceptance and recognition of traditional and ritual authority by the colonial state' – an integral part of the Portuguese (anti-anti-colonial) war, used alongside other repressive operations (71). Partly based on these developments, Frelimo – which would go on to become the sole political party – organized what Bowen calls a regime of 'bureaucratic "moderniz[ation]"' (2000: 8), the goals of which included the 'eliminat[ion of] what it defined as traditional authorities and influence' (Bertelsen 2016: 72). Thus, Frelimo denied the authority of those connected to 'obscurantism (*obscurantismo*)' (73) and prohibited 'ceremonies' related to the *traditional field* (97).

Frelimo's position relative to supernatural paradigms may have contributed to the post-*Portagem* absence of modern ghost stories, and is expressed in literary production of this period. Most clearly, the three editions of *Poesia de Combate*, published in 1971, 1977 and 1980, illustrate this. Generally devoid of references to any supernatural entities, the few poems that do invoke the ghosts or spirits do so disapprovingly. Sérgio Vieira's 'Porque São como Flores Camaradas' [Because We Are Like Flowers Comrades], for example, thematizes the anticolonial struggle and its accomplishments and

Emergence of the Mozambican modern ghost story   113

states these cannot be ascribed to any agency other than humankind: '[N]ão são milagres/deuses e espíritos/o que acontece,/apenas homens [whatever happens/they aren't miracles/gods and spirits,/just men] (Frelimo 1977: 90). In 'Palavras II' [Words II], a voice criticizes a comrade for relying on spirits: 'perguntavas/inutilmente/aos spiritos/aquilo que se passava/ mas os teus espíritos/não sabem escrever' [you asked/the spirits/uselessly/ about what happened/but your spirits/do not know how to write] (75) – although in Agostinho's poem 'Respondam-nos Agora' [Answer us Now], in the third edition of *Poesia de Combate*, a voice somewhat untypically speaks of 'cadaveres' [cadavers] that are 'vivos na Revolução' [alive in the revolution] (Frelimo 1980: 49), possibly invoking a zombie figure.

This would change in the 1980s, under the influence of the capitalist restoration of Mozambique.

CHAPTER 4

The Mozambican modern ghost story

The 1980s saw the resurgence of the Mozambican modern ghost story. The Mozambican social system transitioned several times in the late twentieth century, with formal decolonization in 1974–5, the consolidation of the *Frente de Libertação de Moçambique* [Mozambican Liberation Front] (Frelimo) state in 1975, the failed attempt to create a socialist state in the 1970s and 1980s and the civil war that emerged from that failure. These events created the conditions for Mozambique to become subject to a new phase of primitive accumulation, or capitalist restoration, and to 'transition' back into the periphery of the capitalist world-system. The main claim in this chapter is that the reintegration of Mozambique into the world-system was accompanied by changes in literary production, and that these changes facilitated the formation of a new form of a modern ghost story that is more specifically Mozambican than its predecessors. Couto's 'A História dos Aparecidos' [The Tale of two Apparitions] (henceforth 'História'), first published in the 1986 collection *Vozes Anoitecidas* (2012), was the first such Mozambican modern ghost story, and it will be shown in this chapter how it registers capitalist restoration by drawing on modern ghost story conventions that British and Latin American authors popularized, as well as on narrative strategies used in Mendes's *Portagem* – which it conventionalizes retroactively. In the wake of 'História', several works were published that draw on these Mozambican modern ghost story conventions until they all but disappeared at the beginning of the 1990s, and this chapter provides an overview – short rather than close readings – of those in closing.

Before discussing the case studies, however, it is necessary to outline the political-economic transitions in Mozambique, which form the backdrop

116   CHAPTER 4

and conditions of the Mozambican modern ghost story. This chapter subsequently discusses how scholars commonly analyse 'História' relative to corruption and bureaucratism, and the problems such interpretations create, after which it proceeds to the analysis of 'História'.

Independence, civil war, primitive accumulation

Mozambique gained independence under the leadership of Frelimo. Initially a liberation army, its aims and practices were influenced by its 'left-leaning liberal' leader Eduardo Mondlane (Newitt 2017: 141), but an internal struggle was decided in favour of the socialist 'moderniser' Samora Machel during the 1968 Second Party Congress, and against moderates and traditionalists (Newitt 2017: 141). As a result, Frelimo 'adopted an uncompromising modernist agenda', which included gaining 'independence from Portugal', transforming 'Mozambican society along non-tribal, non-racial, non-capitalist lines' (143) and an opposition to expressions of the *traditional field* or 'obscurantism' (158).

The assassination of Mondlane in 1969, and his succession by Machel, solidified Frelimo's socialist orientation, and – despite the absence of a clear Frelimo victory – Mozambique gained independence in 1975, following the Portuguese revolution of 1974. As sole political party with Machel as its president, it became Marxist-Leninist in name in 1977 and sought to implement its agenda with a focus on collectivism, education, equality and secularization (Newitt 2017: 143–7). Frelimo had some success; it nationalized, inter alia, the housing, healthcare and education sectors (155). Levy writes that, by 1979, a 'national immunization campaign against smallpox, tetanus, and measles had reached an estimated ninety percent of the population and infant mortality had fallen by twenty percent' and, during the first six years of Frelimo rule, 'primary school enrollment doubled from 700,000 to 1,376,000 and secondary education moved from 20,000 to 135,000' (2013: 132). Pitcher describes how, by 1982, 'only 27 percent of firms in industry, commerce and agriculture remained private' (2002: 44), and Bowen shows that, by 1983, the healthcare sector had improved dramatically, as had access to drinking water (2000: 47). Frelimo also reformed the (forced-) labour market, discussed in the previous chapter, by building co-operatives in which the population – and especially peasants – were expected to work. It built communal villages to facilitate housing.

Yet the party also faced 'a crippling crisis' almost 'immediately' after the transition, writes Newitt (2017: 154). The Portuguese withdrew quickly from Mozambique and handed over power to Frelimo after a nine-month period, which proved too brief to train the necessary cadres and experts. No plans for economic aid were established and relations with neighbouring countries were not stabilized – a situation intensified due to Frelimo's support for groups fighting oppressive White-minority governments in South Africa (ANC) and Rhodesia (ZANU) (Newitt 2017: 161). After independence, a large exodus followed, which drained the country of most of its skilled labourers – predominantly Portuguese and those who had co-operated with the colonizer, and had thus had access to education. Leaving settler colonialists and comprador groups actively attempted to destabilize the country through sabotage, by killing cattle stock, destroying equipment, causing production standstills, importing goods that never arrived, exporting goods for which the capital never returned and massively buying up stocks in shops, with the 'depletion of stocks of commodities' as a result (Wuyts 1985: 185).

The immediate post-independence situation meant Frelimo lacked not only the necessary means, expertise and recourses to rule and stabilize an independent, socialist Mozambique, but also a lack of support. Unlike in Cape Verde and São Tomé, where elections were held after independence, Frelimo adopted a strategy of 'taking power first and seeking legitimization afterwards' (Newitt 2017: 152–3), which Bowen demonstrates led to the formation of a 'bureaucratic anti-peasant, one-party state' (2000: 48). The peasantry formed about 80 per cent of the population (Newitt 2017: 157), and supported Frelimo during the liberation struggle because 'poor peasants' were subjected to 'colonial forced labor', and colonial racism severely limited the social mobility of 'middle peasants' (Bowen 2000: 1). However, as Bowen argues, once in power Frelimo represented the interests of the peasantry less and less; instead, it expected poor peasants to work on 'poorly run state farms or join underfinanced cooperatives' (2) and middle peasants to hand over their limited means of production – ploughs, oxen and so on – to the co-operatives, essentially committing 'class suicide' (9). Frelimo's 'agricultural strategy [thus] completely negated what independence meant to the peasantry', namely the possibility of a degree of self-sufficiency and self-determination (2). It instead 'reflected class and bureaucratic interests of those who controlled the state' (11), with the result that, by the beginning of the 1980s, 'there was no social force in the countryside that supported Frelimo's socialist project' (112).

In the face of his failing mission to modernize Mozambique, Machel's anti-capitalism shifted to 'political paranoia' and concerns about sabotage and obscurantism (Newitt 2017: 157–8). The peasantry and their supposedly non-secular, traditionalist ways were a main target of Machel's discontent – but, as Newitt argues, things 'were little better in the city', where Machel suspected 'sabotage' and 'corruption' everywhere and saw the 'traditional superstition' supplemented with 'models of the foreign bourgeoisie' (157). Bowen also argues that, in the 1980s, Frelimo's 'socialist policies' had 'little socialist content to them' (2000: 48), and the party rather 'continued the tradition of an all-powerful administrative structure inherited from the Portuguese' (102). Newitt writes that Frelimo became 'ever more authoritarian' and 'obsessed with ordering the minutiae of daily life' (Newitt 2017: 158). Hence, Derluguian argues that, by 'many indicators, during the 1970s Frelimo was self-consciously transforming itself into a Stalinist party' (213).

The complex conjuncture of post-independence Mozambique shaped the conditions of a civil war that would last until 1992. Frelimo's main opponent – the *Resistência Nacional Moçambicana* [National Mozambican Resistance], or Renamo, initially led by former Frelimo official André Matsangaissa – rapidly grew from a Rhodesia-based radio station, which 'effectively fann[ed] the flames of anti-Frelimo sentiment and regionalism', to a potent military force (Emerson 2019: 64). Rhodesia, and later South Africa, provided 'the means, support, and guidance that allowed Renamo to evolve as quickly as it did' because both had an interest in destabilizing Mozambique, which supported the ANC and ZANU (64). Nevertheless, despite the importance of foreign powers to the war, the USSR and USA were allies of Mozambique and South Africa respectively, the conflict was

The Mozambican modern ghost story	119

not a US–USSR proxy war. Indeed, Morier-Genoud stresses that 'we need to leave behind at once' earlier understandings of the Mozambican war as the 'mere product of the Cold War or of regional dynamics – as if the South African apartheid regime and the Mozambican parties had been mere puppets of the United States and the Soviet Union' (2018: 6). The Cold War 'cannot be ignored of course, but it is clear that it was not the main reason behind the conflict' (7). Rather, 'certain people and certain areas had been marginalized and felt like the coming war could help them address their grievances and status' (7, 9).

The war was, instead, a civil war that 'pitted from the start and in its overwhelming majority members of the same national community – Mozambicans against Mozambicans' (Morier-Genoud 2018: 2). Frelimo was aware of this during the unfolding of the conflict, and Chichava (2018) quotes a communication from the Frelimo Ministry of Defense that reads:

> Our study has concluded that our population is easily won over by the enemy in the communal villages because we are not keeping our promises made to the popular masses during the transfer of populations into communal villages, the conditions for survival such as the stores to buy foodstuffs, hospitals, markets, schools, and even public assistance. (Chichava 2018: 25)

During the conflict, Renamo pursued the destruction of all Frelimo representations (Emerson 29), including expressions of what Cahen labels Frelimo's 'authoritarian modernization' (Cahen 2018: 134). It attacked the schools, healthcare and drinking-water facilities the government had built and targeted rail and road infrastructure, stores, communal villages and co-operatives. Moreover, in an apparent reversal of Frelimo's anti-traditionalism and anti-secularism, Renamo portrayed itself as the protector of the 'traditional field' (Bertelsen 2016: 108). It spoke of its fight against Frelimo as a *'guerra dos espíritos'* [war of the spirits], and Renamo officers were widely considered to have magical powers (Bertelsen 73; see also Wilson 1992). Renamo supported traditional authorities, such as faith healers, soothsayers, *n'angas* and *profetes* – figures Frelimo considered archaic or feudal, and which it argued the so-called secular and modern 'New Man' should replace (Chichava 2018: 29). This relation to the *traditional field* gained them support in the countryside, and some even saw the group as a liberator (Bertelsen 2016: 73). In the areas in which Renamo did not have popular support, it took on the shape of a 'predatory army, terrorizing and plundering the rural population' (Emerson 2019: 99), but even its regular guerrilla warfare and terror campaigns were supplemented with 'traditional resources [such as] ritual healers' (Bertelsen 2016: 73).

The civil war created an unsustainable situation, which worsened with the droughts and famines of the early 1980s, and the failure (often not due solely to Frelimo but also to donors, who demanded the Party open up the country to foreign investors) to gather the necessary aid to mediate the fallout. With the country and its population in ruins, and national debt soaring – a situation worsened due to the global, post-Volcker shock debt-crisis – Frelimo saw itself forced to change its political approach. After the Fourth Party Congress in 1983, Frelimo rolled back many of the nationalizations and partially privatized, decentralized and liberalized its economy. It joined the International Monetary Fund (IMF) and World Bank in 1984 (Bowen 2000: 189).[1] As early as 1984, light industry and the agricultural sector started to be privatized (Pitcher 2002: 44; cf. Pitcher 1996), Frelimo scaled down investment in the healthcare sector and a '[r]edistribution of land and joint-ventures with the private sector' commenced (Pitcher 2002: 110). Considering the results insufficient, and with the war ongoing, Frelimo 'fully embraced and actively courted the support of key Western countries' under the leadership of Joaquim Chissano, who became Frelimo's president after Machel died in 1986 in a plane crash (Emmerson 2019: 177). The party adopted the Program of Economic Rehabilitation (PRE), a form of structural adjustment programme, during the 1987 People's Assembly (Hall and Young 1997: 196). This implied a

---

1   Castel-Branco et al. (2003: 161) point out that privatizations were not only a way to 'raise economic efficiency and the investment rate' but also a condition for joining the Bretton Woods Institutions, the IMF and the Lomé Convention (the European Economic Community's aid/trade agreement with predominantly African countries), which (in part) refused to work with state-owned enterprises. Privatizations were also a way to undermine Renamo by 'adopting one of its demands', a way to divert and prevent criticisms of Frelimo mismanagement and to strengthen the party by enriching its elites (Pitcher 1996: 55).

devaluation of the currency, the lifting of price controls, the cutting of subsidies for state firms and further, far-reaching decentralization and privatization. In turn, this formed the condition for large sums of donor, aid and investment money flowing into the country, and led to devastating austerity for the majority of the population (Hall and Young 1997: 196–7).

Due to this complex combination of circumstances, then, postcolonial Mozambique abandoned – indeed, was forced to abandon – its (nominally) socialist political-economic system and was again integrated into the (periphery of the) capitalist world-system, and into what Kalipeni and Zeleza call 'the deadly embrace' of Western donors (1999: 28–9). Hence, Pitcher metaphorizes that, from 1983 onwards, 'we are seeing the birth of capitalism' in Mozambique (1996: 74) – or, more accurately, primitive accumulation. The end of the Cold War and fall of the USSR symbolically sealed this process, but it had arguably become irreversible with the initial privatizations of 1983. With the weakening of the nominally socialist policy, disapproving attitudes towards the *traditional field* also waned. *N'angas* and *profetes* 'were gradually seen as keys to relegitimize Frelimo [as well as] undermine Renamo's support among rural and urban populations as a custodian of *tradição*' (Bertelsen 2016: 161). In 1986, Frelimo legalized traditional healing, and in 1992 it founded AMETRAMO – an institution that officially aimed to reorder traditional Mozambican medicine but was equally geared 'towards controlling what it could not eradicate' (Bertelsen 2016: 162).

Literary production during Frelimo rule

The primitive accumulation, or capitalist restoration, of Mozambique affected literary production in more and less direct ways. Bortolot argues that Mozambican cultural production was 'guided directly by FRELIMO's ideological position' (2013: 259). Indeed, in their 'The Growth of a New Culture' (1971), the Frelimo officials Guebuza and Vieira insist culture is a way to express the values of the ruling classes. For them, the dominant cultures of post-independence Mozambique are feudal traditionalism and colonial capitalism. In the former, humans are subjected to a hostile nature and the favours of Gods or spirits, and production is organized by a division of labour as it is monopolized by certain artist classes. The latter aims to depersonalize and mentally colonize colonial subjects, and artistic production is reserved (predominantly) for colonialists and settlers (Guebuza and Vieira 10–11). To establish a turn to socialism, the two authors claim, tribal and capitalist culture must be destroyed and replaced by a new culture, which emerges from the socialist struggle. This culture is inclusive and non-individualist; its production is accessible to all, because cultural activity is organized as collective and co-operative activity under the patronage of the state; and the romantic focus on the perceived genius of the individual artist, as it exists in bourgeois artistic production, is replaced by a focus on the 'artisan' (Bortolot 2013: 252). Artisans, the two authors write, are by definition connected to the socialist struggle – not only through the co-operative process of production but also through the content of their works, which must be revolutionary, teach socialism and avoid promoting aestheticism for its own sake (252–4).

Frelimo's notions about culture developed somewhat over time; in 1975, the party aligned them more explicitly with other socialist states, including the People's Republic of China and the USSR. It said the art of the 'Popular Democracy'

> must be an instrument of criticism and self-criticism. As an instrument of combat and education of the great masses, art must adopt socialist realism as its creative method – the true representation of reality. To reflect upon reality, with veracity; to reflect reality, with veracity. (Bortolot 2013: 260)

Frelimo's normative and prescriptive understanding of what culture should be thus roughly shaped the Mozambican cultural landscape along the lines of Zhdanov's prescriptive 1934 'On Literature' (Laranjeira 2001: 262). Zhdanov – who Terry Eagleton describes as 'Stalin's cultural thug', and whose essay on literature was, in fact, 'cobbled together by Stalin and Gorky' (Eagleton 2002: 36) – condemned what he considered the 'orgies of mysticism and superstition [and] the passion for pornography' that characterized bourgeois literature (Zhdanov 1934).

The Mozambican modern ghost story   123

He instead promoted 'truthfulness and historical concreteness of the artistic portrayal' and the teaching of socialism through what he called socialist realism (Zhdanov 1934). Frelimo officials such as Sérgio Vieira, Marcelino dos Santos and Fernando Ganhão oversaw adherence to these prescriptions; this was possible, in part, because – conforming to the idea of state patronage – the government functioned as publisher. It created the possibility of effectively blocking or discouraging the publication of types of works that were not (considered) socialist realist.

The *Poesia de Combate* collections are an example of this type of artistic production. Eventually published by Frelimo, they denounce spirituality and promote the notion of humans as history-making actors: '[N]ão são milagres/deuses e espíritos/o que acontece,/apenas homens' [whatever happens/they aren't miracles/gods and spirits,/just men] (Frelimo 1977: 90). The dominant theme of *Poesia* is the revolutionary struggle, and the collections are co-operative productions in which different artisans are published. Maria-Benedita Basto highlights how the democratization of cultural production is also manifest in these collections. The contributors are mostly new poets, resulting from a 'todos podem escrever' [everyone is allowed to write] policy, and it may not be accidental that the collections have retrospectively been judged to be of poor quality; collective and accessible work promoting the socialist struggle was prioritized over stylistic craftsmanship (2008: 80). Finally, Frelimo removed José Craveirinha's poems, which were part of the original manuscripts, as they deemed them not to be socialist realist (cf. Basto 2012).

As such, the Stalinism that Derluguian sees in Frelimo's politics may arguably have its counterpart in the cultural sphere. However, as the party's grip on the country weakened, so did its ability to shape artistic production. A younger generation of authors began to distance itself from socialist realism and was involved in the foundation of the *Associação dos Escritores Moçambicanos* [Mozambican Writers Association] (AEMO) (1982) and the literary magazine *Charrua* (1984). These provided an institutional basis from which literary production could be changed, which, for Laranjeira (1995), culminated in AEMO's publication of Mia Couto's *Vozes Anoitecidas* in 1986. *Vozes*, argues Mendonça, broke with the 'princípios rígidos do realismo socialista' [ridged principles of socialist realism] and instead drew

124   CHAPTER 4

on what Löwy (2010) would call irrealist literary forms championed by Latin American writers such as Guimarães Rosa, Gabriel García Márquez (Mendonça 2008: 28) and Juan Rulfo, who shall be returned to later in this chapter (Brookshaw 2016: 18). Rather than reflecting 'upon reality, with veracity; to reflect reality, with veracity', as prescribed by socialist realism, *Vozes* 'straddle[d] the dividing line between reality and fantasy' (Chesca Long-Innes 1998: 155).

   Vozes provoked much 'polémica e discussão' [polemics and discussion] (Laranjeira 1995: 262). Mendonça writes that, in 1987, Mbhome Seneia Cuinica criticized Couto for a 'falta de vivência da realidade' [lack of real/ lived experience] and recommended all writers stay close to the experiences of the people (in Mendonça 2008: 29). Nogar – then secretary-general of AEMO but also a supporter of the party line – attacked *Vozes* because of its use of anti-heroes 'modelados por princípios não conformes com as necessidades políticas de momento' [modelled according to principles that are not conform the political necessities of the moment] (in Mendonça 2008: 29). Calana da Silva defended the guiding aesthetics of *Vozes* – its unity, coherence, originality and linguistic innovation (in Mendonça 2008: 29) – and Panguana, defending *Vozes*, argued that '[a] ficção é a única possibilidade que se nos apresenta de abarcamos realidades e lugares nunca vividos e habitados!' [fiction is the only possibility that presents itself to us, in which we can embrace realities and places never lived or inhabited] (in Mendonça 2008: 30–1). Finally, in the 1987 edition of *Vozes*, Craveirinha identified the collection of short stories as the continuation of a literary project that had started with João Dias in the 1950s and continued with Luís Bernardo Honwana in the 1960s. Craveirinha's authority largely ended the debate.

   After *Vozes*, a proliferation of literary styles including neo-symbolism, neo-concretism and neo-surrealism occurred in Mozambique (Laranjeira 2001: 192). For Laranjeira, *Vozes* therefore constitutes the 'fautor de uma mutação literária em Moçambique' [instigator of a literary change in Mozambique] (Laranjeira 1995: 262) and is a 'livro fundador de uma reorgenação literária' [foundational book of literary reorganization] (Laranjeira 2001: 198). Mendonça similarly considers *Vozes* the starting point of a fundamental 'transição' [transition] in Mozambican literature

The Mozambican modern ghost story 125

(2008: 28). The shift in Mozambique's 'general mode of production' was thus accompanied by a shift in the dominant 'literary mode of production' (Eagleton 2006: 45).

'A História dos Aparacidos'

Vozes not only marks a turning point in Mozambican literature but also, it is argued here, contains the first Mozambican modern ghost story, in the form of the short story 'História'. To show how 'História' can be considered a modern ghost story – one that draws on conventions popularized by British and Latin American authors and on narrative strategies used by *Portagem*, and that registers primitive accumulation – it is beneficial to provide a plot summary and a discussion of the ways in which the work could, and has been, understood.

In 'História', characters Luís Fernando and Aníbal Mucavel arrive at a relocated village after a flood wiped out the original one. They are refused entry because the villagers believe the men have died in the flood and are now ghosts. Their fear diminishes when they hear the men's voices, but the villagers remain hesitant to let them in, both because there is a food shortage and because the two men are not accounted for in the rations. However, the character Professor Samuel notes that this is unfair because the local officials '[fazem] candonga com os productos' (Couto 2012: 132) [divert supplies] (Couto 1989: 11), with the result that local officials have enough to eat even when the villagers deal with scarcity. The villagers also argue the men cannot be registered because they fear that, if they try to register two 'fantasmas' [ghosts], the district government will punish them for practising 'obscurantismo' [obscurantism] (Couto 2012: 131). The two men protest that they are not ghosts, but the villagers do not know how to prove this. After three days, which the men spend at Samuel's house, a committee arrives and decides they are to be considered 'populações existentes' [existing population] for now, but that such a dis/reappearance cannot occur again (135).

126   CHAPTER 4

Despite its short length (eight pages), 'História' offers ample possibility for analysis. It could be understood as a socialist realist story that 'reflects' aspects of its historical context of production. The hesitation to register the ghosts, for example, echoes Frelimo's opposition to the *traditional field*; floods and droughts have been an integral part of Mozambican history, plagued Mozambique during the 1980s (cf. Newitt 4) and, under Frelimo rule, led to resettlements as early as 1977 after floods destroyed the Limpopo Valley (Bowen 2000: 12). Keeping in mind the Frelimo censor, the destruction of the village could also be argued to codify the actual practice of Frelimo's '[r]esettlement of the rural population into communal villages after 1984', and the discontent of the villagers in 'História' may reflect the dissatisfaction about the dysfunctionality of those communal villages (Bowen 2000: 14). The flood could even be understood as the dynamic of the civil war, which had taken on aspects of a force of nature. Emerson explains how, by 1984, a stalemate had been established because the Frelimo army relied on heavy firepower, and would gain territory during the dry seasons, but would lose ground to Renamo during the rainy seasons because its heavy machinery was unable to move well over the badly maintained muddy roads. Thus, '[t]owns were lost and recaptured. Lines of communication cut only to be restored' (Emerson 2019: 85). Peasants had no protection from either side, as it would sooner or later be either Frelimo or Renamo 'season'. This, then, caused a general alienation within the population, which the villagers in 'História' possibly express.[2]

Scholars similarly relied on reflection or metaphor to analyse 'História', and predominantly identified it as critical commentary on a bureaucratic and corrupt Frelimo political apparatus.[3] Afolabi claims 'História' is a 'case study in the complex dynamics of Mozambican contemporary reality', in which authorities are 'corrupt' and citizens are denied their 'rights' (124). He understands the ghosts as a metaphor for the 'condemned members

2   Lina Magaia (1987: 26) thematizes this in her work.
3   Other readings of 'História' focus on, inter alia, geography (Feitosa and Manir 2013), memory (Ngoveni 2006) and absurdism (Ferreira 2007). See also Madureira (2006), Afonso (2002), Chabal (1996) and Couto (1990).

The Mozambican modern ghost story 127

of society', who are oppressed by the 'authorities' (124). Luís Gonçalves makes a similar argument and links this to bureaucracy; he says 'História' is an allegory for the 'entire country', that the two ghosts are 'alive' and that their ghosting is a narrative strategy to make the 'bureaucracy of the system' representable in fiction (36–7).

There is little doubt that the above interpretations have a degree of merit, and the summary of 'História' and historical overview above appear to support the corruption and bureaucracy interpretations; yet a more detailed examination of the context that shaped 'História' highlights that such interpretations run the risk of being ahistorical. It is to such an examination this chapter now turns.

Corruption and bureaucratism

Harrison (1999) argues it is 'no exaggeration to say that corruption, or rather the politics of corruption, is a defining issue in the contemporary political discourse in and on Mozambique' (537). Yet he emphasizes that corruption in Mozambique was not uniform, and changed under influence of the history of colonialism, 'socialism, war and liberalization' (537). A consensus appears to exist on corruption in Mozambique being uncommon during the early years of independence (e.g. Harrison 540; Spector 2005), even if the evidence for that claim is considered to be incomplete (Stasavage 2000: 70). On the one hand, Machel had an 'immense hatred' of corruption, which for him was an inherent part of capitalism, and he and his government considered eliminating corrupt practice as part of the desired transition from colonial capitalism to socialism (Harrison 1999: 540). On the other hand, the population's post-liberation 'optimism' and unspoiled faith in the new government also contributed to the relative absence of corruption (Hanlon and Smart 101). As Hanlon and Smart (2010) write, there 'was total trust – a belief that Frelimo was working for you and that everyone was working together to build something new' (101). Elsewhere, Hanlon notes it was simply impossible to accumulate an abundant amount of personal wealth in the newly founded socialist state because it would be 'obvious' if some people had more than others (1997: 186).

This does not mean (government) corruption was absent in the early years of independence; however, according to Bowen, it was 'petty' in form (2000: 198). Two examples: first, when settlers colonialists left Mozambique to return to Portugal, the real estate they owned was nationalized and came under the control of the notoriously favouritist *Administração do Parque Imobiliário do Estado* [State Housing Authority] (APIE) (Rensburg 1981: 45; Simon 1999: 33).[4] Second, the state-run shops, or *lojas do povo* [the people's shops], were infamous sources of unequal distribution of sparsely available foodstuffs and commodities.[5] Machel was aware of this, and organized a presidential offensive in which he cracked down on corruption. He reorganized the APIE (and the national airline, which was also favouritist), introduced rationing systems that improved food distribution and eliminated 'Kafka-esque bureaucratic processes in state organizations' (Marleyn et al. 1982: 115). Frelimo fired responsible ministers and local officials (Rensburg 1981: 220).

Despite Machel's apparent efforts, corruption in Mozambique increased during the 1980s. Post-liberation optimism, faith in the party and 'strong ideological commitment' to long-term socialist goals diminished due to Frelimo mismanagement and the unfolding civil war (Stasavage 2000: 70). With the decline of these 'morals', Frelimo became more 'affected by corruption' (Manning 2002: 125). According to Hanlon and Smart, this initially led to minor inequalities – 'a district administrator [having] cooking oil when there is none in the shop' – and quickly led to the political elites having better 'cars, consumer goods, better houses, and better health care and education' (2010: 103). The chaos of war and the large sums of money involved – about 40 per cent of state budget in 1985 – facilitated the misappropriation of funds, food and fuel for personal benefit and survival; for example, by enlisting 'ghost troops': 12,000 soldiers who were on the pay roll appear to have never existed (Harrison 1999: 541).[6] Finally, Frelimo mismanagement and war often made it impossible to survive

4   The same point is made in Isaacman and Isaacman (1983: 141), Egero (1982), Mittelman (1981: 115) and Harrison (1999: 540).
5   It also became a *topos* in Mozambican literature (e.g. Saúte 2012).
6   For corruption and the military, see also Robinson (2006).

The Mozambican modern ghost story

on public-sector wages, raising the question, for Harrison, of how '*not* to practice corruption' and still subsist (1999: 544).

Yet it was the 'advent of the capitalist market' that gave corruption in Mozambique 'a new scope' (Bowen 2000: 198), and it has even been argued that the structural adjustment programme came to 'define' corruption (Harrison 1999: 538). The loss of faith in the party and its nominally socialist agenda was now accompanied by an official change in rhetoric, replacing the emphasis on collectivism with an emphasis on personal enrichment (Harrison 1999: 542). The policy of privatization and liberalization made such an enrichment especially viable for Frelimo officials. (Donor) money flows into the country increased drastically, and government officials had access to these flows and information about them. They also knew what sectors and companies were going to be privatized, as these had fallen under government control during centralization and nationalization in the first years of independence. Thus, government officials could become the new owners of state properties and businesses, circumventing the market completely – so-called 'silent privatization' (Harrison 1999: 543). The state would also pay officials with land and companies, and had the power to grant or refuse permits (Bowen 2000: 198). Because of the one-party system, these same 'corrupt' Frelimo officials were responsible for holding individuals accountable. After the Fifth Party Congress in 1989, such enrichment was facilitated further by removing all investment restrictions and limitations on employing workers (Bowen 2000: 198). Not incidentally, a popular joke during this period was to refer to the PRE as the PRI, or 'Individual Habilitation Programme' (Roesch 1988: 10).

David Stasavage usefully summarizes that corruption in Mozambique increased 'substantially' due to several factors (2000: 69). Ideological commitment declined, money flows increased and bureaucrats

> retain[ed] extensive control rights over economic activity, with individuals (or individual agencies) often holding monopoly and discretionary power over provision of a particular government-supplied service. At the same time, structures for monitoring bureaucrats and holding them accountable for their actions [were] dramatically weakened. [...] A decrease in real wages for civil service and increasing inequalities in pay between the public and private sectors also contributed to the increase in corruption [as did a] decline in public service. (66)

This situation was to the double detriment of the peasantry, which suffered from the political elite's enrichment and from PRE austerity. Frelimo members, such as Guebuza, were aware of this but noted it was a necessary sacrifice for 'progress' – notably, Guebuza became one of the wealthiest individuals in the country, and succeeded Chissano as president (in Bowen 1992: 271). And while Roesch, in 1988, was careful to compare Mozambique to other African countries in which a new bourgeoisie formed after independence and enriched itself at the expense of the rest of the population – which Fanon warned of (2007 [1961]) – it may now be suggested that definitive similarities exist.

It is essential to emphasize that the corruption in Mozambique was an integral part of the process of primitive accumulation – as it often was – and, even though the case of the USSR is vastly different from that of Mozambique, a brief comparison is clarifying. Mandel shows how, after the 1917 Revolution in the USSR, 'the regime [also] continued to propagate socialist ideas and values, albeit often in a bastardized version, [while] the socialist project itself, whose core is the abolition of exploitation, was abandoned in practice' (2018: 2). When the contradictions eventually contributed to the USSR's collapse, capitalism was restored through a 'revolution from above' *and* with the help of 'international capitalist forces' (2). As in Mozambique, ' "wild privatization" had begun even before the transition was formally launched at the beginning of 1992, with state administrators and their friends illegally transferring public property to private companies in which they were owners' (4). Under Yeltsin, the violent neoliberal transition occurred fast and 'very much to the taste of the pro-Yeltsin forces [which] opened broad horizons for plundering the collective legacy of the Soviet system' (4), leading to the enrichment of political elite and the 'appointment' of 'billionaires' (6).

Large-scale corruption was thus increasingly a problem in Mozambique, and Stasavage demonstrates there is 'partial evidence of an increase in the level of corruption since the beginning of the reform programme' in the early and mid-1980s (2000: 69), although the most significant increase occurred after 1986. This is expected; primitive accumulation arguably started after the 1983 Fourth Party Congress – or, at the latest, after joining the IMF and World Bank in 1984. Yet the decisive turn to capitalism and the large money flows it involved, which facilitated corruption, only started in 1987 under Chissano.

The Mozambican modern ghost story

Returning to 'História' and the risk of analysing it ahistorically: while the theme of corruption is unmistakably a part of the short story, most large-scale corruption occurred after its publication. Moreover, arguing that the story is a commentary on corrupt Frelimo party elites screens out the ongoing process of primitive accumulation, and even provides the condition to argue that the cause of Mozambican corruption was Frelimo's nominally socialist state structure. Teixeira Soares Ferreira indeed comes to this conclusion, and groups together 'a corrupção' [corruption], 'à economia planificada e sua rigidez dogmática' [the planned economy and its rigid dogmatic] and 'à retórica do materialismo dialéctico' [the rhetoric of dialectical materialism] (2007: 391). However, on the one hand – and ignoring the absurd wholesale rejection of dialectical materialism and lack of specificity in describing Frelimo's political-economic system – even though the Frelimo state in its initial years could have generated corruption, this appears not to be what happened, rendering the argument that Frelimo equals corruption mute. On the other hand, Pitcher has pointed out how calling attention to corruption is not a neutral gesture; it has been one of the 'standard features of most neo-liberal agendas (a part of their implicit puritanical moralizing) in developing countries', and has served as a justification for neoliberal interventions, including SAPs (2006: 6–8). Indeed, Teixeira Soares Ferreira (2007), suggesting that Frelimo equals corruption, creates the condition to argue that the neoliberal austerity from the 1980s onwards was justified – or even necessary – rather than a (or even the main) cause of large-scale corruption. Hence, this chapter suggests that a necessary addition to the corruption reading is the specification that 'História' registers the lived experience relative to the formation of a bourgeois elite in pre-PRE Mozambique, under the influence of the onset of primitive accumulation in the early and mid-1980s.[7]

---

7   Couto himself also warns about the corruption reading. 'Journalists', Couto says, 'can't really keep up with the vitality of this type of democracy. Questions of corruption, for instance, make them react rather like politicians making declarations and less like investigative journalists. The nervous and rhetorical criticisms made in the media about corruption have been ridiculous because they don't have the basis of objective research' (1990b: 28).

This leads to the problems with the bureaucratism reading, in which the ghosts in 'História' are considered human beings and villagers are considered simply unable to recognize that the returning men are living humans and not ghosts. Teixeira Soares Ferreira, again, understands 'Historia' as 'sátira política, que se alimenta do *non sense* e do absurdo' [political satire, fed by nonsense and the absurd] (2007: 391). For her, the 'absurdo atinge tais proporções que os próprios "aparecidos" chegam a duvidar da sua condição de vivos' [absurd takes on such proportions that the 'apparitions' themselves start doubting their state of being alive] (391). There certainly is an absurd dimension to the short story. However, this is to miss or understate that 'História' carefully establishes uncertainty about the men's ontological status using *all* characters, not just the government officials. This starts from the title ('Aparecidos' [Apparitions]) and continues in the first paragraphs, in which a narrator clarifies that the dead should stay in their own realm but that some 'teimam em aparecer' [stubbornly keep appearing], as occurred 'naquela aldeia' [in that village] (Couto 2012: 129). The narrator calls the men by their names but also employs terms that indicate they are ghosts, such as 'os mortos' [the dead], 'os falecidos' [the deceased], 'os aparecidos' [the apparitions] and so on (129–33). The villagers enforce the idea that the men are ghosts by arguing they 'morreram' [died], are 'fantasmas' [ghosts] or 'almas' [souls], talk like 'espíritos' [spirits] and do not 'existem' [exist]. The men themselves are initially certain they are 'vivos' [alive] but start doubting this; they say that they are at least 'alguns' [someone] and, as Ferreira notes, eventually consider the possibility that they have indeed died (2007: 130–4).

The uncertainty about the men's status is never resolved. The narrative ends with the commission stating the men 'devem ser considerados populações existentes' (Couto 2012: 135) [should be deemed members of the population in existence] (Couto 1989: 11). Yet the men are never called 'alive' and, even after its judgement, the committee calls them 'os dois aparecidos' [the two apparitions] (135). A sequel to 'História', in which the men (dis)appear again to haunt the village and the commission changes its verdict, is easily imagined.

The Mozambican modern ghost story

In short, it cannot be determined, based on the information provided in the story, that the men are not ghosts. Taking this into account – as well as the careful structuring of the men as ghosts and the influence on Couto of Latin American irrealist authors, whose works were populated by ghost figures – the possibility that the men are indeed ghosts could, and perhaps should, be entertained. If the men are ghosts, this raises the question: is 'História' a ghost story?

'História': A Mozambican modern ghost story

To determine whether 'História' can be understood as a modern ghost story it is necessary to examine whether it draws on the conventions of that genre. Several such conventions are clearly identifiable. 'História' departs from ghost presences from the past, who return although they should not

> os mortos não devem aparecer [mas] há desses mortos que morreram e teimam em aparecer. [...] Foi o que aconteceu naquela aldeia que as águas arrancaram da terra. (Couto 2012: 129)

> the dead ought not to return [but] there are those dead who, having died, persist in coming back. [...] This is what happened in that village which the waters had wrenched from the earth. (Couto 1989: 11)

Characteristically, what happened before the catastrophic event – that is, the past – is inaccessible (129). The ghosts are terrifying to the villagers – '[a]ssustados [...] chamaram os milícias' (Couto 2012: 130) [alarmed [...] they called the militias] (Couto 1989: 11) – and even to the armed forces, to whom they go for protection and who are 'a tremer' [trembling] (130). The villagers believe the ghosts do not belong in the realm of the living; they tell the ghost men to go back 'donde vieram' [whence you came] (129–30), and there is an issue with the law, which the committee solves preliminarily. Narrative closure is refused, taking on the form of a remaining uncertainty about the ontological status of the ghost men and the possibility of them again dis/reappearing. It would be an exaggeration to claim 'História' is a frame narrative, but an extradiegetic narrator does start the story, after which the reader descents into the diegetic crypts. Notably, the theatre adaptation of the short story *was* staged as an archetypal window narrative (Madureira 2016: 31). 'História' is also a class struggle narrative that, as discussed later, climaxes around 75 per cent of the way through the narrative with the men exclaiming the Frelimo rallying cry – 'the struggle continues!' [a luta continua!] – after they become conscious of their class (Couto 2012: 135).

However, other narrative aspects of 'História' are an uncomfortable fit with the modern ghost story genre. There is a clear class struggle aspect, but the ghosts haunt their neighbours and co-villagers instead of a feudal or bourgeois oppressor. In fact, no character embodies an oppressor, and if rage or resentment is shown it is by the villagers, not the ghosts. Finally, the village – as well as everyone in it – may be a ghost, and 'História' is narrated from the perspective of the haunter, not the hauntee.

Yet closer inspection shows these aspects are only seemingly untypical. First, the arrival of the two men separates the ghost men from the villagers, even though they appear to belong to the same class of disenfranchised people. Rather than a class split, though, 'História' thematizes the resolution thereof. When the villagers have overcome their fear, the men wait for the commission's verdict at Samuel's place. The professor says that, even if they are ghosts, ghosts and villagers are not adversaries; rather, their common adversary is an unnamed *they*. Samuel says:

> Esses que vos complicam hão-de cair. São eles que não pertencem a nós, não são vocês. Fiquem, meus amigos. Ajudam-nos no nosso problema. Nós também não somos considerados: somos vivos mas é como se tivessemos menos vida, como se fôssemos metades. Isso não queremos. (Couto 2012: 134)

> These people who bedevil you are bound to fall. It is they who do not belong here, not you. Stay, my friends. Help us in our plight. We too are not being considered: we are alive but it is as if we had less life, it's as if we were only halves. We don't want that. (Couto 1989: 11)

In a somewhat confusing us-and-them construction, the professor creates solidarity between the ghost men and villagers by categorizing the ghost men with the villagers (using the verb *pertencem*) and the villagers with the men (indicating they are not 'considerados' either). In doing so, he

The Mozambican modern ghost story

135

also generalizes the men's experience of being ghosts to the level of the village, which he then doubly reinforces through his description of the villagers as having 'menos vida, commo se fôssemos metades' [less life, it's as if we were only halves]. None of them, he implies, are being considered; all of them have less life, are halves – are ghost men. Of course, the premise of 'História' already suggests this. Like the ghost men, the entire village, including the villagers, disappeared with the flood and reappeared in a new location. 'História' may thus concern a ghost town, which may be inhabited by a community of ghosts.

Although not as clearly as in the case of *Portagem*'s community of miner-ghosts, 'História' specifies the nature of the community of ghosts. Still at Samuel's, Aníbal contemplates his feet and murmurs

> como somos injustos com nosso corpo. De quem nos esquecemos mais? É dos pés, que rastejam para nos suportar. [...] Mas como estão longe dos olhos, deixamos os pés sozinhos, como se não fossem nossos. [...] Assim começa a injustiça neste mundo. (Couto 2012: 132–3)

> how unfair we are to our body. What part of it do we take most for granted? The feet, poor things, which drag themselves along to hold us up. [...] But as they are far from the eyes, we ignore our feet, as if they didn't belong to us. [...] That's how injustice begins in this world. (Couto 1989: 11)

Aníbal continues that 'neste caso, os pés sou eu e Luís' [in this case, those feet are myself and Luís], which now also includes the villagers (Couto 2012: 132–3). The solidarity with the villagers thus makes Aníbal realize he is a member of a class that, based on the comment that it supports everyone, may roughly be understood as a working class – likely a mixture of proletarians and peasants, although no further information is given – constituting the community of ghosts as a community of worker-ghosts. This position of class-consciousness also enables the rage that appeared absent before, and Aníbal's last words are Frelimo's anticolonial rallying cry: 'A luta continua!' [The struggle continues!] (Couto 2012: 135).

It will be noted in passing that 'História' prioritizes this rage over the formal ending of the story – climax over plot – further aligning it with the modern ghost story. The ending, as mentioned, is not a resolution of the ghost question but rather an attempt of, speaking with Bertelsen, 'controlling what [in this case, the district government] could not eradicate' (Bertelsen 162). The commission tries to (re)introduce the two men in a bureaucratic order but cannot decisively say whether they are ghosts or not. Gérard Genette's concepts of discourse time and story time, respectively indicating the time taken to narrate the story and the time passing in the story, highlight how the structure of the narrative reflects this. The initial events – the arrival, the refusal, the stay with Samuel – constitute most of the discourse time and are laced with dialogues and details. Yet the narration of the last four days – including the arrival and verdict of the commission and the men's subsequent actions – which takes up most of the story time takes up less than a page in discourse time. This hurried narration draws attention away from the formal ending and allows the men's battle cry to echo, even as the commission speaks its verdict and provides the men with the 'documentos dos vivos' [documents of the living] that resolve, for the time being, the issue with the law (Couto 2012: 136). All the same, it is questionable how consequential this rage is, as no adversary has been identified.

Finally, 'História' is narrated from the perspective of not the hauntee but the haunter. This perspective appears uncommon, but can be elucidated through a discussion of two works circulating in the same literary ecology as 'História': Mendes's *Portagem* and Juan Rufo's *Pedro Páramo*.

First, an initial relation between *Portagem* and 'História' was suggested above, based on the worker-ghosts, who are the protagonists of *Portagem*'s ghost story and of 'História'. Causality is difficult to determine, but the below section on Mozambican modern ghost stories demonstrates how the figure of the worker-ghost, and particularly of *Portagem*'s miner-ghost variety, has become conventionalized post-'História'. This chapter therefore proposes that 'História' retroactively conventionalizes *Portagem*'s trope of the worker-ghost for the Mozambican modern ghost story. *Portagem* may also clarify 'História's perspective. Focalization through the ghost – or, more specifically, through the haunter – is rare in the modern ghost story genre. Even in a film like *The Others* (Amenábar 2001), which is sometimes erroneously understood as breaking with modern ghost story conventions by taking on the perspective of the ghost (cf. Peeren 2004), this is only seemingly the case. Certainly, the protagonists in *The Others* are ghosts, but the structural relation between haunter and hauntee remains intact.

The Mozambican modern ghost story 137

The Others rather constitutes a reversal in which ghosts are haunted by humans and the latter are eventually exorcized. However, in works of (Mozambican) Neorealism, the perspective *would* be of the working-class hero who in some way engages in the class struggle. In the case of 'História', the workers are the worker-ghosts, and it could thus be proposed that 'História' reverses the narrative perspective of the modern ghost story by introducing the MNR perspective.

Second, Brookshaw (2016) has argued that Juan Rulfo's novella, *Pedro Páramo* (1955), was important for Couto's work. Critics have not failed to notice the importance of *Páramo* for literature at large, which was at the roots of the 'boom' in Latin American fiction, which Márquez could allegedly 'recite front to back' and which is considered to have influenced his *Cien Años de Soledad* (1967) (Márquez 1993: viii; cf. Levine 1973). *Páramo* was also 'widely available' in Mozambique since the 1980s, and Couto 'mentioned on various occasions' how Rulfo was an 'inspiration' for 'his own writing' (Brookshaw 2016: 18). *Páramo*'s main location of Comala, Brookshaw claims, 'is clearly a model for Couto's forgotten deep towns' (18).

Comala may well have been a model for the town in 'História', as a closer look at the novella shows. *Páramo* starts with the arrival of protagonist Juan Preciado in the village of Comala. He is in search of his father, from whom he wants retribution for abandoning him. The arrival occurs at the beginning of the highly fragmented novella[8] but is chronologically (almost) at the end of the story, and the story is constituted by the narration of the life of Juan's father, Pedro Páramo. Pedro grew up in Comala and the village changes during his life, which includes shifts in (rogue) leadership and the death of many characters. In fact, all the characters – including Pedro himself – die over the course of the story, even before Juan gets to Comala. Juan dies in Comala, too, and narrates the novel from the grave.

According to Hay, *Páramo* is a modern ghost story, although in a complex way, and he specifies that it 'sets itself up as a ghost story, or at least [...] encompasses ghost stories' (195, see also Boldy 2016: 67). To make his case, he explains that the novella is 'clearly concerned with a set of relationships between property, class, and temporality', which are mediated

---

8   A correlation between the fragmented structure in *Páramo* and the structure of 'Widow' may be noted here.

138   CHAPTER 4

by 'the figure of the ghost' in the form of narrator Juan (Hay 2011: 195).
Transition is also central to the story, particularly, as Amit Thakkar argues,
'the transition from pre-Revolutionary, isolated caciquismo [in which one
leader dominates one, mostly rural, region] to post-Revolutionary integrated
caciquismo, with the newly propertied el Tilcuate [a militia leader] as the
neo-cacique in the making' (2012: 157). As Hay also claims, Comala is a
'haunted town', 'a town with a traumatic history' of transition by which
it is haunted and in which all the villagers are ghosts (197).

It is not difficult, then, to imagine *Páramo* as a predecessor of 'História'.
They share a haunted village, with a trauma in its past, which is inhabited
by an alienated community. In both villages, all the inhabitants are (possibly) ghosts. Finally, both of the stories are narrated from the perspective
of the ghost. Yet, while it is explicated in *Páramo* that Juan has died, in
'História' the uncertainty about the main characters is sustained – to which
shall be returned below.

Importantly, such a brief discussion of *Páramo* draws attention to an
aspect of the modern ghost story genre that was not mentioned at length
in the discussion of 'História' above: transition. Of course, it was shown
that 'História' registers primitive accumulation in its thematic of corruption. Yet the story registers transition in a more drastic manner. 'História'
starts from the destruction of the past – producing history as inaccessible
and forming the condition for something to return that should not return – and the establishment of the (new) present. The story starts with the
floods that 'arrancaram' [ripped] the old village 'da terra' [from the earth],
and that destroy it to such a degree that 'nem ficou a cicatriz do lugar' [not
even a scar of the place remained] (Couto 2012: 129). The events then take
place in the new village, after the transition, and what happened before can
no longer be accessed other than through the worker-ghosts. Much like in
Portagem, then – where the droughts drove the villagers to the Marandal
mines – transition is the condition for the events of 'História' to unfold,
just as it is a condition for the corruption it thematizes, for the re-emergence of different forms of the supernatural and, indeed, for the production
of the work itself. 'História', in other words, is a narrative of transition.

At this point, this chapter would thus propose 'História' as a modern
ghost story, which – drawing on conventions popularized by British and
Latin American authors (Rulfo in particular) and on narrative strategies

used by *Portagem* – is distinct from earlier variations of that genre. It is suggested, in other words, as a specifically Mozambican modern ghost story, which registers the early stages of the second transition of Mozambique into the periphery of the capitalist world-system, the reappearance of primitive accumulation or *capitalist restoration*; a part of the global institutionalization of neoliberalism that started in the 1970s. It may be added that although primitive accumulation would have been noticed in lived experience at the time, it is unlikely it would have been fully clear what was happening and who its primary actors were. In fact, it could even be suggested that the actors involved are invisible by design – neoliberal domination (in the form of debt imperialism, austerity and so on), unlike colonial domination, was often planned as domination without a face, and the WTO protests of 30 November 1999 would eventually show the danger for the oppressing classes of it having a face. Arguably, the story registers this in the openness at the end of the story and the absence of an identified adversary.

The Mozambican modern ghost story after *Vozes Anoitecidas*

The conventions of 'História' reappeared frequently in Mozambican literature after the publication of *Vozes*, echoing Laranjeira and Mendonça's conception of the collection as marking a transition in Mozambican literary production. This chapter suggests that the genre of the Mozambican modern ghost story is best understood as this body of works, in which these conventions are used and combined in varying ways.[9] The

---

9   The number of published literary works increases in Mozambique in the 1980s and, because the short story decisively overtakes poetry in importance, the emphasis here is on the short-story form. However, Mozambican modern ghost story conventions affected poetry, too. Heliodoro Baptista's work shows the importance of the 'community of ghosts' trope and the Latin American irrealist authors' influence. In the poem 'Cem Anos de Solidão' [Hundred Years of Solitude], referencing Márquez's novel by that name, the model for the community of ghosts is the 'fantasmas em Macondo' [ghosts in Macondo]; that is, the village central to Márquez's novel (1987: 47).

140   CHAPTER 4

work of Suleiman Cassamo is one example of a post-'História' Mozam-bican modern ghost story. Familiar with *Vozes*, Cassamo commented that his work is influenced by many of the same authors as Couto, including the Portuguese Romanticists Garrett and Herculano, and authors from 'das Américas' [the Americas] (Diogo 2012: 184–5). Cassamo names Jorge Amado, Guimarães Rosa, Edgar Allan Poe, 'Jorge Luis Borges, José Lezama Lima, Juan Carlos Oneti, [and] Gabriel García Márquez' (Diogo 2012: 185). Most important, for him, is 'o escasso e espantoso Juan Rulfo' [the scarce and astonishing Juan Rulfo] (Diogo 2012: 184), and he would even dedicate his 2000 *Palestre para um Morto* [Lecture for a Deceased] to the Mexican author ('Juan Rulfo [,] com quem cumungo este obstinando exercício de interpelar os mortos' [Juan Rulfo, with whom I share the ob-stinate exercise of interpellating the dead] (Cassamo 2000: 9)).

Mozambican modern ghost story conventions in Cassamo's writing are clearest in his 1989 collection of short stories, *O Regresso do Morto* [Homecoming of a Deceased]. Cassamo labels the stories 'works of tran-sition' that 'marca' [mark] the period in which the country 'se reargue' [rearranges itself] during the war and the 'carestia de vida' [dearth of life] (Diogo 2012: 186). Like *Vozes*, the collection 'straddle[s] the dividing line between reality and fantasy' (Long-Innes 1998: 155). The story 'Nyeleti' is exemplary, as it thematizes the problems of organized marriage and trans-forms its protagonist into a cactus. Central to 'Nyeleti' is the returned-dead trope, in which character Malatana (the love object of Nyeleti) disappears and 'reappareceu' [reappeared] at dawn after a long absence, characteris-tically towards three-quarters of the way through the narrative (Cassamo 1989: 28). The narrator portrays Malatana as a terrifying, out-of-place ghost figure: a 'Massinguita' [miracle] occurred in the morning, says the nar-rator, 'Malatana reapareceu. […] Chegou como só chegam os fantasmas, de madrugada, palito, dois pirilampos no lugar dos olhos' [Malantana re-appeared. […] He arrived in a way only ghosts arrived, at dawn, thin, two fireflies where the eyes should be] (28).

The story 'Laurinda tu vai Mbunhar' [Laurinda You Will Be Dis-appointed] thematizes the difficulty of subsisting, food scarcity and the concentration of power while also employing the trope of the community of ghosts and the irrealism seen in 'Nyeleti'. It narrates Laurinda, who is

The Mozambican modern ghost story

141

standing in line to buy bread with 'pés nus' [bare feet] on the tarmac, which is heating up in the sun (19). Laurinda, however, is not concerned with her feet; instead, she is fighting a queue that, in her focalization, transforms into a wave. Thus, the process of waiting becomes that of 'nandando contra as ondas da bicha' [swimming against the waves of the queue] (19). The wave, in turn, turns into an animal (in Portuguese, 'animal' and 'queue' share the signifier: 'bicha'), which she can now encourage to walk forwards, although without much effect ('A bicha parou. Anda, bicha. [..] Anda bicha' [The queue/animal stopped. Go animal [...] Go animal] (20)).

The queue/wave/animal is comprised of other beings, who remain invisible until one shape disconnects itself. He takes on the form of a ghost, a shadow, a 'sombra' (20), who asks Laurinda:

'É pessoa?' perguntou a sombra.
'Sim, é'. Repondeu a Laurinda. (20)
'spera o que? Quer pão?
'Sim, quer'.
A sombra pensou um bocado e disse:
'Se quer pode ir com pão, não precisa ir na bicha. E só intender comigo'.

['Are you a person?' the shadow asked.
'Yes, I am'. Laurinda answered.
What are you waiting for? Do you want bread?
'Yes, I do'.
The shadow though briefly and said:
'If you want to leave with bread, it is not necessary to stand in line. Just come with me'.]

Laurinda sees the man as a ghost, but it is implied that he also sees her as such, which is why he needs to confirm whether she is indeed 'pessoa'. 'Laurinda' thus establishes a community of ghosts consisting of those who lack ready access to the means of subsistence. When she realizes the shadow wants her to prostitute herself in exchange for bread, she vehemently turns him down. Only later, when she knows the man does have bread and is abusive, does she realize: 'em cima da sombra, nasceu uma cabeça humana' [above the shadow, a human head was born] (21).

The title story, 'O Regresso do Morto', most clearly draws on Mozambican modern ghost story conventions. At the start of the story, the narrator

142   CHAPTER 4

generalizes that 'mortos, quando regressam' [the dead, when they return]
carry a heavy burden (71). The narrator then zooms in on the ghost central
to the story, whose burden takes the form of a 'mala' [suitcase]. Further, the
ghost is dragging his feet, wears a pair of 'botas sólidas', is covered in dust
from several continents and has a helmet. If the 'mortos se cansam' [dead
get tired], the narrator concludes from the imagery, this ghost 'devia estar
muito cansado' [may be very tired] (71). The narrator follows the ghost,
who continues his walk until he arrives at a house. He looks at the house
'atentamente' [intensely] and sees a woman who 'avivou os olhos mortos'
[brought life to the dead eyes] (71). He screams out at her, but the woman
does not see him. Disappointed, having hoped for a warmer welcome, the
narrator explains: 'nunca ninguém desejou boas-vindas a fantasmas' [no-
body ever welcomes ghosts] (71).

     Using several analepses, the narrator tells the backstory of the ghost,
who he eventually reveals is called Moises. Moises had dreamt of having
access to a lower-middle-class life, with a gramophone, clothes, comfortable blankets and good-smelling bread that stays free from mould for days.
Hence, he had decided to become a miner at a young age, and at 19 years
old he left for South Africa. He never returned, and at some point in time
an unknown man had arrived in the village to report that Moises had died
working in a 'mina' (72). Returning to the present of the arriving ghost, the
dead man, now called 'o Morto', has reached the woman and tells her: 'Não
chores, mãe. Eu não morri ...' [Don't cry, mother, I did not die ...] (72).
His mother, however, does not hear him – and it is not certain whether
she can – as she has fainted at the sight of what is presumably her son.

     Characteristically, the story carefully establishes Moises as a returning
ghost yet sustains uncertainty about his ontological status. Moises is described as belonging to 'os mortos' [the dead] and as a 'fantasma' [ghost];
his dead eyes are mentioned, he is referred to as 'Dead man' ('o Morto'),
in which Morto is capitalized to indicate a proper name (71). The readers
learn of not only Morto's real name but also his supposed death, and the
mother faints when she sees her son, likely because she believes she sees a
ghost. Moreover, even after Moises's name is known, the narrator persists
in calling him 'o Morto' (72). Despite Morto's own claim that he did not
die, then, it can thus not be determined with certainty whether this is true

The Mozambican modern ghost story 143

or not, and it is never revealed whether he is allowed to rejoin his community. Thus, Moises became a ghost though labour in the mines – he leaves for the mines as a 19-year-old and returns a tired ghost. Like the ghosts in *Portagem*, Morto is a worker-ghost of the miner-ghost variety.

The supernatural, in more and less recognizably modern forms, also populates Aldino Muianga's short-story collection *Xitala Mati*. Published in 1987 (a year after *Vozes*), its characters are described as 'morto-vivo' [dead-alive] (40), as located 'entre a vida e a morte' [between life and death] (45) and as the 'espíritos dos […] avós' [spirits of the […] grandparents] (55). Most immediately, the conventions of the Mozambican modern ghost story are recognizable in the story 'O Filho de Mussassa' ['The Son of Mussassa'] (henceforth 'Mussassa').

The protagonist of 'Mussassa', Mussassane, is part of a well-known family of 'longas e nobres tradições' [long and noble traditions] (21). He is known for his 'abastança' [wealth] and philanthropic work, and his family are the de facto 'donos da região' [chiefs of the region] (21). Mussassane's riches, however, are not inherited but earned in the mines of South Africa, where Mussassa has worked since he was 'jovem' [young] (21). One day, when he returns from 'Djone' (a term used to refer to the mines in the Johannesburg region) to his home village, he is 'abastado mas acabado, pronto a entregar o corpo à terra' [wealthy but done for, ready to submit his body to the earth] (22). The villagers at home celebrate his return because they hope to share in the riches after Mussassane's death. In a last speech before dying, he indicates that the suitcase he carries with him has 'muito dinheiro, capaz de comprar todas as terras de Mpissane, gado e as vossas mulheres' [lots of money, enough to buy all the lands of Mpissane, cattle, and your wives] (23). However, he continues, he shall be buried with 'todo o meu dinheiro' [all my money], and crying is not allowed at his funeral (24). Although things initially happen as he prescribes, on the night after the burial a 'vulto' [vulture], who turns out to be Mussassane's 'irmão gémeo' [twin brother], tries to rob the grave (25–6). When prying a last coin from the dead man's mouth, his jaws snap shut, preventing the twin brother from escaping with the money. The following morning, the twin is found in the grave, and the event becomes known as the time when

144   CHAPTER 4

Mussassane 'retonou à vida' [returned to life] to defend the riches he had
worked and died for (27).

The class position of Mussassane, the person returning from the dead,
is not immediately evident. He is described as the 'dono' of the region, part
of an old ruling family, and thus appears to belong to the feudal class; yet
his wealth is not inherited, as it would be in the feudal model, but results
from his work in the South African mines. His money is thus new money,
and his self-confessed ability to buy all the lands, cattle and even women
in the region (whom he apparently considers commodities), as well as his
philanthropic work, would be more characteristic of the capitalist class.
Mussassane, then, is a transitional character who stems from a feudal family
and has transitioned into a capitalist mode of acquiring property. Yet he is
not a capitalist, because although he is wealthy he never owns the means
of production. To build up and sustain his subsistence, he must keep returning to South Africa to sell his labour power and his health, initially
even in the context of forced labour ('chibalo', 21). He never attains the
freedom of being beyond that realm of necessity (which the capitalist class
has), because the South Africa trips last until the very end of his life. When
he returns for the last time, 'abasado mas acabado' [wealthy but done for],
the narrator makes it explicit that getting rich is also what gets him killed
('o pé-de-meia que lhe custara trabalhos e a vida' [the savings that cost him
work and his life] (27)). Despite his wealth, Mussassane's position is thus
characteristic of the working class, and his postmortem return constitutes
the return of a miner-ghost.

An additional observation can be made about Mussassane's wealth.
To rise in the ranks in the mine and acquire his riches, he makes a Faustian
deal. Certainly, he must be buried with his wealth and no one can cry
at his funeral. Yet, as it turns out, it is also demanded that he burns the
hut of his brother to the ground and that his mother dies. The hut of his
brother does go up in flames, and his mother dies under mysterious conditions ('misteriosamente') – young and free of disease (24). While the
wealth Mussassane generates appears the result of some form of alchemy
in the first instance, upon closer examination it is the product of his own
and others' dispossession and sacrifice, mirroring Marx's characterization
of the process of the accumulation of capital as seemingly 'alchemistical'

The Mozambican modern ghost story 145

(Marx 2008a: 73). His wealth does not trickle down, even after his death; his effort to produce his own means of subsistence does not produce the subsistence of the members of his class; nor can his twin brother fortify the foregone status of their feudal family, because Mussassane returned to life to make sure others do not take it from him.

'Mussassa' thus thematizes the shift from feudalism to capitalism, the violent acquisition of wealth in that latter system and the necessary exploitation and laws (of the *traditional field* in this case) involved therein, and mediates them through the ghost-labourer trope in its miner-ghost form. Finally – like the 'História' but in stark contrast to *Portagem* – it is unclear who is ultimately responsible for the exploitation that kills Mussassane and his mother, as the adversaries of the labourers in this process of exploitation remain invisible ('ocultos', 24).

That the figure of the ghost is central to Ungulani Ba Ka Khosa's *Orgia dos Loucos* (2000 [1990]) is evident from its first epigraph, which establishes the ghost as threatening presence: 'A felicidade é frágil, e quando a não destroem os homems ou as circunstâncias, ameaçam-na os fantasmas' [Happiness is fragile, and when men or circumstances do not destroy it, ghosts threaten it] (5). Engagement with the figure of the ghost and its associated characteristics is also expressed on the level of its structure. *Orgia*'s opening story thematizes birth and narrates the way in which a woman tries (and fails) to delay the birth of her child to win a prize. The second-to-last story thematizes death and narrates the passing of the son of a party boss. It ends with the lines: 'Estava morta' [was dead] (83). The temporality suggested by these two stories taken together is a linear one, starting at birth and ending in death, but the short story collection does not end there. In the last-but-one story, 'A Revolta' [The Revolt], the possibility of interruption is suggested through its theme of revolt. The last story, 'Fábula do Futoro' [Fable of the Future], discusses the possibility of repetition through the figure of the 'movimento contínuo' [continuous movement] of the sea (95). The structure of *Orgia* may thus be understood as uprooting linearity and establishing repetition – circularity, haunting.

146   CHAPTER 4

Haunting culminates in the title story 'Orgia dos Loucos', and one
of the ways in which this is expressed is in the style. The following passage
shows this particularly well:

> Olha para o céu de moscas. Estava no círculo. A morte corria no círculo. O sangue
> esmorecia no círculo. Os espíritos corriam no círculo. Os cadavers apodreciam
> no círculo. As moscas dançavam no círculo. Riam no círculo. Viviam no círculo.
> Comiam no círculo. (58)

> [He looks at the fly swarmed sky. He was standing in a circle. Death ran in the circle.
> Blood faded in the circle. Spirits ran in the circle. Cadavers rotted in the circle. Flies
> danced in the circle. Laughed in the circle. Lived in the circle. Ate in the circle.]

Obsessively stressing the circular, haunting and returning, it departs
from the seemingly quotidian flies, who are alive, and move in circles.
The narration then descends into the crypts of death, in which every object circles around, after which it circles back to the flies, as well as to life.

That the story, which narrates the aftermath of an attack on a village, is
a Mozambican modern ghost story becomes explicit when looking closer at
the plot. António Maposse wakes up after the bloodshed and goes in search
of his wife, Maria, and child, João. Passing entire streets filled with scraps
of human remains, Maposse finally finds Maria dead, naked and violated.[10]
He continues his search for his son and is increasingly convinced that he,
himself, has died. Maposse tells himself that 'mataram-nos' [they killed
us] (55), that: 'Estou morto. Sou um fantasma. Estou entre os espíritos'. [I
am dead. I am a ghost. I am among the spirits.] (58). He then continues
to scream 'estou morto' (58), after which, in the words of the narrator, he
'[c]aminhava como um fantasma. Caminhava. Caminhava' [walked like
a ghost. He walked. He walked] (59). When he finally finds his son, who
tells him: 'Sou eu. […] O teu filho. […] Estou vivo' [It's me. […] Your son.
[…] I'm alive], Maposse answers: no, 'Estás morto' [You are dead] (59).
His son again tells Maposse: 'Estou vivo', but his dad replies: 'Não existes'
[You don't exist] and repeats: 'Tu não existes' (59). The son insists: 'Estou
vivo', but Maposse persists in saying: 'Ninguém está vivo. Estamos mortos.

---

10   The style of the story – and the way in which it shifts from short and staccato
      sentences to a stream-of-consciousness-like sentence spanning almost two pages
      (56–7), and then back again to the brief sentences – deserves attention this book
      cannot give it.

Somos espíritos angustiados à porta duma sepultura decente. A vida está com os outros' [Nobody is alive. We are dead. We are tormented spirits without a proper grave. Life is with the others] (59).

'Orgia' is thus populated by the disenfranchised dead – a community of ghosts – who have not had proper burial, even though the uncertainty and disagreement about the ontological status of the ghosts is never resolved. Moreover, it is never clarified who 'the others' (with whom life is) are, and this is even specifically constructed as open question. The story ends with João asking: 'Outros quem?' [what others] and the narrator's comment: 'Maposse não respondeu' [Maposse did not respond] (59).

Aníbal Aleluia's 1988 [2011] collection of short stories, *Contos Do Fantástico* [Tales of the Fantastic], has already been addressed in the introduction and will therefore only be discussed briefly here. The volume, it was argued, adopts the premise that the belief in the supernatural is 'universal' (6); from this perspective, it may not be surprising that it more clearly draws on Mozambican and non-explicitly Mozambican modern ghost story conventions. For example, the collection opens with a variation on the haunted location story, in which haunting is explained by reference to a big battle that took place at the site of the supernatural occurrences. The battle left behind 'tanto cadáver' [so many cadavers] that, 'meio século depois' [half a century later], there were still 'vestígios de ossadas' [remains of bones] to be found, and the drums and maracas of the battle could still be heard (15). Similarly, the next story in the collection, 'Um Pequeno em Chibuto' [A Kid in Chibuto], explicitly draws on Gothic elements to stage a house that is haunted in nights when the 'luar [é] tão vivo que parecia irreal' [moonlight is so radiant that it seems unreal] (35). The brother of the protagonist finally reveals that ghosts are 'frequentes nesta casa' [common in this house] because his 'pai edificou os chalés num cemitério' [father built the chalets on a cemetery] (37). The third story, 'Farida versus Halilo' [Farida versus Halilo] (39), also draws on Gothic imagery. In it, a group of people speaks to an old man called Amade, who tells them about 'aparições' [apparitions] or 'fantasmas' [ghosts] that appeared in great abundance (39–40) in the region, especially 'junto aos cemitérios' [around graveyards] (40). Using a frame narrative structure, the narrator says that, in the case of protagonist Amade, a man has been meeting a woman who, he later finds out, 'morreu há quatro anos' [died four years ago] (49).

148   CHAPTER 4

Aleluia, then, more unambiguously engages with the modern ghost story conventions already seen in the work of British writers. However, he changes the setting to Mozambique and, in some of the stories, often (but not always) changes the type of supernatural entity involved. There are, for example, *guiconós* (dead persons who are called back to earth to do the biddings of a magic wielder), *nguluves* and *muzimos* (ancestral spirits), *mfucuás* (vengeful ghosts, which largely overlap with the modern ghosts of resentment) and *djínis*, or genies, which Aleluia simply classifies as an 'espécie de fantasma' [sort of ghost] (211). Generally, haunting in *Contos* constitutes, in Jameson's words, the 'history [that] hurts' (1983: 88).

A final example is Paulina Chiziane's novel, *Balada de Amor ao Vento* (1992 [1990]) [Love Ballad for the Wind]. Even more so than *Portagem* and *Páramo*, *Balada* contains different ghost figures and stories, which are adapted from what will (somewhat inadequately) be called a gender perspective. The novel narrates the life of protagonist Sarnau from her teenage years to her death at about forty (at the oldest). She grows up in the Mozambican interior and meets a boy called Mwando; they date, she falls pregnant and he does not pay the *Lobolo* – the dowry – but she forgives him because she is in love. He leaves her for – and marries – another woman, but the marriage fails. Sarnau, in the meantime, tries to kill herself – an attempt stopped by her mother, who marries her off to the local king. The king loses interest when she does not bear him a child, leaving her open to Mwando's advances, who now realizes he loves Sarnau after all. They meet in the 'caverna dos fantasmas' [cave of ghosts], where nobody dares enter. Sarnau falls pregnant with a son, and must put a spell on her king husband so that he has intercourse with her, hiding her contact with Mwando. The king falls in love again, making him monogamous, while she sleeps with both men. A jealous sixth wife finds Sarnau out, forcing her to flee with Mwando. They start a new life on the other side of the Save (the river dividing the country in two), and they live happily for a while, until Mwando finds out the king knows he is there and wants to kill him. He tells Sarnau he is leaving her and goes to Angola, where he becomes a priest for the African slaves. He becomes fat and rich, realizes again he loves Sarnau, sells all he has and returns to look for her in the city. He finds her half dead, the mother of two kids, and a prostitute. After a long talk, she takes him back.

What type of ghost story conventions are used? First, when Mwando is in Angola, an archetypal modern ghost story is told. A window narrative told in a campfire setting, it starts from a narrative displacement similar to that of 'Widow', a frame narrative, and is one of several told in this way. The story starts with the line 'contou-se a história' [he told them the story], and ends with: 'Histórias sucediam-se as outras histórias' [stories were followed by other stories] (129). In the story – which takes on the structure of a haunted-house narrative – a character called José, who is about to die, asks a colonizer if he can be buried under the 'figueira' [fig tree] so his soul will not haunt but may find rest (129). The colonizer tells him no, and says 'os fantasmas dos pretos nao lhe metiam medo' [the ghosts of Black people did not scare him] (129). When José dies, the colonizer throws the body onto rocks instead of burying him. Subsequently, 'o fantasma do homem aparecia por todo lado, e um dia entrou em casa do patrão, partiu toda a loiça e esbofeteou toda a gente' [the ghost of the man appeared everywhere, and one day entered the home of the boss, breaking all the dishes and slapping all the people] (129). Finally, the corpse of the man appears on the steps of the colonial mansion, and it is decided that he is to be buried in the location of his choosing. While the narrative is focalized by the haunted colonizer, the actual, hidden narrator is Mwando, allowing the reader to sympathize with the ghosts and against the colonizer – a strategy similar to that of *Portagem*, in which the ghost story is also focalized by the colonizer, after which focalization returns to João Xilim.

A variation on the Mozambican modern ghost story is also found in *Balada*. After Mwando breaks up with Sarnau, she exclaims: 'Eu quero morrer, vou morrer' [I want to die, I am going to die] (31). To clarify, her death wish is not solely a means to end her unhappiness; rather, her plan is to 'germinar fantasma' [sprout as a ghost] after her death (31). The intention of her plan is fully revealed the following morning, when she goes to the lake to drown herself. She hesitates, but then thinks: 'vou, quero morrer, quero ser fantasma para atormentar esse Mwando em todas as noites de lua cheia' [I am going, I want to die, I want to be a ghost, so I can torment this Mwando during all the nights with full moon] (32). Eventually, her mother prevents her death, and Sarnau laments: 'nunca mais serei fantasma' [I will never be a ghost anymore] (33); 'nunca mais serei fantasma. Eu queria tanto ser fantasma!' [I will never be a ghost anymore. I so badly wanted to be a ghost] (34). Nevertheless, as in 'História', this ghost scene in *Balada* is focalized by the ghost figure – or, rather, by the would-be ghost. Being a ghost provides a position from which rage can be exorcized – or, at least, this is how Sarnau sees it.

The novel is dotted with ghost figures, but one last example must suffice. During her affair with Mwando, while married to the king, Sarnau tells her lover to meet up 'na caverna dos fantasmas' [in the cave of ghosts] because there 'ninguém nos incomodará' [nobody will bother us], as the villagers are afraid of the spells that rest on the place (82). One night, she approaches the place, hears a sound and wonders what it is. 'Fantasmas não são, porque só aparecem nas noites de lua cheia' [they cannot be ghosts, because those only appear during nights with full moon], she thinks (85). However, she reconsiders and asks herself: 'Talvez sejam mesmo fantasmas, quem sabe?' [Maybe they really are ghosts, who knows?] (85), after which she sees Mwando and tells him: 'Ah o meu adorável fantasma' [Ah, my beloved ghost] (85). By calling Mwando a ghost and inhabiting the cave of ghosts, she becomes a ghost, too, and they become the fantasmas in the 'caverna dos fantasmas'. Again, being a ghost is considered to be a position of power.

If, as Tavares says, Chiziane sets out to rethink the 'subjugation of feminine subjectivities' as they occurred in Mozambique at the time of writing (2011: 242), *Balada* mediates this – at least in part – through the figure of the ghost and the conventions of the Mozambican modern ghost story.

Conventions of the Mozambican modern ghost story

The Mozambican modern ghost story thus draws on and modifies established conventions and creates new ones. These include the community of ghosts, the figure of the worker- and miner-ghost and the reversal of the narrative perspective, or focalization, from hauntee to haunter. The ghost figures are often vengeful revenants, full of rage or resentment, who (consciously or not) use – or even cherish – their power from beyond (what appears to be) death: their power to haunt. This may also imply a

The Mozambican modern ghost story 151

shift in class position and introduces the aspect of struggle, possibly class struggle, as the figure of the ghost becomes a position from which power can be exorcized, however inconsequential. There are question about the ontological status of the ghost figure, which, conforming to the refusal of narrative closure, may remain unsolved. Ghost figures are not considered to be part of the earthly realm. They are (mostly) linked to the past, which is inaccessible from the present by other means. However, an adversary – those at who the rage is, or should be, directed – is often absent or invisible.

Evidently, although the Mozambican modern ghost story relies on a set of conventions, not all works that may be categorized as such are identical or even draw on all of these conventions. Paradoxically, even in its fixity, a genre is a flexible entity that changes over time as it adjusts to its context of production, as it is streamlined increasingly, as it mixes with other genres and so on. Hay shows this in his exposition of the shift of the modern ghost story from realism to naturalism, modernism and 'magical realism', as discussed in Chapter 1. It is also evident in the difference between Scott's 'The Highland Widow', 'The Tapestried Chamber' and 'Green' as discussed in Chapter 2. In the Mozambican context, as discussed, it shows in how the genre is described as emergent in Chapter 3 and as crystallizing, with conventions of its own, in this chapter.

In line with this, the genre of the Mozambican modern ghost story largely disappears in the beginning of the 1990s, even though isolated instances of the now-familiar Mozambican modern ghost story figures and conventions remain prominent – the community of ghosts, uncertainty about the status of the ghost, the half- or part-person and so on. Marcelo Panguaga's short story 'A Chamada' [The Call] illustrates this well. In the story, protagonist Magul's partner Valentina dies, but one night she '[r]eaparece [...] de forma deslumbrante' [reappears [...] stunningly] (1991: 50). Addressing herself to Magul, Valentina says: 'Eu não morri Magul' [I did not die Magul]. Magul disagrees and says they 'Já não são do mesmo mundo' [are no longer of the same world], but Valentina refuses to believe this (50). Panguana thus relies on the convention of ontological uncertainty, and the conversation clearly recalls the one in 'Louco' between Maposse and his son, the one in 'História' between the villagers and the worker-ghosts and the one in 'Regresso' between the mother and the son. However, unlike in the Mozambican modern ghost story, it is Magul – the living character – through which the story is focalized. Moreover, the main concern of 'Chamada' is the creation of a comic effect at the expense of the figure of the ghost. In the one-liner conclusion of the story, Valentina refers to eternal love in asking Magul how a woman can ever die for a man. Magul, however, misunderstands her question and answers: 'De tuberculose' [Of tuberculosis] (50).

Ontological uncertainty is also created in Couto's *O Último Voo do Flamingo* [Last Flight of the Flamingo] when the narrator says of a group of characters that they did not turn into 'espíritos ou fantasmas, pois essas são criaturas que ocorrem depois da morte. E aquele não haviam morrido. Transmutaram-se em não-seres, sombras à espera' [spirits or ghosts, which are creatures that occur after death. And they had not died yet. They mutated in non-beings, waiting shadows] (Couto 2004: 76). Couto, in fact, makes ample use of the supernatural during this period and employs several of the conventions of the Mozambican modern ghost story. The short story 'Nas Águas do Tempo' [In the Waters of Time], for example, uses a climactic structure at the height of which a ghost appears in the form of the 'namwetxo moha' (1994: 10). This 'fantasma' [ghost] 'feito só de metades: um olho, uma perna, um braço' [was made only of halves: one eye, one leg, one arm] (10) and is characterized as a 'monstro' [monster] (11). However, while the climactic structure is a conventional element of the modern ghost story, and while the description of the *namwetxo moha* resonates with the ghost men and villagers in the 'História', the story is narrated from the perspective of the living, and no community of ghosts is established.

Finally, the figure of the ghost as a metaphor is also common during the 1990–2005 period. There are 'fantasmas do coqueirais' [ghosts of palm trees] (Couto 1994: 56), a 'moço magro' [skinny boy] who 'irrompeu [...] como um fantasma' [interrupted [...] like a ghost] (Couto 2004: 25), narrators who characterize being 'silenciosos, secretos, não faze[r] qualquer ruidão' [silent, secretive, not making any noise] as being 'como fantasmas' [like ghosts] (Azevedo 1997: 8) and so on. During this period, however, more than two conventions are seldom, if ever, found in a story at once.

This would change in 2006, however, under the influence of debates on globalization and world-literature.

CHAPTER 5

Re-emergence of the Mozambican modern ghost story

When the Mozambican modern ghost story re-emerges in 2006, it does so relative to the debates on globalization and world-literature. In the introduction to a special issue of *Comparative Literature Studies* on globalization and world-literature, published in 2004, Kadir writes that the

> re-emergent conjunction between the globalization of the world from decidedly local and uncontestable sites of power and self-interest in ways that fit the pattern of imperial hegemony, on the one hand, and the upsurge of a discourse of/on world literature and globalization among practitioners of comparative literature, on the other hand, is a coincidence that bears examination. (2004: 2)

There exists, he suggests, a connection between the 'globalization of the world' that occurs from 'sites of power' and discussions about globalization and world-literature by scholars of comparative literature. He continues: 'We are now, at the beginning of the twenty-first century, at such a juncture' (2004: 2).

Kadir responds to the renewed traction of the concept of world-literature for studying literature and organizing literary studies around the turn of the millennium, and the debate about globalization that reached its peak around that time. The impact of 'world-literature' is illustrated by the large amounts of scholarship it generated. This includes conferences (e.g. 'World Literature In Between', Istanbul 2008; 'Worlds Within', Sydney 2014), journal articles and monographs (e.g. Moretti 2000; Beecroft 2015; Casanova 1999; Pizer 2006), essay collections (e.g. Prendergast 2004), readers (e.g. D'haen, Domínguez and Thomsen 2012) and anthologies (e.g. Clinton et al. 2009). Similarly, it is illustrated by reports on the state of the discipline. While the 1995 decennial report of the American Comparative

Literature Association barely mentions 'world-literature', the term had become the most central concept – along with 'globalization' and 'translation' – in the Association's subsequent report (Saussy 2006). In the report after that (2014), 'world-literature' is integrated into the fabric of all but two papers, and – again, together with 'translation' and 'globalization' – remains the report's most important term. Finally, world-literature programmes, professors and departments were created in universities from Gottingen to Cornel and from Warwick to Bern and Beijing.

The connection between world-literature and globalization that Kadir suggests is virtually undisputed in debates during this period. Thomsen calls world-literature the 'companion to the central keyword of the times, globalization' (2008: 1), Pizer argues that 'globalization [...] is helping to redefine the very principle of world literature' (2006: 4) and J. Hillis Miller argues it is 'inevitable these days to look at literature globally' – that is, through the concept of world-literature (2011: 253). In fact, Kadir even argues that the connection between world-literature and globalization has existed all along and, he writes, 'Goethe's coinage of Weltliteratur in 1827 was in direct response to his own "globalization" of sorts, when he was responding to a review of one of his works in the *Paris Globe*' (4). Albrow (1998), Harvey (2000), Hassan (2000), Saussy (2006), Pizer (2006), and Gupta (2009) all make similar claims.

If the 'conjunction between the globalization of the world' and the 'upsurge of a discourse of/on world literature and globalization' is indeed a 're-emergent' one, as Kadir suggest – if Kadir's and Goethe's historical moments are comparable on that basis – and if the modern ghost story re-emerges at the same time in Mozambique, a question about the *ideologeme* of the cosmopolitan space is raised. Chapter 2 of this book compared the work of Goethe and Scott to argue that Goethe separated world-literature from its material conditions, which resulted in an optimistic perspective that constitutes an instance of the fantasy of the cosmopolitan space. By contrast, Scott – having recently experienced one (if not the first) of capitalism's financial crises, and who would be living with its consequences until his death – constituted the cosmopolitan space as haunted in his modern ghost stories. Subsequently, this became a standard element of the modern ghost story – the *ideologeme* as the building block for one of modernity's most iconic horror genres. Specifically, then, the question raised is: does the connection (as examined in Chapter 2) between the *ideologeme* of the cosmopolitan space on the one hand and the modern ghost story on the other re-emerge with the debates about globalization and world-literature, particularly in connection to the re-emergence of the Mozambican modern ghost story in 2006? This is the main concern of this chapter.

The claim this chapter puts forth, based on the analysis of Couto's *O Outro Pé da Sereia* (2006) (henceforth *Sereia*), is that the modern ghost story re-emerges in Mozambique in 2006 in a modified form, and registers primitive accumulation as mediated by the conjunctive debates on globalization and world-literature. It does so by merging Mozambican modern ghost story conventions and narrative strategies of globalization, which establish the cosmopolitan space as haunted. Before discussing the novel and its relation to world-literature/globalization and the ghost story respectively, however, it is necessary to unpack the debates on 'globalization' and 'world-literature'.

Globalization, primitive accumulation and the cosmopolitan space

If, as Harvey argues, '"Globalization" is the most macro of all discourses that we have available to us [...] from the standpoint of understanding the workings of society' (2000: 15), it may be no surprise that conceptions of the term differ greatly. Mittelman aptly captures this in his definition of the concept as a 'rubric for varied phenomena' (1996: 2), as does Gupta when he characterizes the term as 'one of the most thickly connotative words in our vocabulary' (2009: 9).

Broadly speaking, a consensus exists that globalization refers to a globe that, in some way, becomes smaller and in which faraway places are somehow connected. Szeman argues, for example, that '[g]lobalization is the moment of mass migration, multiculturalism, and cosmopolitanism' (2003: 84), and Robertson speaks of 'both [...] the compression of the world and the intensification of consciousness of the world as a whole' (1992: 8). Giddens addresses the 'intensification of worldwide social relations which link distant localities in such a way that local happenings are shaped by events occurring many miles away and vice versa' (2013: 64), and Appadurai characterizes globalization as 'cultural processes [that are] products of the infinitely varied mutual contest of sameness and difference on a stage characterized by radical disjunctures between different sorts of global flows and the uncertain landscapes' (1990: 308).[1] Technological developments are often thought to be essential for this 'globalization' to occur (Szeman 2003: 93; Giddens 2013: 17; Robertson 1992: 184; Appadurai 1990: 296).

However, disagreements about what 'globalization' is or means may be more common than consensus. Tellingly, Ritzer observes that '[a]ttitudes toward globalization depend, among other things, on whether one gains or loses from it' (2003: 190). Spectacularly, this is demonstrated by the contrast between Khor's and Moss Kanter's work, who respectively claim that 'globalization' is 'what we in the Third World have for several centuries called colonization' (Khor 1995: 15), and that the 'world is becoming a global shopping mall in which ideas and products are available everywhere at the same time' (Moss Kanter 1997: 37). While there is agreement that 'globalization' is connected to social change on a global scale (Perrons 2004) and to the increased connectivity of people and spaces and the awareness thereof (Castells 2000), ideas on how this must be theorized or conceptualized differ greatly. While there is agreement that 'globalization' involves politics, culture and economy (Gangopadhyay 2005; Laguerre 2006; Gupta 2009), there is no consensus on how these are connected. If some claim the nation state is dying in (the age of) 'globalization' (Brinkman and Brinkman 2008), others maintain the nation is indispensable for 'globalization' but that its functions are redefined (Sassen 2003), while still others argue 'globalization' shields the economy from the democratic parts of the state (Slobodian 2018; Brown 2019). Finally, 'globalization' is argued to have started with humankind, with city-dwelling 5,000–10,000 years ago (Goudsblom 1996), with the beginning of capitalism 500 years ago

---

1   For overviews of the concept of globalization, see, inter alia, Ritzer (2008), Scott (1997) Gupta (2006) and Kilminster (1997).

Re-emergence of the Mozambican modern ghost story

(Wallerstein 2000; Veltmeyer 2008) or with the latest phase of capitalism starting in the 1970s (Harvey 2000; Prempeh 2006).

The myriad of disagreements implies a large number of globalization definitions. Illustratively, Al-Rodhan identified 114 definitions of globalization as early as 2006 – a plurality he attempts to resolve by, yet again, defining globalization anew. Turning to definitions may thus not be the best way to come to understand the term; instead, it may be more useful for the purposes of this book to turn to its history.

One of the best overviews of the history of the concept of 'globalization', arguably, is Gupta's *Globalization and Literature* (2009). 'Globalization', it shows, was first registered in *Webster's Dictionary* in 1961 and then in the *Oxford English Dictionary* in 1974, and gained coinage amongst academics by the end of the 1970s, when it started competing successfully with the (then more popular) terms 'international', 'world' and 'universal' (Gupta 2009: 6–7). The content of 'globalization' in these early stages was either 'the desire to develop the study of sociology in the USA as a world-embracing enterprise' or the wish of 'US business leaders and management gurus to extend US business interests, and exploitation of resources and labour, to a global domain' (7). Until the end of the 1980s, 'the term "globalization" usually appeared unambiguously with the ideological weight of its North American–Western European capitalist associations and affirmations', but this changed with the 'symbolic end of the Cold War' in 1989 (7). Then, the uses of the term 'proliferated exponentially, essentially with the effect of firmly decontextualizing it and neutralizing its ideologically partisan affirmativeness [...] with extraordinary speed' (8). As a consequence, ' "globalization" can now be thrown in apparently meaningfully with regard to almost any kind of issue' that involves 'transaction across boundaries, [in] every encounter and imperial venture [...], everything that passed as "international" or "world"-based or "universal" ' (9). Hence, Gupta writes, citing Fairclough, although ' "globalization" is [both] a set of changes which are actually happening in the world [and] a word [...] in which such changes are represented', those changes and that word do not always necessarily overlap (9).

In his overview of the history of the term, Harvey similarly observes that 'globalization' is now 'one of the most hegemonic concepts for understanding the political economy of international capitalism', as well as culture, politics and even national identity. But the term was in use 'little if at all' until the beginning of the 1970s (2000: 11). Harvey claims 'globalization' was first popularized by an American Express advertisement that promoted its global coverage, and argues it spread like 'wildfire', leading to a proliferation of its denotations, after the financial press started using the term (13). In the process, the changes it supposedly represented were removed from the signifier, as 'globalization' displaced 'the far more politically charged concepts of imperialism and neocolonialism' (Harvey 2000: 13).

Both Gupta and Harvey thus see an increasing rift between the signifier 'globalization' and the processes it is supposed to describe as it competes with more explicitly political terms. The former author is interested in how 'globalization' affects literary production and vice versa; the latter, usefully for this chapter, turns to the world-system to examine the content of 'globalization' further. In the first instance, Harvey argues, globalization represents no 'fundamental revolution' in either the system of production or associated social relations (2000: 68). Nevertheless, there are actual changes in the world-system that may be captured with 'globalization' in the form of a 'quantitative shift', which is based on a series of 'qualitative transformations' (68). The latter include financial deregulation (61), a profound 'technological change and product innovation' (61), the 'so-called information revolution' (62) and, finally, the 'tumbl[ing]' of the 'cost and time of moving commodities and people liberat[ing] all sorts of activities from former spatial constraints, permitting rapid adjustments in locations of production, consumption, populations, and the like' (63).

Harvey stipulates that these transformations, and the 'reorganization of capitalism' they represent, are specific to globalization in their (for him) contemporary form (57). Nevertheless, he also emphasizes that reorganizations of this sort have been intrinsic to the capitalist system of production since '1492' (54). Capitalism, Harvey explains, needs a 'spatial fix' (a metaphor he uses to indicate a necessity that returns periodically); after current markets are saturated, the world-system must expand to be able to reproduce itself (cf. Harvey 2001). Hence, capitalism periodically constructs and reconstructs the geography of the world-system 'in its own image', creating a distinctive geographical landscape, a produced space of transport and communications, of infrastructures and territorial organizations, that facilitates capital accumulation during one phase of its history only to have to be torn down and re-configured to make way for further accumulation at a later stage. (Harvey 2000: 54)

Characterizing this reorganization further, Harvey draws on Marx's phrase 'annihilation of space by time' (Marx 1973: 539) to coin the concept *time–space compression* (cf. Harvey 1989: vii). For him, if the term 'globalization' 'signifies anything about our recent historical geography, it is most likely to be a new phase of exactly this same underlying process of the capitalist production of space' (2000: 52), a 'new round of "time–space compression" in the organization of capitalism' (Harvey 1989: vii). Although Kadir does not specify, his claim that Goethe dealt with his own form of globalization could be understood along the lines Harvey identified – as the recurring reorganization of the world-system, the production of a landscape of 'transport and communications' (2000: 54), the associated liberation of 'all sorts of activities from former spatial constraints' and so on (Harvey 2000: 63).

Harvey's work has consequences for the understanding of globalization relative to what this book has termed 'primitive accumulation'. If, as he suggests, Marx's annihilation of space and his own time–space compression are different instances of the same process, and Marx's concept refers to primitive accumulation, it implies that globalization and primitive accumulation share a social referent. Tony C. Brown makes a similar observation in his analysis of the work of Harvey and Paul Smith. He notes that 'Harvey and Smith both make [it] clear [that] globalization requires acts of expropriation, domestic and international', and that the 'fundamental theoretical formulation' for those acts are found in Marx's 'chapters on the so-called "primitive accumulation"' (Brown 2009: 571–2). He therefore concludes: 'The account Marx provides of primitive accumulation can help us think through the peculiar dynamics of globalization-as-act' (576).

The connection between globalization and primitive accumulation is more direct for Federici (2017). She writes:

I analyze 'Globalization' as a process of primitive accumulation, this time imposed on a global scale. [...] I propose [...] that the pillar of this restructuring has been

> a concerted attack on our most basic means of reproduction, the land, the house, and the wage, aiming to expand the global workforce and drastically reduce the cost of labor. Structural Adjustment, the dismantling of the welfare state, the financialization of reproduction, leading to the debt and mortgage crisis, war: different policies have been required to activate the new accumulation drive [which all] entailed the destruction of our 'common wealth' [and with the aim of forming] a labor-force reduced to abstract labor, pure labor-power, with no guarantees, no protections, ready to be moved from place to place and job to job, employed mostly through short term contracts and at the lowest possible wage. (Federici 2017)[2]

For Federici, then, globalization is primitive accumulation – the latest 'round' of primitive accumulation, this time occurring everywhere on the planet.

Federici's account raises the question: *when* is globalization? Wallerstein argues that, based on the debate, one 'would think' 'globalization' was 'something that came into existence in the 1990s – perhaps only upon the collapse of the Soviet Union, perhaps a few years earlier' (2000: 250). Yet, referencing structural adjustment and financialization, Federici implies, on the one hand, that the phenomenon did not start in the 1990s – or even around the turn of the millennium, when the globalization debate took place – but much earlier; and, on the other, that it is still ongoing.

Indeed, Federici, Harvey and Wallerstein all locate the start of globalization in the 1970s. Certainly, changes occurred in the world-system after the fall of the Iron Curtain and the USSR, if nothing else because the capitalist restoration of the Soviet Union established the United States as the de facto unilateral 'super power' of the world-system, which modified (or intensified) certain US-American polities at home and abroad. As argued in *The 9/11 Commission Report*, 'the American homeland [became] the planet' (Kean 2004: 362; see also Miller 2019). Yet as Wallerstein argues, it would constitute a 'giant misreading of current reality' to consider this the beginning of globalization (2000: 250). The '1990s are not [...] a significant time marker to use if one wants to analyse what is going on' because the *stage* of accumulation did not change in any fundamental

---

2 It may be noted in passing that, under globalization, labour does not flow freely (as capital and goods do), although this is what Federici may be taken to suggest.

Re-emergence of the Mozambican modern ghost story   161

way (Wallerstein 2000: 250).[3] Wallerstein draws attention to the period of '1945 to today', which constitutes a 'typical Kondratieff cycle of the capitalist world-economy', consisting of an A-phase and a B-phase. The first lasted from '1945 to 1967–1973' and represents growth (250). After 1973, as Cooper explains – following a period of rising military and welfare expenditures without an accompanying tax rise under President Johnson; higher raw material prices from the then-recently colonial-turned-independent states; higher percentages of imported oil to the US, which left its economy vulnerable to the Organization of the Petroleum Exporting Countries (OPEC) embargo in 1973; and so on – a consumer price inflation occurred (Cooper 2017: 26). With this, a B-phase – which, according to Wallerstein, is ongoing – started, in which 'profits from production drop[ped] considerably from the levels at which they were in the preceding A-period' (Wallerstein 2000: 253). The B-phase thus represents ongoing decline and, for Wallerstein, overlaps with the changes in society the term 'globalization' aims to capture.

Wallerstein's account – which resonates with those of Harvey, Federici, Cooper and others – is convincing. However, periodizing globalization in this way creates a problem in the context of this book. If globalization started in the 1970s, and if the Mozambican modern ghost story of the 2006 period registers primitive accumulation, it implies that the 2006 form discussed in this chapter registers the same round of primitive accumulation as the 1986 form discussed in Chapter 4. Yet it is argued in this chapter that these two iterations of the Mozambican modern ghost story form are different.

It should be kept in mind at this point that, as addressed in the introduction, primitive accumulation is a 'continuing force' (Harvey 2003: 143); but this appears insufficient to explain the dilemma here. Rather, the explanation of this issue is found in the rift between the actual 'changes' in the world-system and the 'word' ('globalization') in which they are supposed to be represented (Gupta 2009: 8). These 'changes', which

---

3   Of course, Soviet capitalist restoration is an instance of primitive accumulation, and the massive upheaval and consequences it involved should not be underestimated (cf. Mandel 2019; Wood 2018).

started in the 1970s, acutely affected lived experience and were registered by artistic production. This is what Chapter 4 shows. The 'word', as Gupta and Harvey show, took off only in the 1980s and then 'proliferated exponentially' after the collapse of the Soviet Union (Gupta 8). A quick look at 'globalization' in Ngram Viewer provides a similar impression: the use of 'globalization' skyrocketed from around 1989 onwards and peaked in 2006 – not incidentally, the publication year of *Sereia*.[4] Thus, even if no fundamental changes in the world economy occurred after 1989, the *impression* that a new historical era had commenced, with the monumental event of the fall of (what was arguably only the shell of) historical communism, *was* created. Of course, this is also illustrated by scholars writing their fantasies about the end of history, and even by Derrida's *Specters*. Justified or not, the term 'globalization' could function as a vehicle for understanding these events of the end of the 1980s/beginning of the 1990s, just as those events could function to ground the concept and thus solidify the impression that a new historical era had indeed started. This, in sum, is what is meant when it is argued in this chapter that the Mozambican modern ghost story of the first decade of the new millennium registers primitive accumulation mediated through the conjunctive debates on globalization and world-literature.

While this raises questions about the role of 'world-literature', it is first necessary to return briefly to the *ideologeme* of the cosmopolitan space. It was argued in Chapter 2 that the *ideologeme* of the cosmopolitan space separates relatively unobstructed mobility from the system of production of which it is a function. This separation also occurs in the dynamic characterized above as the separation of the word 'globalization' from the actual 'changes' it is supposed to represent – 'globalization' is stripped from its 'liberal capitalist' associations, becomes apparently

---

4   My wager is that the global financial crisis of 2007–8 was detrimental for the concept's attraction because the financial markets' globality also meant a global crisis. While this lies beyond the scope of this book, it will be noted that this may have consequences for the role of the *ideologeme* of the cosmopolitan space – to the extent that the downsides of globalization were now clearly exposed for all to see, as in Scott's case.

Re-emergence of the Mozambican modern ghost story   163

ideologically 'neutral' (Gupta 8) and displaces 'the far more politically charged concepts of imperialism and neocolonialism' (Harvey 2000: 13). This separation is performed by characterizations of 'globalization' as shrinking the globe, as in Szeman, Giddens, Robertson and Appadurai. The annihilation of space is foregrounded – or even considered the essence of globalization – in all these cases, but none of them identifies it as a function of the dominant system of production. The contrast of such accounts with those of Federici and Harvey is striking. The former considers the production of relatively unobstructed mobility as a way to create 'pure labor-power, with no guarantees, no protections, ready to be moved from place to place and job to job' (Federici 2017). The latter consistently addresses the annihilation of space (the liberation of 'all sorts of activities from former spatial constraints' (Harvey 2000: 63), the 'distinctive geographical landscape, a produced space of transport and communications' (Harvey 2000: 54)) and explains it as a function of the recurring reorganization of the capitalist system of production. Harvey, in fact, warns that the elimination of (some) spatial constrains is only one of several 'qualitative transformations' of globalization, but may come to lead a life of its own. He writes that, when

> the history of the globalization process comes to be written, this simple shift in the cost of overcoming space may be seen as far more significant than the so-called information revolution per se (though both are part and parcel of each other in practice). It is, perhaps, invidious to take these elements separately because in the end it is probably the synergistic interactions between them which is of the greatest import. Financial deregulation could not have occurred, for example, without the information revolution, and technology transfer (which also relied heavily on the information revolution) would have been meaningless without a much greater ease of movement of commodities and people around the world. (Harvey 2000: 63)

Harvey thus appears to anticipate the cosmopolitan space, and it is also worth recalling at this point how Lazarus noted 'globalization is in these terms a dream: more concretely we might qualify it as the name given to the "reactionary utopia"' (1999: 44). Indeed, what are some of the seemingly ideologically neutral definitions of globalization but instances of the fantasy of the cosmopolitan space?

164   CHAPTER 5

World-literature, globalization and the cosmopolitan space

Considering the conjuncture of globalization and world-literature, and
in light of the second chapter of this book, it is worth examining the
ideologeme of the cosmopolitan space relative to the re-emergence of
world-literature concepts around the turn of the millennium.

The conjuncture between 'globalization' and the re-emergence of
'world-literature' was already evident in the 1980s, when the former concept was in the process of gaining coinage. Aldridge's *The Reemergence of
World literature* (1986) demonstrates this well. In the years following the
Second World War, comparative literature's focus on national characteristics were problematized by scholars such as Wellek. Wellek observed that
the national paradigm in comparative literature should serve 'as a reaction
against narrow nationalism', but that it instead facilitated nationalisms by
allowing an emphasis on the accomplishments of particular nations and
the influence of some cultures on others (1958: 284). Unwilling to leave
behind the category of the national altogether, Wellek suggested shifting
the focus to the universal; to study 'all literature from an international
perspective, with a consciousness of the unity of all literary creation and
experience' (294). He reformulated his idea several years later by proposing
an 'international perspective which envisages a distant ideal of universal
literary history and scholarship' without 'ignor[ing] or minimiz[ing] the
existence and vitality of the different national traditions' (1970: 36).

However, Aldridge observes, roughly thirty years later, that works
from the 'East and the Third World' were still often neglected, despite debates about universality, and asks how there could be 'universal standards'
if there is no 'universal coverage' (1986: 9–10). Similarly, he problematizes
the signifier 'world' in 'world-literature', which appears to imply all-inclu-
siveness, and was generally understood as 'simply all literature [...] or [as]
a canon of excellent works from many languages' (Wellek 1970: 15), but
in practice 'consisted almost exclusively of masterpieces of the Western
world' (Aldridge 1986: 9). The non-European works that were included,
he writes, were deemed as mere precursors, not as cultural achievements
in their own right (10).

The representational gap in the 'world' of 'world-literature' as he conceives of it is problematic on the one hand, according to Aldridge, because it attests of a 'colonialist mentality' that is no longer tenable in the 'present time' (10). On the other hand, it is problematic due to what Harvey calls the *qualitative transformations* of globalization. Aldridge writes that the

> new technological and political developments – particularly jet travel, the media of mass communication and commercial links between Japan, China, and the West – have stimulated a revived awareness of world literature and the need of a new definition, one that recognizes Africa and Asia as equal partners. (Aldridge 9)

Technology, politics and economy create the necessity for Aldridge to rethink world-literature, and he suggests three interventions that may give literary studies 'a truly global dimension' and enable it to become more egalitarian (9). First, redefine world-literature as 'the great works or classics of all times selected from all of the various national literatures' (55). Second, coin the category of universal literature, which he defines as 'the sum total of all texts and works throughout the world, or the combination of all national literatures' (55–6). Third, allow translations to be used in the discipline of comparative literature, so that works written in languages not widely taught in American and European universities can also be included in the curriculum (56).

The post-1989 combination of the increased integration of the term 'globalization' in quotidian and analytical discourse and the obfuscation of its content affected the globalization–world-literature conjuncture. In 1986, Aldridge still addresses the 'new technological and political developments' that create the impression of the globe's compression and necessitate a more inclusive world-literature (9). In 1994, Lawall already assumes the world-as-globe – as already actualized whole – and she directly proceeds to the methodological problems this poses for the practice of (comparative) literary studies. She observes that '[p]romising the world is risky business' because the 'disappointment is all the more severe when the "world" of world literature turns out to be much smaller than the globe' (1). In solution thereof, she calls for a novel reading practice, or 'new literacy' (284). World-literature, she writes, 'involves a look outward towards other regions of the globe' (67) and thus correlates to 'read[ing] the world' (1). It

166   CHAPTER 5

constitutes a 'negotiation between familiar and unfamiliar, or between
a reading subject and a world – generally seen as "other" – with which it
must come to terms' (x). Moreover, for her, world-literature also means the
promise of 'personal growth', the 'excitement of an aesthetic voyage' and
a way to 'prepare broadly informed, self-confident and adaptable citizens'
(1). World-literature, for Lawall, is thus a voyage during which educated
cultural encounters may take place.

Neither Lawall nor Aldridge appear to have been immensely important
for the start of the re-emergence of 'world-literature' around the turn of
the millennium, although some of their ideas remained prominent in the
debate.[5] Roughly, the world-literature debate that took place around the
turn of the millennium – and that Kadir situates relative to that of globalization – may be divided in two groups: difference (reading the unfamiliar)
on the one hand and totality (methodology) on the other (arguably, a
different way to put this would be idealist and materialist). Due to their
relation to the *ideologeme* of the cosmopolitan space, it is worth looking
closer at these two approaches.

The first group of world-literature studies may be exemplified by the
work of Pizer, and would include Lawall and the figures of what could be
called the 'Harvard school' of world-literature. Pizer's study provides an
overview of world-literature, from Goethe onwards, in which three aspects
are central: globalization, translation and pedagogy. He cites Goethe to
argue that world-literature is inevitable because of the 'increasing globalization of commerce and culture' (Pizer 2006: 30). While he does not
explicate what 'globalization' means to him, he does indicate it involves
migration, which makes it more difficult to assign works to one nation only
(and therefore also necessitates a category of world-literature), and that it
has downsides. For him, the most 'obvious' downside of globalization is
the 'trend towards homogeneity' (4), 'the homogenizing effects of globalization' (129), or 'globalized homogeneousness' (129), which appear to be
synonyms for 'Americanization' (91). He explains that, 'at least superficially',
what one sees when surfing through 'foreign Websites' is 'America' (5) – a

---

5   Prendergast (2004: vii) argues that the contemporary world-literature debate took
     off only with the publication of Casanova's *The World Republic of Letters*.

Re-emergence of the Mozambican modern ghost story

'perception' that is 'interrupted only' when 'acts of terror committed by foreigners take place' (5). Even those who are 'eager to experience and appreciate cultural diversity, to know the "Other" as other, generally must make substantial efforts, such as gaining a genuine knowledge of foreign languages', to do so (5).

The solution to this supposed 'superficial homogenization' caused by globalization, for Pizer, is found in world-literature – which, for him, must be based in translation and pedagogy. The issue of translation largely overlaps with Aldridge's ideas from twenty years before. Pizer's pedagogy is based on his

> belie[f] that one of the fundamental desiderata of a World Literature course should be the inculcation of an appreciation for the nuances of alterity, of a belief that life and literature outside the United States are inscribed by unique linguistic/cultural matrices perhaps no longer defined at the national level, but capable of being glimpsed through the filter of the subnational–transnational dialectic. (15)

Doubling down on this point, and connecting world-literature, globalization, translation and alterity, he writes:

> A genuinely relevant engagement with Weltliteratur in the World Literature classroom must be rooted in a focus on Goethe's prophetically global, non-nationalistic understanding of the term, an understanding grounded in a principle of radical alterity based on a novel view of translation. Only thus will this engagement both make sense to American students reared in an age of globalization dominated by the United States and help them to appreciate and learn from the alterity they will encounter, in translation, in world literature. (46)

In brief, then: for Pizer, globalization creates the solution (world-literature) to the problem it also creates (homogenization), as world-literature facilitates or constitutes a type of cultural encounter with the 'other' through which alterity is displayed and its appreciation is, or can be, promoted.

Pizer's historical overview of the world-literature concept is useful and informative, but his study also raises questions. His use of the term 'foreign' to indicate 'non-US American', and his emphasis on 'American students' as users of world-literature, anchors world-literature's gaze so solidly within the United States that, on the one hand, 'Americans' (a

168   CHAPTER 5

population that deserves to be treated as non-monolithic) appear to be the main victims of (their supposedly self-inflicted) globalization. Consequently, on the other hand, world-literature appears to become a tool for specifically American scholars, students and classrooms – world-literature as an American response to American 'homogenizing globalization' (137) or 'Americanization' (91); an American solution to an American problem for Americans. Pizer thus creates a 'hierarchy of looking', of the appreciator/appreciated, of those who have the power to appreciate the nuances of what he calls the 'foreign' or 'Other' and those who are (labelled) 'foreign' or 'Other' and are the object of appreciation. World-literature, in this way, becomes a form of (unilateral) tourism; a way of commodifying alterity so it may be consumed.

An extensive critical tradition has problematized this (in Hooks's words) 'idea that there is pleasure to be found in the acknowledgment and enjoyment of racial difference. The commodification of Otherness' (1992: 366). And because the appreciator in Pizer is located squarely within the United States – for him also the dominant force of globalization – the question of whether this dominance is also the very condition for his world-literature appears inevitable. In Said's words, it is questionable whether this issue of appreciating ' "otherness" and "difference" can 'easily be distinguished from the process of empire' (1989: 214).

Pizer appears to avoid speaking of, or is unaware of the importance of, the system of production and uses the word 'capitalism' only once in his book – namely to describe, in the briefest of ways, Marx and Engels's account of world-literature – and does not relate it to globalization (Pizer 2006: 144). Consequently, he can apparently never fully explain the effects of globalization, leading to the opaque formulation of what he calls superficial homogenization (91). He thus fails to take into account conceptualizations of capitalism as a force of creation and destruction (as explained in Marx's *Grundrisse*): that it creates 'isomorphy' rather than homogeny (Deleuze and Guattari 2005: 436), that it to homogenizes *and* diversifies (Wallerstein 1974: 407) and that, as Hall said, 'the thing about modern capitalism is that it loves difference' (in Akomfrah et al. 1989). On a different occasion, Hall pointed out:

Re-emergence of the Mozambican modern ghost story 169

> We used to think at an earlier stage, that if one could simply identify the logic of capital, that it would gradually engross everything in the world. It would translate everything in the world into a kind of replica of itself, everywhere; that all particularity would disappear; that capital in its onward, rationalizing march would not in the end care whether you were black, green or blue so long as you could sell your labor as a commodity. It would not care whether you were male or female, or a bit of both, provided it could deal with you in terms of the commodification of labor. But the more we understand about the development of capital itself, the more we understand that that is only part of the story. That alongside that drive to commodify everything, which is certainly one part of its logic, is another critical part of its logic which works in and through specificity. [...] [C]apital has had to negotiate and by negotiate I mean it had to incorporate and partly reflect the differences it was trying to overcome. It had to try to get hold of, and neutralize, to some degree, the differences. It is trying to constitute a world in which things are different. (Hall 1997: 22–8)

Pizer also fails to take into account that a 'global literary marketplace' to which all authors have equal access does not exist; that, rather, global publishing is an uneven system of production and circulation that involves the commodification of cultural difference (cf. Huggan 2001).

Pizer's rather optimistic conception of world-literature thus mystifies and reproduces these structures and creates a familiar image, which is already announced in his designation of Goethe's mystifying notion as 'prophetic' (Pizer 2006: 46). Relying heavily on the condition of circulation, which supposedly creates the solution to its own problems, Pizer – like Goethe – isolates the annihilation of space from the system of which it is a function. His account of world-literature is thus grounded in the fantasy of the cosmopolitan space and draws on the *ideologeme* for its construction.

This brings us to the second group of world-literature studies – which, unlike the first, does take into account the way in which literary production and circulation are organized, and relies on this structure to devise a methodology that may allow for overcoming the potential immensity of the world-literature corpus. Illustrative is Casanova's *Republic*, which opens (similarly to Lawall) with the question: is it 'legitimate to speak of world literature? If so, how are we to take in so huge a body of work and to make sense of it? Must one speak of literature, or of literatures' (Casanova xi)? Rejecting Aldridge's proposal for inclusion and Lawall's mode of reading, she argues it is not enough to geographically enlarge the corpus of works needing to be studied, or to import economic theories of globalization into the literary universe – still less to try to provide an impossibly exhaustive enumeration of the whole of world literary production. It is necessary instead to change our ordinary way of looking at literary phenomena. (Casanova 2007: xi)

Specifically, Casanova argues that, to understand world-literature, one must look at literature 'as a whole' (3). Basing herself on Fernand Braudel's concept of 'unequal structure' (Casanova 2007: 83), she leaves the concept of world-literature behind in favour of 'international literary space', or 'the world republic of letters' (xii). For her, this republic constitutes not an egalitarian space in which one can neutrally read the 'other' but a literary field as a 'world of rivalry, struggle and inequality' (4).

Similarly, Moretti writes that 'comparative literature' is still 'fundamentally limited to Western Europe' (2000: 54) but that, to solve this problem, the 'question is not really *what* we should do – the question is *how*' (55, emphasis in the original). As such, reading

'more' seems hardly to be the solution. Especially because we've just started rediscovering what Margaret Cohen calls the 'great unread'. 'I work on West European narrative, etc…'. Not really, I work on its canonical fraction, which is not even one per cent of published literature. And again, some people have read more, but the point is that there are thirty thousand nineteenth-century British novels out there, forty, fifty, sixty thousand – no one really knows, no one has read them, no one ever will. And then there are French novels, Chinese, Argentinian, American. Reading 'more' is always a good thing, but not the solution. (55)

World-literature thus cannot be 'literature, bigger'; rather, the 'categories have to be different' (2000: 55). Like Casanova, Moretti looks at the whole of literature. Drawing on Wallerstein's theory of the world-system, he argues that there is a world-literature – as in world-system, with a hyphen – and that, as the world-system, it 'is simultaneously one, and unequal' (56). The term 'world-literature' in Moretti eventually disappears into the background in favour of his term 'distant reading' (cf. Moretti 2013).

Finally, in what is arguably the single most important study on world-literature to date, the WReC explains world-literature 'in the broadest

Re-emergence of the Mozambican modern ghost story   171

sense as the literature of the modern capitalist world-system' (2015: 15), characterized by 'combined and uneven development' (11).

As in Goethe's time, then, the fantasy of the cosmopolitan space still plays an important role for theorizations of world-literature around the turn of the millennium, and largely takes on the shape of a celebration of the consumption of difference, without an elaboration of the role difference play in the system in which it is embedded. Unlike in Goethe's lifetime, there is now also a broad understanding of the role of the world-system for literary production – and thus for world-literature – in which, following Marx and Engels, capitalism is theorized as the condition of world-literature. This raises the question: 'If and how are these two strands of thought registered in the Mozambican modern ghost story of this period?'

Sereia and globalization

In 2006, the Mozambican modern ghost story re-emerges in the form of Couto's *O Outro Pé da Sereia*, João Paulo Borges Coelho's *Crónica da Rua 513.2* [Chronicle of 513.2 Street] and Guita Jr's *Os Aromas Essenciais* [The Essential Aromas], followed in 2012 by Lucilio Manjate's *O Contador de Palavras* [Counter of Words]. All of these works draw on ghost story conventions in different ways. Manjate, for example, draws on the construction of ghosts and on the half-alive trope; Guita Jr on the vengeful ghost; and *Sereia* and *Rua* explicitly thematize transition, which they mediate through the figure of the ghost and (Mozambican) modern ghost story conventions, such as the *ideologeme* of the cosmopolitan space, the community of ghosts, the haunted structure, the perspective of the ghost and so on. In all of these cases, they are refracted through the debate on globalization and the related debate on world-literature. Because *Sereia* is the clearest of these examples, the remainder of the chapter focuses on that novel.

Sereia, according to Madureira, 'represents a noticeable departure from Couto's earlier fiction' (2008: 208). Previously, Couto's language was so characterized by neologisms – allegedly to Mozambicanize the Portuguese language – that it led to 'Couto dictionaries' (cf. Cavacas 1999). In *Sereia*, however, neologisms are rarer, leading Madureira to argue that 'Couto's engagement with the national narrative has [...] changed significantly' (2008: 212). Instead, he argues, *Sereia* engages with 'the global economic logic [of neoliberal capitalism]' (224). Madureira is not alone in considering *Sereia* relative to 'globalization'. Brugioni (2012) argues the novel reflects on a 'globalized world', while Monteiro and Nevevé (2012) suggest it shows that 'cultural globalization is also a form of colonization'.

A focus on globalization in analyses of *Sereia* is not unexpected; 'globalization' (understood as primitive accumulation) lent analytical force not only for the Mozambican context, as demonstrated in Chapter 4, but also as a post-1989 phenomenon. Before 1989, Mozambique could play its US and Western European allies off against their USSR and Eastern European allies. This provided a means of control over the foreign policy demands imposed on the country. After the capitalist restoration of the USSR, however, this was no longer possible, which increased the influence international organizations (including NGOs and donors) had over Mozambican policy. In what Cramer (2006) has called a 'reckless [...] post-conflict experiment' (266), the IMF, World Bank and so on could more forcefully demand the reduction of government size and the minimization – or even complete elimination – of state intervention in the economic realm. Import tariffs were removed and subsidies on food and fuel, 'on which the poorest sections of the population depended', were stripped (Newitt 2017: 207). According to Cramer, the privatization/expropriation programme imposed on Mozambique did not lead to improvements for most of the population. It 'acted partly as a mechanism for corrupt accumulation and asset stripping, but was not backed by an industrial policy of the kind that has always been necessary genuinely to nurture structural change in poor economies', producing a Mozambique as a 'weak state' (Cramer 2006: 266). The UN's 2000 Millennium Development Goals, which should have replaced the (by then considered insufficient) structural adjustment programmes with the new Poverty Reduction Plans (PRPs), did not drastically change this. As Newitt argues, the PRPs had 'no focus' and merely 'solemnly proclaim[ed] the obvious' (2017: 209). Thus, as Cramer

Re-emergence of the Mozambican modern ghost story 173

writes, the expropriation globalization represented, which had started in the 1980s but accelerated post-1989, led to growing inequality in Mozambique between the political elite and the rest of the country (2006: 183), creating – in Newitt's terms – a few 'palaces of global capitalism', outside of which 'live the poor' (2017: 222). The process of globalization as primitive accumulation and as post-1989 phenomenon may thus be said to be part of the raw material on which *Sereia* draws and, as addressed in the analysis below, the novel is indeed structured by global unevenness.

On the other hand, a focus on globalization in discussions on *Sereia* are not unexpected because the globalization debate may be said to be part of its raw material. By 2006, when the novel was published, the term circulated widely in analytical and quotidian discourse, and (as shown above) even reached its peak use in that year. Characters participate in this debate, address the different ways in which globalization has been theorized (specifically, they speak on different occasions of economic globalization, Coca-Cola-ization, the global village, creolization, cosmopolitanism and pan-Africanism) and perform the way in which 'globalization' has lost its stable referent. When the Southmans – American tourists – arrive in Mozambique for their holiday, husband Benjamin 'balbuciou [...] com a voz prisioneira da emoção' [stammered, with a voice imprisoned by emotion] 'Oh, Africa! My forgotten land!' (Couto 2006: 168). Benjamin's outcry seems ambiguous; it reiterates the colonial discursive formation of Africa as a dark continent on the one hand while also drawing on the homeland paradigms of Aimé Césaire's *Cahier d'un Retour au Pays Natal* [*Return to my Naitve Land*] (1939) – or, perhaps more accurately, Salman Rushdie's *Imaginary Homelands* (1991). However, Casuarino – the village businessman who is part of the welcoming committee – identifies the comments for what they are. Casuarino steps on a 'uma grade de coca-cola' [a case of Coca-Cola] and, mimicking Benjamin's pathos, 'em tom solene e eufórico, proclamou: – Isto é a globalização, my friends! A globalização mundial! Vila Longe é a capital da aldeia global!' [in a solemn and euphoric tone, proclaimed: – this is the globalization, my friends. Worldwide globalization! Vila Longe is the capital of the global village!] (Couto 2006: 169). Casuarino, in other words, responds to the emptiness of Benjamin's quasi-pan-Africanist pathos

174   CHAPTER 5

by performing the overdeterminedness of the signifier 'globalization', as
well as the idea of globalization as 'reactionary utopia' (Lazarus 1999: 44).

Sereia thus quite bluntly registers globalization, which in light of
the discussion above may be understood as primitive accumulation, in its
themes, characters, dialogues and so on. It does so as well using a set of narrative strategies that mutually enforce each other – tropes of globalization.

Tropes of globalization in Sereia

The four main tropes of globalization in *Sereia* are what are called here
the journey trope, locale enumeration, spatial jumps and entrelacement.
Starting with the first, *Sereia* consists of three journeys, divided over
three narrative strands and (roughly) alternating chapters, which have
different paper colours and fonts, of which two take place in 2002 and
one in 1560–1. The protagonist of the first 2002 journey is a woman called
Mwadia, who lives in exile in a place called Antigamente (meaning 'for-
merly' or 'in the past') with her husband, Zero Madzero. At the start of
the novel, the couple sees what they think is a star crash, but when they
try to find it they instead find 'uma caixa' [a box] of documents and a
statue of 'uma mulher branca' [a White woman], which they identify as
'Nossa Senhora' [Maria] (Couto 2006: 46–7). Because they want the
statue to have a home, Mwadia takes her to Vila Longe, the village in
which she grew up (48); but the village turns out to be largely destroyed,
so Mwadia lays the statue to rest under an 'embondeiro' [baobab] at the
end of the novel, ending her mission and allowing her to transition away
from Antigamente and Vila Longe and towards a destiny that lies outside
of the narrative (379).

The second journey is that of the Brazilian Afro American couple
Rosie and Benjamin Southman, who fly from New York to Mozambique
in 'menos de treze horas' [less than thirteen hours] (161) and then drive to
Vila Longe with the aim of experiencing their imagined homeland – an
exoticized, commodified image of Africa. There, their narrative strand
crosses and joins with that of Mwadia, and over the course of their stay
their aims are revealed to the villagers.

Re-emergence of the Mozambican modern ghost story 175

Finally, the sixteenth-century narrative strand describes the journey of Portuguese missionary Silveira, who travels by ship from Goa to the Monomotapa kingdom (located in what is now Mozambique). His colonial mission is to 'realizer a primeira incursão católica na corte do Império de Monomotapa' [complete the first Catholic incursion in the court of the Monomotapa Empire], and the 'estátua de Nossa Senhora' [statue of the Holy Mary] aboard the ship is the 'símbolo maior desta peregrinação' [most important symbol of that pilgrimage] (61). Silveira 'jurou' [swore] to bring this statue to the 'corte do Monomotapa' [court of Monomotapa], where it can 'repousar' [rest] (61). When Silveira's Congolese translator, Nimi Nsundi, cuts the foot off the 'Santa' [saint] (231) – because he says it is, in fact, a water goddess trapped in the saint's body – Silveira wants to kill him for his actions. Nimi, however, commits suicide before Silveira can execute the punishment, and Nimi's diary passes on to his girlfriend, Dia – also a translator – who continues to document the trip. Silveira eventually ends up in the Monomotapa kingdom, where he is killed. The statue and documents are the same ones Mwadia finds roughly 442 years later.

Sereia thus performs the globe and creates an impression of mobility on the local, regional, trans-Atlantic and trans-(Indian) Oceanic levels, which is relatively unobstructed due to the available technology (boat, car, plane, etc.). It performs, in other words, the annihilation of space through technological inventions/innovation that eliminate time and through which the globe can be apprehended. The second narrative strategy, that of *locale enumeration* – a concept I use to describe the almost obsessive enumeration of the names of geographical locations – has similar aims. *Sereia* mentions North America, Africa, Europe, Mozambique, Kenya, Zimbabwe, France, Spain, Congo, Japan, Nigeria, the Netherlands, Tanzania, Goa, Camuendje, Cahora Bassa, Coast of Mozambique, North of Mozambique, Coast of Africa, Ilha de Moçambique, Madeira, Bragança, Passagem, Antigamente, Vila Longe, Damau, Diu, Chicoa, Tete, Chinde, Bemba, Panaji, New York, Dar-es-Salaam, Nampula, Lisbon, São Paulo, Rome, the Indian Ocean, the Atlantic Ocean, the Margin of the Zambezi river, Mussenguezi and Mandovi. In enumerating this many place names, an attempt to apprehend the enormity of the globe is again constituted and its accessibility again implied. Of course, despite the number of places

176   CHAPTER 5

Sereia enumerates, it barely scratches the surface of the enormity of the globe's locales; this strategy may therefore be considered the narrative equivalent of Moretti's 'reading more', which, for Moretti, seems 'hardly to be the solution' (Moretti 55).

A third narrative strategy, which has a similar function to the first two, is what was called *spatial jumps* in Chapter 2. The strategy is used throughout *Sereia* but is clearest in the following three examples. First, when Mwadia bathes Zero, the narrator zooms out and says: 'Madzero não podia saber que longe, mais longe que o outro lado do mundo, uma mão nervosa viria a redigir a seguinte mensagem' [Madzero could not know that far away, even farther than the other side of the world, a nervous hand was editing the following message] (19). Second, when Benjamin and Rosie fly to Mozambique, the narrator emphasizes the trip's short duration, saying it takes 'menos de treze horas' [less than thirteen hours] (161). Finally, *curandeiro* Lazaro Vivo has a cellphone that is not yet connected to the 'serviços internacionais' [international service] (30) – at least, not in his house in the mountains. In Vila Longe it is, however, and when Benjamin disappears at the end of the novel a police officer calls Lazaro to tell him the American is in Zimbabwe. When the villagers wonder how he acquired that information, the narrator describes the cellphone as the 'secreto vencedor da distância' [secret conqueror of distance] (341). As with the Simplon passage in Scott's 'Highland Widow', these passages present distance in order to bridge or eliminate it, using, respectively, narration, (narration of) modes of transportation and (narration of) information technology.

This leads to a fourth and final narrative strategy: multi-strand narration, or *entrelacement*. In his seminal work on world-literature, Beecroft (2008, 2015) suggests considering all the literatures of the world as 'world literature' (without a hyphen), and dividing this large category into different modes based on how literature circulates. Each mode, he argues, has different forms associated with it. The last, not-fully-realized mode is that of the 'global literary ecology', which would consist of 'literary circulation that truly knows no borders' – a 'fantasy of a world without borders' that contains the 'fantasy [of] equal access to the literary world for all' – the same fantasy that is the content of the cosmopolitan space (2015: 41). The most important form or trope of that global literary ecology is what he calls

Re-emergence of the Mozambican modern ghost story　　177

the '"plot of globalization", the use of multi-strand narration to convey on a formal level our interconnected and polycentric world' (41). And, while this technique is not new in itself, what is novel is the 'use of this device as a way to project onto the level of form the paranoiac interconnectedness of life in a globalized era and the expansion of the scale on which these narratives are interwoven to the level of the planet itself' (2015: 302). Indeed, *Sereia* uses entrelacement to show how 'everything is connected' across not only space (the Southmans and Vila Longe) but also time (Silveira and Mwadia/the Southmans).

Sereia employs these four narrative strategies to perform and apprehend a globe as unified and accessible – for, in Gupta's words, 'the apprehension of the world itself, as a whole, as a complex function of parts and levels' (2009: 2). In doing so, it prominently draws on the narrative building block of the *ideologeme* of the cosmopolitan space, along the lines of the globalization and world-literature debates. Yet Beecroft's observation has implications for *Sereia* and for the *ideologeme*; *Sereia's* narrative strategies may be specific neither to it nor to Mozambican literature in general. Indeed, Beecroft (2015) gives the example of Iñárritu's 2006 *Babel* as an entrelacement narrative but other examples of works that use this technique and are published around the same time are plentiful – for example, *The Nature of Blood* (Phillips 1997), *Fountain at the Center of the World* (Newman 2003), *Cloud Atlas* (Mitchell 2004) and *World War Z* (Brooks 2006) – all of which use entrelacement to demonstrate interconnectedness. Moreover, *Locale enumeration*, these examples show, is equally common. *Babel's* narrative strands are set in Mexico, Japan and Morocco, in a shared present, and they converge in the circulation of a rifle. *Blood's* are set in Cyprus, Venice, Germany, London and Palestine in the years 1480, 1930 and around 2000, and they converge around European tribalism. *Cloud's* are set in the Pacific, Cambridge, Edinburgh, San Francisco, London and the fictional Neo Seoul and Big Isle, in the years 1849, 1936, 1973, 2012, 2144 and a year that is not on the Christian calendar, and they converge through the technique of the frame narrative. The narrative strands in *Fountain* are set in London and Tonalacapan, and they converge in Seattle. *World War Z's* narrative strands are set in Lhasa, Meteora, the Amazon rainforest, Barbados, Tel Aviv, Bethlehem, Langley, Vaalajarvi, the Antartica Vostok

178   CHAPTER 5

Station, Amarillo, Troy (Montana), Memphis, Alang, Topeka, Khuzhir, Ice City, Denver, Robben Island, Armagh, Odessa, Manitoba, Rajasthan, Taos, Burlington, Wenatchee, Malibu, Tennessee, Bohemia, Micronesia, South Korea, Kyoto, Cienfuegos, Beijing, Sydney, Ancud, Siberia, Hawaii, Quebec and Ainsworth, and converge on a ship in the ocean.

What these examples also show is that both (what we may call) *spatial entrelacement* and (what we may call) *temporal entrelacement* are shared narrative conventions.

Finally, *spatial jumping* is also a common narrative convention in these works. This is implied in the connection to Scott's Simplon passage, but is particularly helpfully demonstrated by the film *The Bourne Identity* (Liman 2002), which, using a moderate form of *locale enumeration*, is set in the Mediterranean Sea, Zürich, Langley Virginia, Nigeria, Paris and Greece. *Bourne* revolves around the trope of the protagonist-as-secret-weapon, who the government can no longer control and who must find out who he is while staying out of the hands of that government. In doing so, he and the government that is attempting to track him down use several tools to annihilate space through *spatial jumping*. For example, phone conversations are central to the film and constitute spatial jumps by being shot at both sides of the line. This creates a rapid sequence of consecutive shifts, bringing the viewer unobstructedly from one part of the Earth to the other and back. The telephone here is clearly the mediator, or eliminator, of space – as it was for Lazarus. On another occasion, a computer is used to locate secret agents all over the world; again, it is a piece of technology that eliminates space. The camera zooms in on the screen, which then merges with it to the extent that the computer screen becomes one with the frame of the movie – the viewers' screen. From this perspective, with lines of code running through the screen, the viewer is unobstructedly taken from one city to another. Last, as in *Sereia*, there is an emphasis on the variety of means of transportation, and the protagonist uses (or attempts to use) trains, planes, trams, cars and boats. Even if public transport is not an option, because the authorities are looking for the protagonist and can easily find him there, protagonist Bourne has the option of paying a (then-unknown) woman $20,000 to drive him by car; and, despite the slowness of that means of transportation being emphasized by briefly focusing on the journey itself, he falls asleep, misses most of the journey and simply wakes up in a different country.

Sereia thus taps into a narrative tradition that is prominent at the time of its publication, and of which *Babel, Z, Cloud, Bourne* and *Blood* are examples. This tradition consists of a set of narrative strategies that register and perform 'globalization', and in which that term refers primarily to a world in which space is no longer relevant (or not as relevant as it once was), although without a material explanation thereof – the cosmopolitan space. However, there is an essential difference between works such as *Sereia* on the one hand and *Bourne* on the other, which plays out along similar poles as seen in the globalization debate and which recalls Pizer's world-literature conceptualization (as characterized above): in *Sereia* unobstructed mobility is unequally distributed. Lazaro refers to his phone as an eliminator of space, as shown above; however, a closer look shows that Lazaro has a phone, and can be contacted, but is unable to make a call himself. The Southmans can travel to Vila Longe with ease, while the villagers emphasize their own inability to travel to the United States to visit the couple. In another example, when Mwadia and her friend Matambira talk in the post office where he works, and which is the hub for (inter)national exchange between the village and the outer world, the narrator notices it is located 'junto à arruinada central de telefones' [next to the destroyed telephone office] (371). The mail itself does *appear* to function properly; letters have been arriving, throughout the novel, addressing supposed terrorist threats in the region. Mwadia therefore attempts to cheer up her friend, who laments the state of the village, telling him that, in his function at the post office, he 'costura distâncias' [sews distances together] (371). Matambira then confesses the post office is, in fact, out of order: 'nada functiona [...] as linhas estão cortadas, roubaram os postes, os cobres, os isoladores' [nothing works [...] the telephone lines are cut, they robbed the posts, the copper, the isolators] (371). Thus, although Vila Longe is just a phone call away from Zimbabwe – or a thirteen-hour flight away from New York, for the Americans – the villagers have no way of 'sewing' distances together; where Bourne can pay $20,000 to get to Switzerland, the villagers of Vila Longe barely have the means to leave their village.

180   CHAPTER 5

Couto's novel thus repurposes the tropes of globalization to establish
that relatively unobstructed mobility is unequally distributed – a world that
is, to use the WReC's formulation, 'single but radically uneven' (2016: 535).
This is escalated even further through modern ghost story conventions,
including the structure of debt, the community of ghosts (expanded to
real estate and objects), ontological uncertainty and so on.

Haunted cosmopolitan spaces in Sereia

That the novel is dotted with aspects relating to ghosts is evident from
the opening epigraphs onwards. The first epigraph consists of a poem
by the Senegalese poet Birago Diop, which announces the presence
of ghosts: 'Os que morreram/ não se retiram' [those who die/do not
withdraw themselves] (7). The second epigraph is a quote by Maestro
Arcanjo (the Vila Longe barber) and similarly announces the presence
of ghosts: 'em todo o mundo é assim: morrem as pessoas, fica a História.
Aqui, é o inverso: morre apenas a História, os mortos não vão' [in the
whole world it is like this: people die, History stays. Here, it is the other
way around: only History dies, the dead do not go] (15). Both epigraphs
thus hint at the presence of ghosts, and even of communities of ghosts, before the main narrative has started, incidentally recalling the connection
between the historical novel and the (modern) ghost story as referred to
by Hay (2011) and as cited at the start of the second chapter of this book.

The epigraphs also signify structurally, for which it is necessary to
briefly recall Genette's theorization of the paratextual device. Genette
argues that the epigraph has several functions, including commenting on
the title, commenting on the text, backing the text with the authority of
the epigraph's author and, finally, the 'epigraph effect', or the fact that the
presence of the epigraph itself aids in defining the work's genre. In addition, he argues, because the epigraph 'is a quotation' it raises questions
about who its author is and who chooses or proposes the epigraph (Genette
1997: 150–1). To better understand the device, he distinguishes between
the allographic epigraph (a quote from someone who is not the author of

Re-emergence of the Mozambican modern ghost story   181

the work) and the autographic epigraph (a quote from someone who *is* the author of the work).

Sereia's epigraphs are chiefly allographic – their sources include critics, poets, proverbs and historical documents – and the device's formal characteristic, of raising questions about its speaker/author, are indeed instrumentalized. This is most clearly illustrated by an epigraph in which, in archetypal modern ghost story fashion, a frame narrative is constructed: it cites Edward Said, who cites Eric Auerbach, who quotes Hugo de St Victor (Couto 2006: 59). Yet the novel also uses epigraphs that quote characters from the novel. Genette does not have a category for these, although he approaches it with his subcategory of the 'anonymous epigraph' (Genette 1997: 151); his example is the epigraph of F. Scott Fitzgerald's *The Great Gatsby*'s by Thomas Parke D'Invilliers – a pen name of F. Scott Fitzgerald and a character in his semi-autobiographical novel. I will therefore call this type of epigraph a *character epigraph*. It is important to distinguish between anonymous and character epigraphs because they affect the relation between narrative and epigraph in different ways. Elmer has argued the epigraph has a 'doubtful status' because it raises the question, for the reader, of whether it is 'internal or external' to the 'tale proper' (Elmer 1993: 67) – a characteristic that holds true for paratext in general (Genette 1997: 2). The anonymous epigraph does not affect this ambiguous status but the character epigraph does, because characters belong to the narrative proper and do not exist outside it. Simultaneously, however, by placing characters in the paratextual realm they obtain a 'life' outside the narrative – it is not difficult to imagine a reader who would search for information about the speaker of the epigraph. What that reader would find, however, is a voice from nowhere – a voice-without-body – or, at least, not a material body other than the novel. This voice-without-body has the same effect as the structure of debt, in that it mystifies who is speaking. Of course, the voice-without-body is also a characteristic of the ghost. And, while this type of metaphorical use of 'ghost' is generally resisted in this book, it is mentioned here because (as will be shown below) the characters in these epigraphs may indeed be ghosts.

According to Genette, the epigraph gained in popularity at the end of the eighteenth century and was exported via the Gothic genre from

182   CHAPTER 5

England (1997: 147). If the export vessel of the epigraph was the Gothic narrative, *Sereia* certainly has Gothic elements. When Mwadia arrives in Vila Longe, she finds the village in terrible shape. Her first destination is the church, which she believes is a good place to lay the statue to rest, yet she finds '[o] edifício estava em ruínas. Não havia telhado, janelas, portas. Restavam paredes sujas' [the building was in ruins. There was no roof, windows, doors. All that was left were dirty walls] (Couto 2006: 111). Continuing this Gothic imagery, the narrator describes how even the 'cemitério' [cemetery] was 'distru[ido]' [destroyed], so 'não seria na igreja de Vila Longe que a imagem [...] podia ganhar um nicho seguro' [the statue could not find a safe space in the church of Vila Longe] (111). Other public buildings are similarly unsuitable, Mwadia finds, and are characterized as 'tumba' [tombs] (146) or no more than 'uma parede arruinada' [a ruined wall] (141). Summarized from the viewpoint of the Southmans, the 'estado de destruição dos edifícios' [destroyed state of the buildings] made it appear as if they were 'mastigados por uma apocalíptica voragem' [chewed up by an apocalyptic vortex] (167). When Rosie Southmans asks Mwadia if this is all the result of the war, Mwadia confirms it is, and adds that these 'casas não foram destruídas. Estas casas morreram' [Those houses were not destroyed. Those houses died] (167).

Vila Longe is thus a ghost town, and its houses are ghosts. Reminiscent of Rulfo's *Pedro Páramo*, *Portagem* and 'História' alike, it is also inhabited by a community of ghosts – the villagers. That this is so is suggestive in the case of some characters, such as *curandeiro* (or witch doctor) Lazaro Vivo [Lazarus Alive]. It is never explicitly claimed that Lazaro is a ghost, but he can be understood as one based on the double biblical reference in his name. The first biblical Lazarus is used in a story in which Jesus wants to illustrate the totality of Christian life and afterlife. In life, Lazarus is a beggar, which means he can be all he desires in the afterlife. Conversely, the rich man who refuses to feed Lazarus in life will be hungry in the afterlife (Luke 16: 1931). The second Lazarus figure concerns a man who is awoken from the dead (John 11: 1–44). Lazaro is thus associated with death, and may even refer to a man who has died.

Lazaro Vivo may be a ghost himself and, because he insists he 'fico a fazer companhia aos mortos' [keeps the dead company], he hints that the other

Re-emergence of the Mozambican modern ghost story   183

characters are also ghosts (28). And while his case may be uncertain, less doubt exist about Mwadia's husband, Zero Madzero, who, from the outset, is described as resembling 'um fantasma, magro e sujo' [a ghost, skinny and dirty] (Couto 2006: 17). Due to his appearance, Mwadia entertains the possibility that her husband is a ghost; she asks him: 'me confesse: você já morreu?' [confess: did you already die?] (17). Zero does not reply, but when Mwadia bathes him shortly afterwards, her suspicion is enforced; she sees 'sangue' [blood], originating from wounds on his neck, stain the water (18). The narrator contributes to the uncertainty about Madzero's state of being, describing Zero as 'a esquecer' [forgetting] himself (20) and saying: 'aproximava do próprio nome, ele se anulava' [he approximated his own name, he annulled himself] (19). Finally, Madzero cannot leave Antigamente – that is, the past – and, while the reason for this is never spelled out, it could be assumed that it is because, having died, he only exists in the past.

The uncertainty about Madzero plays a role throughout the novel and involves minor and major characters. In a conversation with one of the villagers, Mwadia is asked where Zero is, to which she answers that her husband stayed in Antigamente. The villager misunderstands:

> [Villager] Em quê?
> [Mwadia] Em Antigamente
> [Villager] Morreu?
> [Mwadia] Não, Antigamente é o lugar onde vivemos
> [Villager] Nunca ouvi falar.
> [Mwadia] Fico de lado de lá do rio, do lado de lá da montanha.
> [Villager] A propósito de lado de lá: os meus irmãos também faleceram, você
>   sabe? (143)

> [[Villager] Where?
> [Mwadia] In the past.
> [Villager] He died?
> [Mwadia] No. Antigamente is the name of the place where we live.
> [Villager] Never heard of it.
> [Mwadia] It is on the other side of the river, on the other side of the mountain.
> [Villager] Speaking of the other side: my brothers died too, did you hear?]

The villager (mis)understands living in Antigamente as a euphemism for being dead, and – even when Mwadia explains that Zero did not

184   CHAPTER 5

die – cannot let go of this idea, partly due to Mwadia's inability of describing her home in words not related to death.

Mwadia's mother attempts to get her daughter to admit Madzero is dead, without success. She asks Mwadia if, after having found a home for the statue, she is going back to 'nesse lugar que não existe?' [that place that does not exist?], to which Mwadia responds: 'Antigamente e o meu lugar' [Antigamente is my place] (Couto 2006: 106). Her mother retorts: 'O seu lugar é este. […] Sabe o que eu ouvi dizer? […] Que o seu marido já tinha morrido. Morreu ou não?' [Your place is this one. […] You know what I heard? […] That your husband has already died. Did he die or not?] (107). Mwadia says it is 'tudo mentira [all lies] (107). Her mother insists she married a 'fantasma' [ghost] (107), after which Mwadia asks if she really thinks 'o seu homem é menos fantasma que o meu Zero?' [your husband is less of a ghost than my Zero is?] (107) – and, indeed, her mother's husband is also described as a 'fantasma' [ghost] (105). The narrator intervenes in the discussion and notices that the mother is not 'a única pessoa que insistia que Zero já se havia retirado da Vida' [the only person who insisted that Zero had already withdrawn himself from Life] (107). The narrator introduces a number of possibilities for what might have happened to Zero, but ends by saying the 'verdade é que ninguém possuía a certeza de que se tratava de Zero Madzero' [truth is that nobody could know for sure what happened with Zero Madzero] (107). Mwadia closes the discussion by asking: 'Que importa se ele está vivo ou morto?' [Why does it matter if he is a ghost or not?] (107). The possibility that Zero is a ghost is perpetuated in this way throughout the novel, but certainty about his ontological status is never offered.

If Lazaro, Madzero and Mwadia's stepfather may all be ghosts, Mwadia's friend at the post office escalates this possibility to the entire village, suggesting that 'esta gente aqui, em Vila Longe, é que está morta' [the people here, in Vila Longe, they are the ones who are dead] (148). Mwadia's mother later affirms that 'a gente nunca sabe quando está morte' [people never know when they are dead] (170). The villagers may thus indeed be ghosts, although they are unaware that they are. Even Mwadia later admits this may be the case, recalling how, when she was young, 'deixaram me ver o mundo inteiro morrer' [they let me see the entire world die] (282). It is these could-be ghosts, then, who speak in the epigraphs.

Re-emergence of the Mozambican modern ghost story　　　　185

Like the buildings and the characters, the main object of *Sereia* (which I have argued elsewhere is an *object protagonist*: Maurits 2020) are also constructed as ghosts. The statue is initially in the care of Silveira, who aims to bring it to the Monomotapa kingdom, where she can 'repousar' [rest] (Couto 2006: 61). He fails in his mission, after which the statue mysteriously appears in Mwadia's Antigamente. She is then tasked with the 'missão' [mission] to 'encontrar um lugar sagrado' [encounter a sacred place] for the statue, and only when the statue has been found a resting place does the novel end (224). The presence of the statue is disturbing to the villagers – although not to Mwadia, who lives in the past (in Antigamente) because she is likely unable to accept the present, in which her husband has died (which is why the appearance of the statue is not problematic to her). The villagers, however, disavow the past. As one of the shop owners puts it, 'o passado é coisa mal morta, o melhor é não mexer nele' [the past is a thing undead, it is best not to mess with it] (151). The villagers even have a ritual for forgetting the past: they circle the 'arvore do esquecimento' [tree of forgetting] thrice, after which they forget everything (320–1). As in *Portagem* and 'História', this forms the very condition of the ghost story, because only if the past is (apparently) inaccessible can its presence in the present be frightening. The statue, in other words, is modelled on the motif of the restless ghosts, who can only rest after finishing an unresolved task and who linger in the present until this is done.

Even the documents Mwadia finds are constructed as ghosts. When Mwadia first opens the box in which she finds them, she feels its contents might somehow be a threat, and the narrator remarks that she opens it '[c]om infinito cuidado […] como se temesse que dali emergissem fantasmas' [with infinite care, as if she feared that ghosts would emerge from it] (Couto 2006: 49). It is unclear for some time in the novel what precisely happens to the documents, although the impression is created that a villager takes them to the library. Meanwhile, the entertainment for the Southmans is prepared, and Casuarino tells Mwadia she will have to play 'um papel central' [a central role] in the construction of an experience the couple will hopefully consider authentic (155). Specifically, he wants Mwadia to 'finger ser visitada pelos espíritos' [pretend to be visited by spirits] (155). It is clear, then, that Casuarino counts on a ritual that is not real and does not

186   CHAPTER 5

actually involve spirits. The narrator confirms this, and says Mwadia will
not actually be possessed by spirits but that 'tratava de uma encenação' [it
concerned a staging] (276), and that the stories told during the séance are
'inventa[d]os' [made up] (281). The Southmans believe they are viewing
an authentic ritual and, when Mwadia's stepfather interrupts the séance,
Benjamin sneers at him ('o que é isso, homem? [...] Você não pode falar,
ela está visitada' [what is up with you, man? You cannot talk, she is being
possessed] (275)). At the end of the session, both of the Southmans are
'como Casuarino previra, [...] fascinados' [as Casuarino foresaw, [...] fas-
cinated] – so much so that they 'repetiam deleitados' [repeated delight-
edly]: 'Eis África autêntica' [this is authentic Africa] (276). The Southmans,
in some sense, take the Pizer position of world-literature.

The villagers are informed about Casuarino's plans and know they are
staged. Yet Mwadia is so convincing the villagers get scared, and it is for this
reason that Mwadia's stepdad interrupts her – he wants to ask if she is doing
well. Over the following days, during which séances take place repeatedly,
the villagers wonder whether she 'realmente [tinha] poderes' [really had
powers] and, finally, Mwadia's family calls a 'reunião de emergência' [emer-
gency meeting] (277). Her mother demands to know what is going on, and
implores her to 'não me faça sofrer mais' [not make me suffer more] (278).

Mwadia thus also constructs a voice-without-body, and she finally
admits she has been possessed – but not by spirits:

> Mwadia respondeu vagamente: os livros e os manuscritos eram as suas únicas
> visitações. De dia, ela abria a caixa de D. Gonçalo da Silveira e perdia-se na leitura
> dos velhos documentos. De noite, Mwadia ia ao quarto dos americanos (Couto
> 2006: 278)

> [Mwadia responded vaguely: the books and manuscripts were her only visitations.
> During the day, she opened the box of D. Gonçalo da Silveira and she lost herself
> in the reading of the old documents. At night, Mwadia went to the room of the
> Americans]

Mwadia's cautiousness in opening the box thus seems to have been in
vain: ghosts did emerge and haunt both the Americans – although in
part for entertainment, or rather, as Hooks (1992) described, the production and consumption of difference – and the villagers, through
Mwadia.

Re-emergence of the Mozambican modern ghost story 187

This haunting by the documents is not restricted to the intradiegetic world. To show this, it is necessary to return to *Sereia*'s macrostructure of entrelacement – which, as mentioned, is one of Sereia's main narrative tropes of globalization. In studies on *Sereia*, the multi-strand narration has usually been understood as a commentary on history and a bridge between past and present. For example, Brugioni argues that, because the 1560–1 narrative is based on actual historical events, history and fiction are merged, and Madureira considers the function of the double narrative structure a device for drawing a parallel between the colonial attitude on the one hand and (what he considers) the neocolonial behaviour of some (non-government) organizations on the other. He highlights how, in Silveira's gaze, the inhabitants of Mozambique are reduced to savages, and how the Southmans reduce the contemporary Mozambicans to mythical and authentic Africans, in order to argue that 'the novel repeatedly suggests the two enterprises end up mirroring each other's logic' (215). The novel clearly supports such understandings, and one villager actually accuses Rosie Southman of wanting to 'apresentar como criaturas exóticas, vivendo de crenças e tradições. Não era essa a imagem que os colonos faziam de nós?' [present us as exotic creatures, living of beliefs and traditions. Was this not the image the colonizers created of us?] (339). However, most accounts do not consider the way in which the strands relate – or, to be more precise, the fact that these two chronotopes alternate. To explicate, starting in the present of 2002, the narrative is interrupted by the chronotope of the sixteenth century. In other words, the past repeatedly interrupts the present in the novel in the form of sixteenth-century chronotopes, which is to say, in the form of the documents Mwadia finds. It is also for this reason that the narrative (necessarily) starts in 2002. Mwadia must find the documents first and let the 'fantasmas' out. Only then can they haunt both the characters in the diegetic world and the very structure of the novel.

Sereia's macrostructure, established by what Beecroft identifies as the most important plot of globalization, is haunted in *Sereia*.[6] Thus, *Sereia* not only constructs 'globalization' as the unequal distribution of unobstructed

---

6   It may be pointed out that Couto also used – and distorted – multi-strand narration in his *Terra Sonâmbula* (1992), in which the anti-journey is also thematized and the two narrative strands are never joined.

188   CHAPTER 5

mobility, using conventional tropes of globalization and combining them with the conventions of the Mozambican modern ghost story, but also constructs this already-compromised cosmopolitan space as haunted. While this may be understood as a registration of the horror of the primitive accumulation of the 1980s and 1990s, *Sereia*, as in the case of the Mozambican modern ghost story, is unable to indicate what constitutes it as unequal – what haunts it – those who enact inequality remain invisible; in the Mozambican modern ghost story, the consequential actors of primitive accumulation remain hidden.[7]

7   A similar view of 'globalization' is constructed in Couto's 2006 poem, 'Globalização' (2007: 5152), in which peasants are opposed to a politician, an anthropologist and a geologist figure. All three of these characters rely on the peasants to produce, respectively, the party, authenticity and inauthenticity. The Southmans, in the same way, rely on the villagers to produce authenticity for them to satisfy their aim of consuming cultural difference. It could be wagered, then, that *Sereia* suggests the totality of 'globalization' is its relations of production.

Conclusion

The main thesis of this book is *there exists a Mozambican modern ghost story and it registers primitive accumulation*. Its history may be characterized as emerging and re-emerging in different moments of primitive accumulation, starting with the proto-form of Campos de Oliveira's Gothic poetry, followed by the more recognizable modern ghost story in Mendes' *Portagem*, by the recognizably *Mozambican* modern ghost stories of the 1980s – with, and following, the publication of Couto's *Vozes Anoitecidas* – and, finally, by the globalization debate influenced ghost-story form of the 2000s, for which the example of Couto's *O Outro Pé da Sereia* is used in this book, but to which other works, like Borges Coelho's *Crónica da Rua 513.2*, also belong. As this book only has begun to show, the genre has predecessors in the British modern ghost story, in Latin American irrealism, in Portuguese Romanticism and Gothic literature, French horror and supernatural fiction, Portuguese and Mozambican Neorealism, the global novel, and so on. All of these forms have complex genre histories, and while some of them have been researched and others have not, all of these histories lie beyond the scope of this book.

The Mozambican modern ghost story changes over time, in part due to its context, and relative to the different predecessors on which it draws, as is manifest formally. Certainly, there exists a set of genre conventions that modern ghost stories have in common, which is somewhat consistent over decades and even centuries, and which includes frightening supernatural figures, a climactic structure, the refusal to narrative closure, issues with the law, empire, class identity and class struggle. Most importantly, these conventions include something (traumatic) returning from an otherwise inaccessible past, and a transition. Yet these conventions are modified and reinterpreted over time, as other – both contemporary and non-contemporary – forms and (raw) materials are combined with existing ones. Thus, Mendes' *Portagem* draws on the haunted-house trope and on the, for him, contemporary form of Mozambican Neorealism; the focalization by a worker who fails in his class struggle. In the 80s, this is used to switch the focalization in the Mozambican modern ghost story from hauntee to haunter, a switch which is also encouraged by the circulation of Rulfo's *Pedro Páramo* in the Mozambican literary ecology during this period. Nevertheless, at the same time, archetypal expressions of the haunted-house trope, which could indeed be at home in any literature, at any time, as the (flawed) omnipresence thesis discussed in the introduction suggests, also occur, for example, in the framed narrative in Chiziane's *Balada de Amor ao Vento*. *Sereia*, finally, combines the Mozambican modern ghost story conventions as they materialized in the 80s with narrative strategies of, what could be called, the 'global novel'. The most prominent conventions of this specifically Mozambican modern ghost story include the community of ghosts, the figure of the worker- and specifically miner-ghost, the focalization by the figure of the ghost who uses its power to haunt, the uncertainty about the ghost's ontological status and the absence of the object of its rage – of the 'oppressor'.

There are several noteworthy aspect beyond this book's main thesis. On a general level, the book shows the complexity of the formation of genres – much more complex, even, than the amorphous blob of something like Ward Shelley's attempt to visualize the history of science fiction in his artwork 'The History of Science Fiction' manages to express. Because it is unlikely that all contacts can be traced, much of the study of genres may necessarily focus on symptoms – forms that are similar. However, this method is also limited as it is difficult to determine where even a certain symptom comes from. Is, for example, the focalization by the figure of the ghost that is common to the Mozambican modern ghost story more the result of *Portagem* or of *Páramo*?

Further, even though the British modern ghost story is clearly influential for the modern ghost story in general, this book has found no reason to claim the Mozambican modern ghost story is the result of straightforward cultural Imperialism. Certainly, that Britain was once an imperial power may, and likely will, have contributed to the circulation of the genre, but its foundations were formed before the British Empire came into existence. Moreover, even if the selection and shaping of form may in part be

Conclusion   191

an unconscious process, it is not impossible that the choices authors make are for specific reasons, which are at least at odds with forthright cultural Imperialism – *Portagem*'s ghosts haunt the colonial ruler, Chiziane's Sarnau character wants to be a ghost so she can haunt her former lover, and so on. Consequently, the notion that culture will necessarily – and particularly considering Imperialism and later globalization – become increasingly homogeneous (or, conversely, heterogeneous), and the notion that something like a Mozambican modern ghost story is necessarily symptomatic of a problem, may not have a foundation. Of course, similar arguments have been made on many occasions before, yet such claims are persistent in returning.

On a general level, the book shows that despite *Portagem*, the Mozambican modern ghost story only really takes shape or proliferates in the 1980s. This results in part from the particularities of Mozambican (literary) history but, even so, it could be proposed that this makes the Mozambican modern ghost story a genre of particularly neoliberalism. Indeed, the primitive accumulation that it registers in the 80s and 2000s is that of neoliberalism. While this is a reductive assessment, it may nevertheless be important to highlight that the genre consistently fails to identify the consequential actors of the primitive accumulation of neoliberalism. This would raise new questions about the cultural work that the Mozambican modern ghost story does in particular, about its relation to genres with which it is contemporary and about cultural strategies under neoliberalism more generally. These, however, must remain for a later moment.

Bibliography

Abraham, Nicolas, and Maria Torok, *The Shell and the Kernel: Renewals of Psycho-analysis* (Chicago, IL and London: University of Chicago Press, 1994).

Afolabi, Niyi, *Golden Cage: Regeneration in Lusophone African Literature and Culture* (Trenton, NJ: Africa World Press, 2001).

Afonso, Maria Fernanda, *O Conto Moçambicano: Escritas Pós-Coloniais* (Lisbon: Caminho, 2002).

Alba, Sebastião, *O Ritmo do Presságio* (Lisbon: Edição 70, 1981).

Albrow, Martin, 'Auf Dem Weg zu einer globalen Gesellschaft?', in Ulrich Beck, ed., *Perspektiven der Weltgesellschaft* (Frankfurt am Main: Suhrkamp, 1998), 411–35.

Albuquerque, Orlando de, and José Ferraz Motta, *História da Literatura em Moçambique* (Braga: APPACDM Distrital de Braga, 1998).

Aldridge, Alfred Owen, *The Reemergence of World Literature: A Study of Asia and the West* (London and Toronto: University of Delaware Press, 1986).

Aleluia, Aníbal, *Contos do Fantástico* (Maputo: AEMO, 2011).

——, *Mbelele e Outros Contos* (Maputo: AEMO, 1987).

Allen, Walter Ernest, *The Short Story in English* (Oxford: Clarendon Press, 1981).

Al-Rodhan, Nayef, *Definitions of Globalization: A Comprehensive Overview and a Proposed Definition* (Geneva: Geneva Centre for Security Policy, 2006).

Amaral, João Fonseca, *Poemas* (Lisbon: Casa da Moeda, 1999).

American Comparative Literature Association, 'State of the Discipline Report' (2014), <https://stateofthediscipline.acla.org/>, accessed 24 November 2014.

Anderson, W. E. K., 'Introduction', in W. E. K. Anderson, ed., *The Journal of Sir Walter Scott* (Edinburgh: Canongate, 1998), xxiii–xlvi.

Appadurai, Arjun, 'Disjuncture and Difference in the Global Cultural Economy', in Mike Featherstone, ed., *Global Culture: Nationalism, Globalization and Modernity* (London: Sage, 1990), 295–310.

Arendt, Hannah, *The Origins of Totalitarianism* (San Diego, New York and London: Harcourt, 1976).

Arrighi, Giovanni, *The Geometry of Imperialism* (London: Verso, 1983).

Auerbach, Nina, 'Ghosts of Ghosts', *Victorian Literature and Culture* 32/1 (2004), 277–84.

Azevedo, Licínio, *O Comboio de Sal e Açúcar* (Maputo: Ndjira, 1997).

Bibliography

Bagnol, Brigitte, 'Lovolo e Espíritos no Sul de Moçambique', *Análise Social* xi.iii/ 2 (2008), 251–72.

Bakhtin, M. M., and P. M. Medvedev, *The Formal Method in Literary Scholarship: A Critical Introduction to Sociological Poetics*, trans. A. J. Wehrle (Cambridge, MA: Harvard University Press, 1981).

Bakhtin, Mikhail, *The Dialogic Imagination: Four Essays* (Austin: University of Texas Press, 2008).

Baptista, Heliodoro, *Por Cima de Toda a Folha* (Maputo: AEMO, 1987).

Basto, Maria-Benedita, 'Writing a Nation or Writing a Culture? Frelimo and Nationalism during the Mozambican Liberation War', in Eric Morier-Genoud, ed., *Sure Roads? Nationalisms in Angola, Guinea-Bissau and Mozambique* (Leiden, the Netherlands, and Boston, MA: Brill, 2012), 103–26.

Baylor University, 'The Baylor Religion Survey, Wave II' (Waco, TX: Baylor Institute for Studies of Religion 2007).

Beecroft, Alexander, *An Ecology of World Literature* (London: Verso, 2015).

——, 'World Literature Without a Hyphen: Towards a Typology of Literary Systems', *New Left Review* 54 (2008), 87–100.

Beinart, William, and Karen Brown, *African Local Knowledge and Livestock Health* (Woodbridge: James Curry, 2013).

Bender, Helmut, and Ulrich Melzer, 'Zur Geschichte des Begriffes "Weltliteratur"', *Aeculum* IX/1 (1958), 113–23.

Berczik, Árpád, 'Zur Entwicklung des Begriffs "Weltliteratur" und Anfänge der Vergleichenden Literaturgeschichte', *Acta Germanica et Romanica* 2 (1967), 3–22.

Bergland, Renée L., *The National Uncanny: Indian Ghosts and American Subjects* (Hanover and London: University Press of New England, 2000).

Bertelsen, Bjørn Enge, *Violent Becomings. State Formation, Sociality, and Power in Mozambique* (New York, NY: Berghahn Books, 2016).

Berthin, Christine, *Gothic Hauntings: Melancholy Crypts and Textual Ghosts* (Houndmills, Basingstoke: Palgrave Macmillan, 2010).

Birus, Hendrik, 'Goethes Idee der Weltliteratur. Eine historische Vergegenwärtigung', in Manfred Schmelling, ed., *Weltliteratur heute. Konzepte und Perspektiven* (Würzburg: Königshausen and Neumann, 1995), 5–28.

——, 'The Goethean Concept of World Literature and Comparative Literature', *CLCWeb* 2/4 (2000).

Boldy, Steven, *A Companion to Juan Rulfo* (Woodbridge: Tamesis, 2016).

Borges Coelho, João Paulo, *Crónica da Rua 513.2* (Lison: Caminho, 2006).

Bortolot, Alexander, 'Artesãos da Nossa Patria', in Sidney Littlefield Kasfir and Till Forster, eds, *African Art and Agency in the Workshop* (Bloomington: Indiana University Press, 2013), 252–73.

Bibliography

Borwein, Naomi Simone, 'Vampires, Shape-Shifters, and Sinister Light: Mistranslating Australian Aboriginal Horror in Theory and Literary Practice', in Kevin Corstophine and Laura R. Kremmel, eds, *The Palgrave Handbook to Horror Literature* (New York: Palgrave MacMillan, 2018), 61–76.

Bowen, Merle L., 'Beyond Reform: Adjustment and Political Power in Contemporary Mozambique', *The Journal of Modern African Studies* 30/02 (1992), 255–79.

——, *The State Against the Peasantry: Rural Struggles in Colonial and Postcolonial Mozambique* (Charlottesville and London: University Press of Virginia, 2000).

Bown, Nicola, Carolyn Burdett, and Pamela Thurschwell, *The Victorian Supernatural* (Cambridge: Cambridge University Press, 2004).

Boyd, Colleen E., and Coll Thrush, eds, *Phantom Past, Indigenous Presence: Native Ghosts in North American Culture and History* (Lincoln: University of Nebraska Press, 2011).

Brandt Corstius, J. C., 'De Ontwikkeling van het Begrip Wereldliteratuur', *De Vlaamse Gids* 41 (1957), 582–99.

Brewster, Scott, and Luke Thurston, *The Routledge Handbook of the Ghost Story* (New York, NY, and Abingdon: Routledge, 2018).

Briggs, Julia, *Night Visitors: The Rise and Fall of the English Ghost Story* (London: Faber, 1977).

Brinkman, Richard L., and June E. Brinkman, 'Globalization and the Nation-State: Dead or Alive', *Journal of Economic Issues* 42/2 (June 2008), 425–33.

Brogan, Kathleen, *Cultural Haunting: Ghosts and Ethnicity in Recent American Literature* (Charlottesville: University Press of Virginia, 1998).

Brooks, Max, *World War Z* (New York, NY: Three River Press Books, 2006).

Brookshaw, David, 'Mia Couto in Context', in Grant Hamilton and David Huddart, eds, *A Companion to Mia Couto* (Woodbridge: James Currey, 2016), 17–24.

Brown, Tony C., 'The Time of Globalization: Rethinking Primitive Accumulation', *Rethinking Marxism: A Journal of Economics, Culture & Society* 21/4 (2009), 571–84.

Brown, Wendy, *In the Ruins of Neoliberalism: The Rise of Antidemocratic Politics in the West* (New York, NY: Columbia University Press, 2019).

Brugioni, Elena, 'O Outro Pé da Sereia: História[s] na Pós-Colonialidade', *Luso-Brazilian Review* 49/1 (2012), 46–62.

Buescu, Helena Carvalhão, 'The Transition from Romanticism to Realism', in Stephen Parkinson, Cláudia Pazos Alonso, and T. F. Earle, eds, *A Companion to Portuguese Literature* (Woodbridge: Tamesis, 2009), 109–19.

Bunson, Margaret, *Encyclopedia of Ancient Egypt* (New York, NY: Facts on File, 2002).

Cabral, Ricardo, *The Development of Teacher Education in Portuguese Goa, 1841–1961* (New Delhi: Concept, 1957).

Cahen, Michel, 'Indigenato Before Race?', in Francisco Bethencourt and Adrian J. Pearce, eds, *Racism and Ethnic Relations in the Portuguese-Speaking World* (New York, NY: Oxford University Press, 2012), 149–71.

——, 'The War as Seen by Renamo Guerrilla Politics and the "Move to the North" at the Time of the Nkomati Accord, 1983–1985', in Eric Morier-Genoud, Michel Cahen, and Domingos Manuel do Rosário, eds, *The War Within: New Perspectives on the Civil War in Mozambique, 1976–1992* (Woodbridge: James Currey, 2018), 100–46.

Callinicos, Alex, 'England's Transition to Capitalism', *New Left Review* 207 (September–October 1994), 124–33.

Carvalho, Lourenço de, *Minha Ave Africana* (Maputo: Tempográfica, 1972).

Casanova, Pascale, *The World Republic of Letters*, trans. M. B. DeBevoise (Cambridge, MA: Harvard University Press, 2007).

Casares, Adolfo Bioy, 'Prologo', in Jorge Luis Borges, Adolfo Bioy Casares, and Silvina Ocampo, eds, *Antología de la Literatura Fantástica* (Buenos Aires: Sudamericana, 1940), 7–15.

Cassamo, Suleiman, *O Regresso do Morto* (Maputo: AEMO, 1989).

Castel-Branco, Carlos, Christopher Cramer, and Degol Hailu, 'Privatization and Economic Strategy in Mozambique', in Tony Addison, ed., *From Conflict to Recovery in Africa* (Oxford: Oxford University Press, 2003), 155–70.

Castle, Terry, *The Female Thermometer: Eighteenth-Century Culture and the Invention of the Uncanny* (Oxford and New York, NY: Oxford University Press, 1995).

Cavacas, Fernanda, *Mia Couto: Brincação Vocabular* (Lisbon: Mar Além, 1999).

Césaire, Aimé, *Discourse on Colonialism* (New York, NY: Monthly Review Press, 1972).

——, *Notebook of a Return to the Native Land* (Middletown, CT: Wesleyan University Press, 2000).

Chabal, Patrick, *The Postcolonial Literature of Lusophone Africa* (London: Hurst and Company, 1996).

Chapman, Paul M., 'Introduction', in Sheridan Le Fanu, ed., *The House by the Churchyard* (Hertfordshire: Wordsworth Editions, 2007), 11–17.

Checkland, S. G., *Scottish Banking: A History 1695–1973* (Glasgow: Collins Publishers, 1975).

Chichava, Sérgio, 'The Anti-Frelimo Movements & the War in Zambézia', in Eric Morier-Genoud, Michel Cahen, and Domingos Manuel do Rosário, eds,

Bibliography 197

The War Within: Perspectives on the Civil War in Mozambique 1976–1992 (Woodbridge: James Currey, 2018), 17–45.

Chiziane, Paulina, *Balada de Amor ao Vento* (Lisbon: Caminho, 1992 [1990]).

Clinton, Jerome W., and Sarah Lawall, *The Norton Anthology of World Literature* (New York, NY: W. W. Norton & Company, 2009).

Conway, Stephen, 'Transnational and Cosmopolitan Aspects of Eighteenth-Century European Wars', in Dina Gusejnova, ed., *Cosmopolitanism in Conflict: Imperial Encounters from the Seven Years' War to the Cold War* (London and New York, NY: Palgrave Macmillan, 2018), 29–55.

Cooper, Melinda, *Family Values: Between Neoliberalism and the New Social Conservatism* (New York, NY: Zone Books, 2017).

Cooppan, Vilashini, 'Ghosts in the Disciplinary Machine: The Uncanny Life of World Literature', *Comparative Literature Studies* 41/1 (2004), 10–36.

Couto, Mia, *Idades, Cidades, Divinidades* (Maputo: Ndjira, 2007).

——, 'Lack of Access Makes the Press More Bureaucratic', *Index on Censorship* 19/5 (May 1990b), 28.

——, *O Outro Pé da Sereia* (Lisbon: Caminho, 2006).

——, *O Último Voo do Flamingo* (Lisbon: Caminho, 2004).

——, 'Tale of the Two Who Returned from the Dead', trans. David Brookshaw, *Wasafiri*, 5/1 (1989), 10–11.

——, *Terra Sonâmbula* (Lisbon: Caminho, 1992).

——, *Voices Made Night* (Oxford: Heinemann, 1990a), 70–6.

——, *Vozes Anoitecidas* (Lisbon: Caminho, 2012).

Cox, Michael, 'Introduction', in M. R. James, ed., *Casting the Runes and Other Ghost Stories* (Oxford and New York, NY: Oxford University Press, 1999), xi–xxx.

Cramer, Christopher, *Civil War Is Not a Stupid Thing: Accounting for Violence in Developing Countries* (London: Hurst and Company, 2006).

Craveirinha, José, *Karingana ua Karingana* (Lisbon: Edições 70, 1982).

——, *Xigubo* (Maputo: AEMO, 1995).

Darwin, John, 'Conclusion: Decolonisation and Diaspora', in Eric Morier-Genoud and Michel Cahen, eds, *Imperial Migrations: Colonial Communities and Diaspora in the Portuguese World* (New York, NY, and Basingstoke: Palgrave 2013), 316–26.

Dasgupta, R. K., 'Lenin on Literature', *Indian Literature* 13/3 (September 1970), 5–25.

Davis, Colin, *Haunted Subjects: Deconstruction, Psychoanalysis and the Return of the Dead* (Houndmills, Basingstoke: Palgrave Macmillan, 2007).

Deleuze, Gilles, and Felix Guattari, *A Thousand Plateaus* (Minneapolis and London: University of Minnesota Press, 2005).

Derluguian, Georgi M., 'Mozambique in the 1980s: Periphery Goes Postmodern', in Eric Morier-Genoud, Michel Cahen, and Domingos Manuel do Rosário, eds, *The War Within: New Perspectives on the Civil War in Mozambique, 1976–1992* (Woodbridge: James Currey 2018), 203–20.

Derrida, Jacques, *Specters of Marx: The State of Debt, the Work of Mourning and the New International*, trans. Bernd Magnus and Stephen Cullenberg (London and New York, NY: Routledge, 2006 [1993]).

D'Haen, Theo, et al., *The Routledge Companion to World Literature* (New York, NY: Routledge, 2012).

Dias, João, *Godido e Outros Contos* (Lisbon: Casa dos Estudantes do Império, 1952).

Dick, Alexander, *Romanticism and the Gold Standard: Money, Literature, and Economic Debate in Britain 1790–1830* (New York, NY: Palgrave Macmillan, 2013).

Dickerson, Vanessa D., *Victorian Ghosts in the Noontide: Women Writers and the Supernatural* (Columbia and London: University of Missouri Press, 1996).

Diogo, Rosália Estelita Gregório, 'Suleiman Cassamo: A Voz do Povo pela Boca do Povo', *Scripta* 14/27 (2012), 183–6.

Domínguez, César, 'Gualterio Escoto: A Writer across World-Literatures', in Susan Bassett, ed., *Translation and World Literature* (Oxon and New York, NY: Routledge, 2018), 75–92.

Dorn Brose, Eric, *German History* (Oxford: Berghahn, 1997).

Drazen, Patrick, *A Gathering of Spirits: Japan's Ghost Story Tradition from Folklore and Kabuki to Anime and Manga* (Bloomington, IN: iUniverse, 2011).

Duffy, James, 'Portuguese Africa (Angola and Mozambique): Some Crucial Problems and the Role of Education in Their Resolution', *The Journal of Negro Education* 30/3 (Summer 1961), 294–301.

Eagleton, Terry, *Criticism and Ideology: A Study in Marxist Literary Theory* (London: Verso, 2006).

——, *Marxism and Literary Criticism* (London and New York, NY: Routledge, 2002).

Edmundson, Mark, *Nightmare on Main Street: Angels, Sadomasochism, and the Culture of Gothic* (Cambridge, MA, and London: Harvard University Press, 1999).

Egero, Bertil, 'Mozambique before the Second Phase of Socialist Development', *Review of African Political Economy* 25 (September 1982), 83–91.

Elmer, Jonathan, 'Poe, Plagiarism, and the Prescriptive Right of the Mob', in Christoph K. Lohmann, ed., *Discovering Difference: Contemporary Essays in American Culture* (Bloomington and Indianapolis: Indiana University Press, 1993), 66–87.

Emerson, Stephen, *Mozambican Civil War: Marxist-Apartheid Proxy, 1977–1992* (Barnsley: Pen and Sword, 2019).

Bibliography 199

Eppers, Arne, ' "Berührungen aus der Ferne" – Goethe und Walter Scott', in Werner Frick, Jochen Golz and Edith Zehm, eds, *Goethe Jahrbuch 123* (Weimar: Faust et Wallenstein, 2006), 152–67.

Erickson, Lee, *The Economy of Literary Form: English Literature and the Industrialization of Publishing, 1800–1850* (Baltimore, MD: Johns Hopkins University Press, 1996).

Esherick, Joseph, 'On the Restauration of Capitalism', *Modern China* 5/1 (January 1979), 41–78.

Fanon, Frantz, *The Wretched of the Earth* (New York, NY: Grove Press, 2007).

Federici, Silvia, 'On Primitive Accumulation, Globalization and Reproduction', *Medium* (10 September 2017), <https://friktionmagasin.dk/on-primitive-accumulation-globalization-and-reproduction-c299e08c3693>, accessed 12 November 2020.

Feitosa, Miguel, and Márcia Manir, 'Os Mortos Estão Voltando …: O Sentimento de Lugar e a Perspectiva da Experiência em "A História dos Aparecidos", de Mia Couto', *Geograficidade* 3/1 (July 2013), 50–8.

Felton, Debby, *The Ghost Story in Classical Antiquity* (Austin: University of Texas Press, 1999).

Ferreira, Ana Maria Teixeira Soares, *Traduzindo Mundos: Os Mortos na Narrativa de Mia Couto* (Aveiro: Universidade de Aveiro, 2007).

Ferreira, Manuel, *No Reino de Caliban III: Antologia Panorâmica da Poesia Africana de Expressão Portuguesa* (Lisbon: Plátano Editora, 1997).

——, *O Mancebo e Trovador Campos Oliveira* (Lisbon: Casa da Moeda, 1985).

Ferriar, John, *An Essay Towards a Theory of Apparitions* (London: Cadell and Davies, 1813).

Fillafer, Leander Franz, and Jürgen Osterhammel, 'Cosmopolitanism and the German Enlightenment', in Helmut Walser Smith, ed., *The Oxford Handbook of Modern German History* (Oxford: Oxford University Press, 2011), 119–43.

Finucane, Ronald C., *Appearances of the Dead: A Cultural History of Ghosts* (New York, NY: Prometheus Books, 1984).

Frank, Armin Paul, 'Translation and Historical Change in Post-Renaissance Europe', in Harald Kittel et al., eds, *Traduction: Encyclopédie internationale de la recherche sur la traduction* (Berlin: De Gruyter, 2007), 1460–1520.

Frelimo, *Poesia de Combate 2* (Maputo: Frelimo, 1977).

——, *Poesia de Combate 3* (Maputo: Frelimo, 1980).

Frier, David, 'The Transition from Romanticism to Realism', in Stephen Parkinson, Cláudia Pazos Alonso, and T. F. Earle, eds, *A Companion to Portuguese Literature* (London: Tamesis, 2009), 120–30.

Funada-Classen, Sayaka, *The Origins of War in Mozambique: A History of Unity and Division* (Tokyo: African Minds, 2012).

Gagnier, Regenia, 'The Global Circulation of Charles Dickens's Novels', *Literature Compass* 10/1 (2013), 82–95.

Gangopadhyay, Partha, ed., *Economics of Globalisation* (Aldershot, UK and Burlington, VT: Ashgate, 2005).

Genette, Gerard, *Paratexts: Thresholds of Interpretation*, trans. Jane E. Lewin (Cambridge: Cambridge University Press, 1997).

George, A. R., *The Babylonian Gilgamesh Epic: Introduction, Critical Edition and Cuneiform Texts* (Oxford: Oxford University Press, 2003).

Giddens, Anthony, *The Consequences of Modernity* (Hoboken, NJ: John Wiley & Sons, 2013).

Goethe, Johann Wolfgang von, *Conversations with Eckermann* (Washington and London: Walter Dunne, 1901).

——, *Goethe's poetische und prosaische Werke in zwei Bänden* (Tübingen: Cotta'sche Verlagsbuchhandlung, 1836).

——, *Kunsttheoretische Schriften und Übersetzungen. Band 18* (Berlin: Aufbau, 1960).

Gonçalves, Luís, 'Mia Couto and Mozambique: The Renegotiation of the National Narrative and Identity in an African Nation', PhD thesis (Chapel Hill: University of North Carolina, 2009).

Goudsblom, Johan, *Human History and Social Process* (Exeter: University of Exeter Press, 1996).

Guebuza, Armando, and Sergio Vieira, 'The Growth of a New Culture', *Mozambique Revolution* 49 (1971), 10–11.

Günther, Horst, *Versuche, Europäisch zu Denken: Deutschland und Frankreich* (Frankfurt am Main: Suhrkamp, 1990).

Gupta, Suman, *Globalization and Literature* (Cambridge: Polity, 2009).

Habjan, Jernej, 'The Eighteenth Brumaire of Jacques Derrida', in Jernej Habjan and Jessica Whyte, eds, *(Mis)Readings of Marx in Continental Philosophy* (New York: Palgrave Macmillan, 2014), 128–44.

Hall, Margaret, and Tom Young, *Confronting Leviathan: Mozambique since Independence* (Athens: Ohio University Press, 1997).

Hall, Stuart, 'The Local and the Global: Globalization and Ethnicity', in Anthony King, ed., *Culture, Globalization, and the World-System: Contemporary Conditions for the Representation of Identity* (Minneapolis: University of Minnesota Press, 1997), 19–40.

Hamilton, Russel G., *Voices of an Empire: History of Afro-Portuguese Literature* (New Berlin, WI: Burns and MacEachern, 1975).

Hanlon, Joseph, 'Mozambique: Under New Management', *Soundings* 7 (Autumn 1997), 184–94.

——, and Teresa Smart, *Do Bicycles Equal Development in Mozambique* (Woodbridge: James Currey, 2010).

Bibliography

Harootunian, Harry, *History's Disquiet. Modernity, Cultural Practice, and the Question of Everyday Life* (New York, NY: Columbia University Press, 2000).

Harrison, Graham, 'Corruption as "Boundary Politics": The State, Democratisation, and Mozambique's Unstable Liberalisation', *Third World Quarterly* 20/3 (June 1999), 537–50.

Hartley, Daniel, *The Politics of Style* (Chicago, IL: Haymarket Books, 2017).

Harvey, David, 'Globalization and the "Spatial Fix"', *Geographische Revue* 2 (2001), 23–30.

——, *Spaces of Hope* (Berkeley: University of California Press, 2000).

——, *The Condition of Postmodernity* (Oxford and Cambridge: Blackwell, 1989).

——, *The New Imperialism* (Oxford and New York, NY: Oxford University Press, 2003).

Hassan, Wail S., 'World Literature in the Age of Globalization: Reflections on an Anthology', *College English* 63/1 (September 2000), 38–47.

Hay, Simon J., *A History of the Modern British Ghost Story* (New York, NY: Palgrave Macmillan, 2011).

Hebmüller, Paulo, 'Escutas de Mia Couto', *Vermelho* (19 December 2017), <https://vermelho.org.br/2017/12/29/escutas-de-mia-couto/>, accessed 8 December 2020.

Hedges, David, and Aurélio Rocha, 'Moçambique Durante o Apogeu do Colonialismo Português, 1945–1961: A Economia e a Estrutura Social', in David Hedges, ed., *História de Moçambique: Moçambique no Auge do Colonialismo, 1930–1961* (Maputo: Livraria Universitária – UEM, 1999), 29–64.

Heller, Agnes, 'Marx and Modernity', *Thesis Eleven* 8/1 (1984), 44–58.

Hibbert, Samuel, *Sketches of the Philosophy of Apparitions: Or, An Attempt to Trace Such Illusions to Their Physical Causes* (Cambridge: Cambridge University Press, 2011 [1825]).

Homer, *The Iliad* (London: Bohn, 1851).

——, *The Odyssey* (Boston, MA: J. R. Osgood, 1871).

Honwana, Alcinda Manuel, 'Spiritual Agency & Self-Renewal in Southern Mozambique', PhD thesis (London: University of London, 1996).

Honwana, Luís Bernardo, 'Préfacio', in *Ninguém Matou Suhura* (Maputo: AEMO, 1988), 1–2.

Huggan, Graham, *Postcolonial Exotic: Marketing the Margins* (London and New York, NY: Routledge, 2001).

Iñárritu, Alejandro González, *Babel* (Paramount, 2006).

Isaacman, Allen, 'Colonial Mozambique, an Inside View: The Life History of Raúl Honwana', *Cahiers d'Études africaines* 109 (1988), 59–88.

202   *Bibliography*

——, and Barbara Isaacman, *Mozambique: From Colonialism to Revolution, 1900–1982* (New York, NY: Westview Press, 1983).

James, M. R., *Complete Ghost Stories* (London: Collector's Library, 2007).

Jameson, Fredric, *A Singular Modernity: Essay on the Ontology of the Present* (New York, NY: Verso, 2002).

——, *Archaeologies of the Future* (London and New York, NY: Verso, 2005).

——, 'Marx's Purloined Letter', *New Left Review* 209 (1995), 75–109.

——, *The Political Unconscious: Narrative as a Socially Symbolic Act* (London and New York, NY: Routledge, 1983).

Jay, Martín, *Cultural Semantics: Keywords of Our Time* (Amherst: University of Massachusetts, 1998).

Jin, Gracie, 'Q&A with Mia Couto, The Writer Who Just Won the "American Nobel Prize"', *Mic* (4 November 2013), <http://mic.com/articles/71373/q-a-with-mia-couto-the-writer-who-just-won-the-american-nobel-prize>, accessed 18 February 2015.

Jr, Guita, *Os Aromas Essenciais: Poesia* (Lisbon: Editorial Caminho, 2006).

Kadir, Djelal, 'To World, To Globalize: Comparative Literature's Crossroads', *Comparative Literature Studies* 41/1 (2004), 1–9.

Kahn, Sheila, 'O Exílio Pátrio e Identitário', *Scripta* 11/20 (2007), 137–54.

Kalipeni, Ezekiel, and Tiyambe Zeleza, *Sacred Spaces and Public Quarrels: African Cultural and Economic Landscapes* (Trenton, NJ: Africa World Press, 1999).

Kanter, Rosabeth Moss, *World Class* (New York, NY: Simon and Schuster, 1997).

Kean, Thomas, et al., *The 9/11 Commission Report* (New York, NY: Government Printing Office and W. W. Norton & Company, 2004).

Keese, Alexander, *Living with Ambiguity: Integrating an African Elite in French and Portuguese Africa, 1930–61* (Stuttgart: Franz Steiner Verlag, 2007).

Khor, Martin, 'Globalization and the Need for Coordinated Southern Policy Responses', *Cooperation South* (May 1995): 15–18.

Khosa, Ungulani Ba Ka, *Orgia dos Loucos* (Maputo: Imprensa Universitária, Fundação Universitária, 2000 [1990]).

Kilminster, Richard, 'Globalization as an Emergent Concept', in Alan Scott, ed., *The Limits of Globalization: Cases and Arguments* (London: Routledge, 1997), 257–83.

Knopfli, Rui, *Obra Poética* (Lisbon: Casa da Moeda, 2003).

Kristeva, Julia, *Desire in Language: A Semiotic Approach to Literature and Art*, trans. Thomas Gora and Alice Jardine, ed. Leon S. Roudiez (New York, NY: Columbia University Press, 1980).

Lang, Andrew, 'The Comparative Study of Ghost Stories', *The Nineteenth Century* 17 (1885), 623–32.

Bibliography

Laranjeira, Pires, *Literaturas Africanas de Expressão Portuguesa* (Lisbon: Universidade Aberta, 1995).

——, 'Mia Couto e as Literaturas Africanas de Língua Portuguesa', *Revista de Filología Románica* 2 (2001), 185–205.

Lawall, Sarah, *Reading World Literature: Theory, History, Practice* (Austin: University of Texas Press, 2010).

Lazarus, Neil, 'Cosmopolitanism and the Specificity of the Local in World Literature', *The Journal of Commonwealth Literature* 46/1 (March 2011), 119–37.

——, *Nationalism and Cultural Practice in the Postcolonial World* (Cambridge and New York, NY: Cambridge University Press, 1999).

——, 'The Fetish of "the West" in Postcolonial Theory', in Crystal Bartolovich and Neil Lazarus, eds, *Marxism, Modernity and Postcolonial Studies* (Cambridge and New York, NY: Cambridge University Press, 2002), 43–64.

Le Fanu, Sheridan, *Green Tea: In a Glass Darkly* (Oxford and New York, NY: Oxford University Press, 1999).

Leite, Ana Mafalda, 'Tópicos para uma História da Literatura Moçambicana', in Maria Paula Meneses and Margarida Calafate Ribeiro, eds, *Moçambique: Das Palavras Escritas* (Lisbon: Afrontamento, 2008), 47–77.

Lenin, Vladimir Ilyich, ' "Report on the Work of the Council of People's Commissars" (December 22, 1920)', in John Hinshaw and Peter N. Stearns, eds, *Industrialization in the Modern World: From the Industrial Revolution to the Internet* (Santa Barbara, CA, Denver, CO, and Oxford: ABC-CLIO, 2014), 563–5.

——, *State and Revolution* (Mansfield Centre, CT: Martino, 2011).

Levine, Suzanne Jill, 'One Hundred Years of Solitude and Pedro Páramo: A Parallel', *Books Abroad* 47/3 (Summer 1973), 490–5.

Levy, Brian, 'Seeking the Elusive Developmental Knife Edge: Zambia and Mozambique – A Tale of Two Countries', in Douglass C. North, John Joseph Wallis, Steven B. Webb, eds, *In the Shadow of Violence: Politics, Economics, and the Problems of Development* (Cambridge and New York, NY: Cambridge University Press, 2013), 112–48.

Liman, Doug, *The Bourne Identity* (Universal Pictures, 2002).

Lincoln, Andrew, *Walter Scott and Modernity* (Edinburgh: Edinburgh University Press, 2007).

Lisboa, Eugínio, and Helder Macedo, *The Dedalus Book of Portuguese Fantasy* (New York, NY: Dedalus, 1994).

Liu, Andrew B., *Tea War: A History of Capitalism in China and India* (Austin, TX: Yale University Press, 2020).

Long-Innes, Chesca, 'The Psychopathology of Post-colonial Mozambique: Mia Couto's "Voices Made Night" ', *American Imago* 55/1 (Spring 1998), 155–84.

Lopes, Maria Alexandra Ambrosia, *Poéticas da Imperfeição* (Lisboa: Faculdades de Ciências Humanas, 2010).

Löwy, Michael, 'The Current of Critical Irrealism: "A Moonlit Enchanted Night"', in Matthew Beaumont, ed., *A Concise Companion to Realism* (Malden, MA: Wiley-Blackwell, 2010), 193–206.

Luckhurst, Roger, 'The Contemporary London Gothic and the Limits of the "Spectral Turn"', *Textual Practice* 16/3 (2002), 527–46.

Luxemburg, Rosa, *The Accumulation of Capital*, trans. Agnes Schwarzschild (New Haven, CT: Yale University Press, 1951).

Lynch, Eve M., 'Spectral Politics: The Victorian Ghost Story and the Domestic Servant', in Nicola Bown, Carolyn Burdett, and Pamela Thurschwell et al., eds, *The Victorian Supernatural* (Cambridge and New York, NY: Cambridge University Press, 2004), 67–86.

Lyotard, Jean-François, *The Inhuman: Reflections on Time* (Stanford, CA: Stanford University Press, 1991).

Machado de Sousa, Maria Leonor, 'Dickens in Portugal', in Michael Hollington, ed., *The Reception of Charles Dickens in Europe* (London: Bloomsbury, 2013), 197–213.

Macherey, Pierre, and Susan Lanser, 'The Problem of Reflection', *SubStance* 5/15 (1976), 6–20.

Madureira, Luís, *Imaginary Geographies in Portuguese and Lusophone–African Literature: Narratives of Discovery and Empire* (Lewiston: E. Mellen Press, 2006).

——, 'Nation, Identity and Loss of Footing: Mia Couto's O Outro Pe da Sereia and the Question of Lusophone Postcolonialism', *Novel: A Forum on Fiction* 41/2–3 (June 2008), 200–28.

——, 'Uma Coisa Fraterna: Mia Couto & the Mutumbela Gogo Theatre Group', in Grant Hamilton and David Huddart, eds, *A Companion to Mia Couto* (Suffolk and Rochester: James Currey 2016), 25–48.

Magaia, Lina, Dumba Nengue, *Histórias Trágicas do Banditismo-I* (Maputo: Imprensa Nacional, 1987).

Maia Gouveia, Maria Margarida, *Vitorino Nemésio* (Lisbon: Instituto de Cultura e Língua Portuguesa, 1986).

Mandel, David, 'Primitive Accumulation in Post-Soviet Russia', in Matt Vidal, Tony Smith, Tomás Rotta, and Paul Prew, eds, *The Oxford Handbook of Karl Marx* (New York: Oxford University Press, 2019), 739–54.

Manjate, Lucilio, *O Contador de Palavras* (Maputo: Ndjira, 2012).

Manning, Carrie, *The Politics of Peace in Mozambique: Post-Conflict Democratization, 1992–2000* (Westport, CT: Praeger/Greenwood, 2002).

Bibliography

Marleyn, O., David Wield, and Richard Williams, 'Notes on the Political and Organizational Offensive in Mozambique and its Relationship to Agricultural Policy', *Review of African Political Economy* 24 (1982), 114–20.

Márquez, Gabriel García, *Cien Años de Soledad* (Buenos Aires: Editorial Sudamericana, 1976 [1971]).

——, 'Foreword', *Pedro Páramo* (London: Serpents Tail, 1993), v–xii.

Marx, Karl, *Capital* (Oxford: Oxford University Press, 2008a).

——, *Grundrisse: Foundations of the Critique of Political Economy*, trans. Martin Nicolaus (London: Vintage Books, 1973).

——, *The 18th Brumaire of Louis Bonaparte* (New York, NY: International Publishers, 2008b).

——, and Friedrich Engels, *The Communist Manifesto* (London: Penguin Classics, 2002).

Mason, Nicholas, ' "The Quack has Become a God": Puffery, Print, and the "Death" of Literature in Romantic-Era Britain', *Nineteenth-Century Literature* 60 (2005), 1–31.

Maurits, Peter J., 'The Mozambican Ghost Story: Local Genre or Global Form?', in Jernej Habjan and Fabienne Imlinger, eds, *Globalizing Literary Genres* (New York, NY, and London: Routledge, 2015), 180–95.

——, 'Worlds of Mia Couto: The Aesthetic of the Global', in Kristian van Haesendonck, ed., *The Worlds of Mia Couto* (Oxford: Peter Lang, 2020), 61–82.

Mawere, Munyaradzi, *African Belief and Knowledge Systems: A Critical Perspective* (Mankon, Bamenda: Langaa, 2011).

McKinstry, Sam, and Marie Fletcher, 'The Personal Account Books of Sir Walter Scott', *Accounting Historians Journal* 29/2 (2002), 59–89.

McNally, David, *Monsters of the Market: Zombies, Vampires, and Global Capitalism* (Leiden: Brill, 2011).

Medeiros, Paulo de, 'Ghosts and Hosts: Memory, Inheritance and the Postimperial Condition', *Diacrítica* 24/3 (2010), 201–14.

Mendes, Orlando, *Depois Do Sétimo Dia* (Lourenço Marques: Publicações Tribuna, 1963).

——, *Lume Florindo na Forja* (Maputo: Inld, 1980).

——, *Portagem* (Lisbon: Edições 70, 1981).

——, *Véspera Confiada* (Lourenço Marques: Livraria Academica, 1968).

Mendonça, Fátima, *Literatura Moçambicana* (Maputo: Faculdade de Letras, Universidade Eduardo Mondlane, 1988).

——, 'Literaturas Emergentes, Idades e Cânone', in Margarida Calafate Ribeiro and Maria Paula Meneses, eds, *Moçambique: Das Palavras Escritas* (Lisbon: Afrontamento, 2008), 19–33.

Miles, Robert, *Gothic Writing 1750–1820* (Manchester and New York, NY: Manchester University Press, 2002).

Miller, J. Hillis, 'Globalization and World Literature', *Neohelicon* 38/2 (December 2011), 251–65.

Miller, Todd, *Empire of Borders* (London and New York, NY: Verso, 2019).

Millgate, Jane, 'Archibald Constable and the Problem of London: "Quite the Connection We Have Been Looking For"', *The Library* 6–18/2 (1996), 110–23.

Mitchell, David, *Cloud Atlas* (London: Sceptre, Hachette UK, 2004).

Mitchell, Geoffrey S., '(Lost) Love, Eros and Metaphor: Colonialism, Social Fragmentation and the "Burden" of Race in *Portagem* by Orlando Mendes', in Phillip Rothwell, ed., *Reevaluating Mozambique* (Dartmouth: University of Massachusetts Press, 2003), 69–86.

Mittelman, James H., ed., *Globalization: Critical Reflections* (Boulder, CA: Lynne Rienner Publishers, 1996).

——, *Underdevelopment and the Transition to Socialism: Mozambique and Tanzania* (New York, NY: Academia Press, 1981).

Moisés, Massaud, *A Literatura Portuguesa Através os Textos* (São Paolo: Cultrix, 1968).

Monteiro, Lucineide Rodrigues, and Miguel Nenevé, 'O Outro Pé da Sereia, de Mia Couto: a Desconstrução da Visão Eurocêntrica Sobre Moçambique', *Polifonia* 19/26 (2012), 52–62.

Moretti, Franco, 'Conjectures on World Literature', *New Left Review* 1 (2000), 54–68.

——, *Distant Reading* (London and New York, NY: Verso, 2013).

Morier-Genoud, Eric, Michel Cahen, and Domingos M. do Rosário, *The War Within: Perspectives on the Civil War in Mozambique 1976–1992* (Woodbridge: Woodbridge, 2018).

Moser, Gerald, M., 'Lume Florindo na Forja by Orlando Mendes: Portagem by OrlandoMendes', *World Literature Today* 56/2 (1982), 395.

Moser, Robert H., *The Carnivalesque Defunto: Death and the Dead in Modern Brazilian Literature* (Athens: Center for International Studies, Ohio University, 2008).

Muianga, Aldino, *Xitala Mati* (Maputo: AEMO, 1987).

Nally, Claire, 'Protestant Suspicions of Catholic Duplicity: Religious and Racial Constructs in Le Fanu and Yeats', in Paddy Lyons and Alison O'Malley-Younger, eds, *No Country for Old Men: Fresh Perspectives on Irish Literature* (Oxford: Peter Lang, 2009), 215–32.

Neal, Larry, 'The Financial Crisis of 1825 and the Restructuring of the British Financial System', *Federal Reserve Bank of St. Louis Review* 80 (1998), 53–76.

Bibliography

Newitt, Malin, *A Short History of Mozambique* (New York, NY: Oxford University Press, 2017).

Ngoveni, Lawrence, *Inclusivity and the Construction of Memory in Mia Couto's Under the Frangipani* (Witwatersrand: University of the Witwatersrand, 2006).

Nicolai, Christoph Friedrich, 'A Memoir on the Appearance of Spectres or Phantoms Occasioned by Disease, with Psychological Remarks', *Nicholson's Journal of Natural Philosophy, Chemistry, and the Arts* (1803), 161–79.

Noa, Francisco, 'Literatura Moçambicana: Os Trilhos e as Margens', in Margarida Calafate Ribeiro and Maria Paula Meneses, eds, *Moçambique: Das Palavras Escritas* (Lisbon: Afrontamento, 2008), 35–46.

Nordstrom, Carolyn, *A Different Kind of War Story* (Philadelphia: University of Pennsylvania Press, 1997).

Noronha, Rui de, *Sonetos* (Lisbon: Texto Editores, 2006).

Ogilvie, Sheilagh, 'Proto-Industrialization in Germany', in Sheilagh Ogilvie and Markus Cerman, eds, *European ProtoIndustrialization* (Cambridge: Cambridge University Press, 1996), 118–36.

Panguana, Marcelo, *A Balada dos Deuses* (Maputo: AEMO, 1991).

Pavanello, Mariano, ed., *Perspectives on African Witchcraft* (Abingdon and New York, NY: Routledge, 2017).

Peeren, Esther, 'Everyday Ghosts and the Ghostly Everyday in Amos Tutuola, Ben Okri, and Achille Mbembe', in María del Pilar Blanco and Esther Peeren, eds, *Popular Ghosts: The Haunted Spaces of Everyday Culture* (New York, NY: Continuum, 2004), 106–17.

Penvenne, Jeanne, *African Workers and Colonial Racism: Mozambican Strategies and Struggles in Colonial Mozambique, 1877–1962* (London: James Currey, 1995).

——, *Attitudes Toward Race and Work in Mozambique: Lourenco Marques, 1900–1974* (Boston, MA: African Study Center, 1979).

——, 'Settling against the Tide', in Caroline Elkins and Susan Pedersen, eds, *Settler Colonialism in the Twentieth Century* (London and New York, NY: Routledge, 2005), 79–94.

Penzoldt, Peter, *The Supernatural in Fiction* (New York, NY: Humanities Press, 1952).

Perrons, Diane, *Globalization and Social Change: People and Places in a Divided World* (London and New York, NY: Routledge, 2004).

Petrus, T. S., and D. L. Bogopa, 'Natural and Supernatural: Intersections between the Spiritual and Natural Worlds in African Witchcraft and Healing with Reference to Southern Africa', *Indo-Pacific Journal of Phenomenology* 7/1 (2007), 1–10.

Phillips, Caryl, *The Nature of Blood* (London: Faber and Faber, Random House, 1997).

Pitcher, M. Anne, 'Forgetting from Above and Memory from Below: Strategies of Legitimation and Struggle in Postsocialist Mozambique', *Africa* 76/1 (February 2006), 88–112.

——, 'Recreating Colonialism or Reconstructing the State? Privatisation and Politics in Mozambique', *Journal of Southern African Studies* 22/1 (March 1996), 49–74.

——, *Transforming Mozambique: The Politics of Privatization, 1975–2000* (Cambridge: Cambridge University Press, 2002).

Pizer, John, *The Idea of World Literature: History and Pedagogical Practice* (Baton Rouge, LA: Louisiana State University Press, 2006).

Postone, Moishe, 'Specters of Marx', *History and Theory* 37/3 (1998), 370–87.

Prempeh, E. Osei Kwadwo, *Against Global Capitalism: African Social Movements Confront Neoliberal Globalization* (Aldershot and Burlington, VT: Ashgate Publishing, 2006).

Prendergast, Christopher, *Debating World Literature* (London: Verso, 2004).

Quayle, Eric, *The Ruin of Sir Walter Scott* (New York, NY: C. N. Potter, 1968).

Queiroz, Eça de, *O Crime de Padre Amaro* (Porto: Lello & Irmao, 1912).

Rabaté, Jean-Michel, *The Ghosts of Modernity* (Gainesville: University Press of Florida, 1996).

Redding, Sean, *Sorcery and Sovereignty: Taxation, Power, and Rebellion in South Africa, 1880–1963* (Athens: Ohio University Press, 2006).

Redol, Alves, *Gaibéus* (Lisbon: Caminho, 1992).

Reis, Carlos, *O Discurso Ideológico do Neo-Realismo Português* (Coimbra: Almedina, 1983).

Rensburg, A. P. J. Van, *Africa's Men of Destiny* (Pretoria: De Jager-Haum, 1981).

Ribeiro de Mello, Fernando, *Antologia do Conto Fantástico Português* (Lisbon: Tipografia Peres, 2003).

Riberio Cruz, Clauber, *O (Re)nascer de uma Nação: Portagem e o Destino de um Mulato* (Riga: Novas Edições Acadêmicas, 2017).

Rigney, Ann, *The Afterlives of Walter Scott: Memory on the Move* (Oxford and New York, NY: Oxford University Press, 2012).

Rio, Knut, Michelle MacCarthy, and Ruy Blanes, *Pentecostalism and Witchcraft: Spiritual Warfare in Africa and Melanesia* (Cham: Palgrave McMillan 2017).

Ritzer, George, *The Blackwell Companion to Globalization* (Malden, MA: John Wiley & Sons, 2008).

——, 'The Globalization of Nothing', *SAIS Review* 23/2 (2003), 189–200.

Bibliography

209

Robbins, Bruce, ' "The Don't Much Count, Do They?": The Unfinished History of The Turn of the Screw', in Peter G. Beidler, ed., *The Turn of the Screw* (Boston, MA and New York, NY: Bedford/St Martins, 2010), 333–46.

Robertson, Roland, *Globalization: Social Theory and Global Culture* (London: Sage, 1992).

Robinson, David Alexander, *Curse on the Land: A History of the Mozambican Civil War* (Perth: The University of Western Australia, 2006).

Rocha, Hugo, *Histórias Fantasmagóricas* (Lisbon: Livraria Civilização, 1969).

Rodrigues, Lia Noêmia Rodrigues, *Garrett and the English Muse* (Woodbridge: Tamesis, 1983).

Roesch, Otto, 'Classes in Formation?' *Southern Africa Report* 4/2 (October 1988), 6–28.

Royle, Nicholas, *After Derrida* (Manchester and New York, NY: Manchester University Press, 1995).

——, *Deconstructions: A User's Guide* (New York, NY: Palgrave Macmillan, 2000).

Sabiron, Céline, 'Exhuming the Vestigial Antique Body in Walter Scott's Caledonia', *Miranda* 11 (November 2015), 1–12.

Sá-Carneiro, Mario de, *Lucio's Confession*, trans. Margaret Jull Costa (Langford Sawtry: Daeldalus, 1993).

Sadlier, Darlene J., *The Portuguese-Speaking Diaspora: Seven Centuries of Literature and the Arts* (Austin: University of Texas Press, 2016).

Sahlins, Marshall, *Waiting for Foucault, Still* (Chicago, IL: Prickly Paradigm Press, 2002).

Sassen, Saskia, 'The State and Globalization', *Interventions* 5/2 (2003), 241–8.

Saussy, Haun, ed., *Comparative Literature in an Age of Globalization* (Baltimore, MD: John Hopkins University Press, 2006).

Saúte, Nelson, *Rio dos Bons Sinais* (Maputo: Marimbique, 2012).

Saville, John, 'Primitive Accumulation and Early Industrialization in Britain', *The Socialist Register* 6 (March 1969), 247–71.

Savoye, Jeffrey, 'Sinking Under Iniquity', *Edgar Allan Poe Review* 8/1 (2007), 70–4.

Scarborough, Dorothy, *The Supernatural in Modern English Fiction* (New York, NY, and London: G. P. Putnam's Sons, 1917).

Schivelbusch, Wolfgang, *Tastes of Paradise: A Social History of Spices, Stimulants, and Intoxicants* (New York, NY: Vintage Books, 1992).

Scott, Alan, *The Limits of Globalization: Cases and Arguments* (London: Routledge, 1997).

Scott, Walter, *Chronicles of the Canongate* (London and New York, NY: Penguin, 2003).

——, 'On the Supernatural in Fictitious Composition', *Foreign Quarterly Review* 1/1 (1827), 60–98.

——, 'Story of an Apparition', *Blackwood's Edinburgh Magazine* (April 1818), 705–7.

——, *The Bride of Lammermoor and Keepsake Stories and Chronicle of Canongate* (New York, NY: R. F. Fenno and Company Publishers, 1900).

——, *The Journal of Sir Walter Scott* (New York, NY: Harper and Brothers, 1891).

Shapiro, Stephen, 'Transvaal, Transylvania: Dracula's World-System and Gothic Periodicity', *Gothic Studies* 10/1 (2008), 29–47.

Silva, Manoel de Souza e, *Do Alheio ao Próprio: A Poesia em Moçambique* (São Paulo: Editora da Universidade Federal de Goiás, 1996).

Silva, Raul Calane da, 'Língua e Literatura em Moçambique: Evolução e Integração', *Grial* 49/189 (2011), 146–51.

Simões Alberto, Manuel, *Contribuição para o Estudo da Mestiçagem Moçambicana. Tese Apresentados ao Primeiro Congresso Realizado de 8 a 13 Setembro de 1947* (Lourenço Marques: Tipografia Minerva Central, 1947).

Simon, David, 'Rethinking Cities, Sustainability and Development in Africa', in Ezekiel Kalipeni and Tiyambe Zeleza, eds, *Sacred Spaces and Public Quarrels: African Economic and Cultural Landscapes* (Trenton, NJ, and Asmara: Africa World Press, 1999), 17–41.

Siskind, Mariano, 'The Genres of World Literature: The Case of Magical Realism', in Theo d'Haen, David Damrosch, Djelal Kadi, eds, *The Routledge Companion to World Literature* (New York: Routledge, 2012), 345–55.

Slobodian, Quin, *Globalists: The End of Empire and the Birth of Neoliberalism* (Cambridge, MA: University of Harvard Press, 2018).

Smajić, Srdjan, *Ghost-Seers, Detectives, and Spiritualists: Theories of Vision in Victorian Literature and Science* (Cambridge: Cambridge University Press, 2010).

——, 'The Trouble with Ghost-Seeing: Vision, Ideology, and Genre in the Victorian Ghost Story', *ELH* 70/4 (2003), 1107–35.

Smith, Andrew, and William Hughes, eds, *The Victorian Gothic: An Edinburgh Companion* (Edinburgh: Edinburgh University Press, 2012).

Soares, Bruno, *O Modo Fantástico em Mário de Sá-Carneiro* (Rio de Janeiro, Bonecker, 2019).

Solomon, Courtney, *An American Haunting* (After Dark Films, 2005).

Spector, Bertram, 'Corruption Assessment: Mozambique: Final Report', Maputo: United States Agency for International Development (2005), <http://www1.worldbank.org/publicsector/anticorrupt/MozambiqueCorAsm.pdf>, accessed 8 December 2015.

Bibliography

Spencer, J., 'Colonial Language Policies and Their Legacies in Sub-Saharan Africa', in Joshua A. Fishman, ed., *Advances in Language Planning* (The Hague and Paris: Mouton, 1974), 163–75.

Spivak, Gayatri, *An Aesthetic Education in the Era of Globalization* (Cambridge, MA: Harvard University Press, 2013).

Stasavage, David, 'Causes and Consequences of Corruption: Mozambique in Transition', in Alan Doig and Robin Theobald, eds, *Corruption and Democratisation* (London and Portland, OR: Frank Cass, 2000), 65–97.

Strich, Fritz, *Goethe und die Weltliteratur* (Marburg: Francke, 1946).

Sullivan, Jack, *Elegant Nightmares: The English Ghost Story from Le Fanu to Blackwood* (Athens: Ohio University Press, 1978).

Sumich, Jason, *The Middle Class in Mozambique: The State and the Politics of Transformation in Africa* (Cambridge: Cambridge University Press, 2018).

Swayne, Matthew L., *Haunted Rails* (Woodbury, MI: Llewellyn Publications, 2019).

Szeman, Imre, 'Culture and Globalization, or, the Humanities in Ruins', *CR: The New Centennial Review* 3/2 (Summer 2003), 91–115.

Tavares, Maria, 'Women Who Give Birth to New Worlds: Three Feminine Perspectives on Lusophone Postcolonial Africa', PhD thesis (University of Manchester, 2011).

Thakkar, Amit, *The Fiction of Juan Rulfo: Irony, Revolution and Postcolonialism* (Woodbridge: Tamesis, 2012).

Thomsen, Mads Rosendahl, *Mapping World Literature: International Canonization and Transnational Literatures* (London: A&C Black, 2008).

Todorov, Tzvetan, *The Fantastic: A Structural Approach to a Literary Genre*, trans. Richard Howard (Ithaca, NY: Cornel University Press, 1970).

Van Doren Stern, Philip, *The Pocket Book of Ghost Stories* (New York, NY: Pocket Books, 1947).

Varga, Zsuzsanna, 'Sporadic Encounters: Scottish-Portuguese Literary Contacts since 1500', in Tom Hubbard and Ronald D. S. Jack, eds, *Scotland in Europe* (Amsterdam and New York, NY: Rodopi, 2006), 203–21.

Vazsonyi, Nicholas, *Lukács Reads Goethe: From Aestheticism to Stalinism* (Columbia, SC: Camden House, 1997).

Veltmeyer, Henry, *New Perspectives on Globalization and Antiglobalization: Prospects for a New World Order?* (Aldershot and Burlington, VT: Ashgate Publishing, 2008).

Wallerstein, Immanuel, 'Globalization or the Age of Transition: A Long Term View of the Trajectory of the World-System', *International Sociology* 15/2 (June 2000), 249–65.

——, 'The End of What Modernity?', *Theory and Society* 24/4 (August 1995), 471–88.

—, *The Modern World-System IV: Centrist Liberalism Triumphant, 1789–1914* (Berkeley and London: University of California Press, 2011).

—, 'The Rise and Future Demise of the World Capitalist System: Concepts for Comparative Analysis', *Comparative Studies in Society and History* 16/4 (September 1974), 387–415.

Warwick, Alexandra, 'Victorian Gothic', in Catherine Spooner and Emma McEvoy, eds, *The Routledge Companion to Gothic* (New York, NY, and London: Routledge, 2007), 29–37.

Weitz, Hans-J., ' "Weltliteratur" Zuerst bei Wieland', *Arcadia* 22 (1987), 206–8.

Wellek, René, *Discriminations: Further Concepts of Criticism* (New Haven, CT: Yale University Press, 1970).

—, 'The Crisis of Comparative Literature', in Stephen Nichols, ed., *Concepts in Criticism* (New Haven, CT: Yale University Press, 1958), 282–95.

Williams, George S., 'Croftangry's Castle and the House of Usher: Scott, Poe, and "Decayed and Lingering Exotics" ', *Studies in Scottish Literature* 44/2 (2019), 142–51.

Wilson, Kenneth, 'Cults of Violence and Counter-Violence in Mozambique', *Journal of Southern African Studies* 18/3 (1992), 527–82.

Wiredu, Kwasi, 'Introduction', in Okot p'Bitek, ed., *Decolonizing African Religions: A Short History of African Religions in Western Scholarship* (New York, NY: Diasporic Africa Press, 2011), xi–xxxvii.

Wolfreys, Julian, *Victorian Hauntings: Spectrality, Gothic, the Uncanny and Literature* (Basingstoke: Palgrave Macmillan, 2001).

Wood, Claire, 'Playful Spirits: Charles Dickens and the Ghost Story', in Scott Brewster and Luke Thurston, eds, *The Routledge Handbook to the Ghost Story* (New York, NY: Routledge, 2017), 89–97.

Wood, Tony, *Russia without Putin: Money, Power, and the Myths of the Cold War* (London and New York, NY: Verso, 2018).

WReC (Warwick Research Collective), *Combined and Uneven Development: Towards a New Theory of World-Literature* (Liverpool: Liverpool University Press, 2015).

WReC, 'WReC's Reply', *Comparative Literature Studies* 53/3 (2016), 535–50.

Wuyts, Marc, 'Money, Planning and Rural Transformation in Mozambique', *Journal of Development Studies* 22/1 (1985), 180–207.

Young, Matthew, 'Paranormal Tax-ivity! Mum Refuses to Pay Tax on Haunted Room', *Daily Star* (9 September 2014), <http://www.dailystar.co.uk/news/lat est-news/394094/Ghost-in-spare-room-mum-refuses-to-pay-bedroom-tax>, accessed 13 August 2014.

Zhdanov, Andrei, 'Soviet Literature: The Richest in Ideas, the Most Advanced Literature' (1934), <http://soviethistory.msu.edu/>, accessed 12 November 2020.

Index

African ghost thesis 28–9, 36–7
Aleluia, Aníbal 1, 3, 10–3, 33, 36, 96, 147–8
annihilation of space by time 44–5, 48–9, 159, 163, 169, 175
bureaucratism 116, 127, 132

Borges Coelho, João Paulo 171

capitalism 3–7, 9, 18–9, 39, 41–2, 45, 49–50, 53, 65, 68, 74–5, 77, 82, 84, 95, 98, 103, 105, 118, 121–2, 127, 130, 145, 157–9, 168, 171–3
Cassamo, Suleiman 140–3
Chiziane, Paulina 148, 150, 190–1
corruption 116, 118, 127–32, 138
cosmopolitan 47–8, 51, 53, 70
    haunted 60–5, 67–8, 73, 155, 180, 188
    space 42–6, 49, 51, 55, 69, 105, 154–5, 162–4, 166, 169, 171, 173, 176–7, 179
Couto, Mia 35–7, 131, 140, 152
    'A História dos Aparecidos' (short story) 35, 115, 123–6, 132–9
    O Outro Pé da Sereia (novel) 155, 171–2, 180–8
Craveirinha, José 93, 111, 123–4

debt 54–5, 64, 120, 139, 160
    structure of 42, 57–8, 60, 62, 65, 67, 180–1
Derrida, Jacques 19–22, 28, 30, 162
Dias, João 89–90, 124

entrelacement *see* tropes of globalization
epigraph 10, 145, 180–2, 184
exotic 37, 81, 90, 174, 187
exorcism 15, 17, 20, 22, 32–5, 137, 150–1

Federici, Silvia 7, 159–63
Frelimo 75, 112–13, 115–23, 126–31, 134–5

ghost
    ghostly 4, 10, 20, 22, 29, 30–5, 38–9, 62, 89, 94–5
    miner-ghost 108–10, 135, 136, 142–5, 150, 190
    worker-ghost 135–8, 143, 152
globalization 3, 46, 152–74, 177, 179, 181, 187–9, 191
Goethe, Johannes Wolfgang von 25, 42–51, 53, 63–5, 73, 154, 159, 166–7, 169, 171
Gothic 3–4, 11, 14–18, 20, 23, 25, 39, 42, 56, 58, 67, 75, 83–7, 89–90, 94, 147, 181–2, 189

Honwana, Alcinda 30, 34
Honwana, Luís Bernardo 96, 124

Jr, Guita 171

Khosa, Ungulani Ba Ka 145
Knopfli, Rui 92–3, 111

Le Fanu, Sheridan 26, 66, 68, 71
    'Green Tea' (short story) 17, 66, 71–4
locale enumeration *see* tropes of globalization

Mendes, Orlando 25, 64, 102, 106, 109, 111, 115, 136, 189
    Portagem (novel) 75, 93–7, 99–102, 105–11
miner-ghost *see* ghost

214 · *Index*

mobility 44–5, 52–6, 60–1, 65, 67, 70,
    73–4, 95, 105, 117, 162–3, 175,
    179–80, 188
modernity 3–6, 9, 13–6, 41, 52, 62, 74, 95,
    109, 155
Moretti, Franco 23, 27–8, 38, 46, 153,
    170, 176
Muianga, Aldino 143–5

narrative closure 16, 39, 133, 151, 189
neoliberal 130–1, 139, 172, 191
Neorealism
    Mozambican 75, 95–6, 99, 110,
        137, 189
    Portuguese 95–6

Oliveira, Campos de 75, 79, 81, 83–6,
    89–90, 189
omnipresence thesis 10–3, 22, 27, 190

primitive accumulation 3, 6–9, 18–19, 39,
    42, 44–5, 49, 51, 63, 68, 72, 75,
    83, 95, 103, 105–6, 109, 111, 115–16,
    121, 125, 130–1, 138–9, 155, 159–63,
    172–4, 188

Renamo 30, 34, 118–21, 126
Rulfo, Juan 24, 124, 137–8, 140,
    182, 190

Scott, Walter 2, 14–17, 24, 26, 43, 73, 85,
    109, 154, 156, 162, 178
    'The Highland Widow' (short
        story) 23–5, 41–2, 45, 51–67, 69,
        74, 137, 149, 151, 176

'Tapestried Chamber' (short
    story) 3, 17, 31–2, 58–9, 66–70,
    88, 151
spatial jumps *see* tropes of globalization
spirit 2, 4, 15, 30–6, 70, 71, 109, 112–13,
    119, 122–3, 132, 143, 146, 147, 148,
    152, 185–6

time-space compression 159
traditional field 10, 21, 28, 33, 37–9, 82,
    90, 109, 112, 116, 119, 121, 126, 145
transition 36, 62, 84, 88–9, 144, 174, 189
    capitalist restoration 115, 130, 138–40
    from feudalism to capitalism 16, 18–
        19, 39, 41–2, 50, 52, 68, 73–4, 82,
        127, 171, 189
    to colonial capitalism 3, 97–8, 102–3,
        109, 124
    to socialism 117, 127
tropes of globalization
    entrelacement 174, 176–8, 186
    locale enumeration 70, 174–5,
        177, 178
    spatial jumps 51, 174, 176, 178
    journey trope 174

Wallerstein, Immanuel 4–5, 15, 78, 157,
    160–1, 168, 170
worker-ghost *see* ghost
world-literature 3, 9, 42–51, 53, 64–5,
    73, 152–5, 162, 164–71, 176, 177,
    179, 186

RECONFIGURING IDENTITIES IN THE PORTUGUESE-SPEAKING WORLD

Edited by

Paulo de Medeiros and Cláudia Pazos-Alonso

The series publishes studies across the entire spectrum of Lusophone literature, culture and intellectual history, from the Middle Ages to the present day, with particular emphasis on figurations and reconfigurations of identity, broadly understood. It is especially interested in work which interrogates national identity and cultural memory, or which offers fresh insights into Portuguese-speaking cultural and literary traditions, in diverse historical contexts and geographical locations. It is open to a wide variety of approaches and methodologies as well as to interdisciplinary fields: from literary criticism and comparative literature to cultural and gender studies, to film and media studies. It also seeks to encourage critical dialogue among scholarship originating from different continents.

Proposals are welcome for either single-author monographs or edited collections (in English and/or Portuguese). Those interested in contributing to the series should send a detailed project outline to oxford@peterlang.com.

VOL. 1   Ana Margarida Martins: Magic Stones and Flying Snakes:
         Gender and the 'Postcolonial Exotic' in the Work of Paulina
         Chiziane and Lídia Jorge.
         ISBN 978-3-0343-0828-1. 2012

VOL. 2   Ana Mafalda Leite, Hilary Owen, Rita Chaves, Livia Apa (eds):
         Narrating the Postcolonial Nation: Mapping Angola and
         Mozambique.
         ISBN 978-3-0343-0891-5. 2014

VOL. 3 Ana Mafalda Leite, Sheila Khan, Jessica Falconi, Kamila Krakowska (eds): Speaking the Postcolonial Nation: Interviews with Writers from Angola and Mozambique.
ISBN 978-3-0343-0890-8. 2014

VOL. 4 Francisco Bethencourt (ed.): Utopia in Portugal, Brazil and Lusophone African Countries.
ISBN 978-3-0343-1871-6. 2015

VOL. 5 Ana Luísa Amaral, Ana Paula Ferreira, Marinela Freitas (eds): New Portuguese Letters to the World: International Reception. ISBN 978-3-0343-1893-8. 2015

VOL. 6 Fernando Beleza and Simon Park (eds): Mário de Sá-Carneiro, A Cosmopolitan Modernist.
ISBN 978-3-0343-1885-3. 2017

VOL. 7 Eleanor K. Jones: Battleground Bodies: Gender and Sexuality in Mozambican Literature.
ISBN 978-1-78707-317-3. 2017

VOL. 8 Maria do Carmo Piçarra and Teresa Castro (eds): (Re)imagining African Independence: Film, Visual Arts and the Fall of the Portuguese Empire.
ISBN 978-1-78707-318-0. 2017

VOL. 9 Maria Manuel Lisboa: A Heaven of Their Own: Heresy and Heterodoxy in Portuguese Literature from the Eighteenth Century to the Present.
ISBN 978-3-0343-1962-1. 2018

VOL. 10 Doris Wieser and Ana Filipa Prata (eds): Cities of the Lusophone World: Literature, Culture and Urban Transformations.
ISBN 978-1-78874-251-1. 2018

Vol. 11 Paulo Pepe and Ana Raquel Fernandes (eds): Beyond Binaries, Sex, Sexualities, and Gender in the Lusophone World.
ISBN 978-1-78707-615-0. 2019

Vol. 12 Ana Mafalda Leite, Jessica Falconi, Kamila Krakowska, Sheila Khan, and Carmen Tindó Secco (eds): Voices, Languages, Discourses: Interpreting the Present and the Memory of Nation in Cape Verde, Guinea-Bissau and São Tomé and Príncipe.
ISBN 978-1-78707-585-6. 2020

Vol. 13 Ana Mafalda Leite, Hilary Owen, Ellen Sapega and Carmen Tindó Secco (eds): Postcolonial Nation and Narrative III: Literature & Cinema. Cape Verde, Guinea-Bissau and São Tomé e Príncipe.
ISBN 978-1-78707-581-8. 2019

Vol. 14 Elena Brugioni, Orlando Grossegesse, and Paulo de Medeiros (eds): A Companion to João Paulo Borges Coelho.
ISBN 978-1-78707-986-1. 2020

Vol. 15 Kristian Van Haesendonck (ed.): The Worlds of Mia Couto.
ISBN 978-1-78874-594-9. 2020

Vol. 16 Peter J. Maurits: The Mozambican Modern Ghost Story (1866–2006): The Genealogy of a Genre.
ISBN 978-1-78997-541-3. 2022